T0294048

Kerry-Anne Walsh was in the Canberra press gallery for twenty-five years occupying senior posts in print, radio and TV. Disenchanted with political spin and the nature of political reporting, she left the gallery in 2009 to establish her consultancy KA Communications. Her book *The Stalking of Julia Gillard* won the 2014 Australian Book Industry Award for the best non-fiction book of the year. Kerry-Anne and her son Kieran live in Canberra, and she continues to be a keen questioner of Australian politics.

# hoodwinked

## how pauline hanson fooled a nation

### kerry-anne walsh

ALLEN&UNWIN
SYDNEY • MELBOURNE • AUCKLAND • LONDON

Allen & Unwin
83 Alexander Street
Crows Nest NSW 2065
Australia
Phone:    (61 2) 8425 0100
Email:     info@allenandunwin.com
Web:      www.allenandunwin.com

 A catalogue record for this book is available from the National Library of Australia

ISBN 978 1 76011228 8

Set in 12/16pt Adobe Caslon by Midland Typesetters, Australia
Printed and bound in Australia by Griffin Press

10 9 8 7 6 5 4 3 2 1

 MIX
Paper from responsible sources
FSC® C009448

The paper in this book is FSC® certified. FSC® promotes environmentally responsible, socially beneficial and economically viable management of the world's forests.

# CONTENTS

'I wouldn't mind if there were more Asians in Australia than Anglo-European Australians, as long as they [the Asians] spoke English.'

An insert by Pauline Hanson into a 1996 parliamentary speech on immigration that was deleted by her adviser John Pasquarelli before she delivered it

# AUTHOR'S NOTE

Very few public figures can claim the level of fame, or infamy, that Pauline does. So much so, her surname isn't needed. Everyone knows her, or knows of her, and nearly everyone has a passionate viewpoint about her; she doesn't engender indifference. She's been a looming presence since she accidentally wandered onto the political set and brought the house down with her cameo appearance between 1996 and 1998, and even though by mid-2018 she'd only ever been in parliament a collective four years.

I didn't set out to write an academic paper on Pauline or an 'on the one hand, on the other' treatise. I wanted to know what made her tick, and it took me in directions I'm sure she and her ardent fans won't like. So be it. She's had a dramatic effect on the body politic even though many of her utterances are knowingly ill informed and clearly aimed at stirring up anger and resentment rather than creating a stronger, forward-looking, unified nation.

She thus deserves critical scrutiny, even though she labels it witch-hunting and an amorphous biased media 'out to get her'. The reality of her time in the limelight, including this parliamentary incarnation, is, in fact, the opposite. Her supporters at News Limited, including the well-read tabloids, on commercial radio broadcasting to big audiences and on Sky News give her an uncritical airing not extended to other politicians. I stand by for the usual suspects in those quarters to have their say about this book and me.

This is a narrative formulated after extensive research, including numerous interviews and conversations with those who know and have dealt with her. (Only those who went on the record have been quoted; other background information informed my views and have been absorbed into the narrative.)

I am grateful to other authors whose works I have either quoted or which helped me understand more about her and the times including David Marr's Quarterly Essay *The White Queen*, Anna Broinowski's *Please Explain*, Margo Kingston's *Off the Rails* and Royce Kurmelov's *Rogue Nation*. John Pasquarelli's *The Pauline Hanson Story by the Man Who Knows* was illuminating, as was Pauline's memoir, *Untamed and Unashamed*, and extracts from the book she allegedly co-authored then avowed she didn't, *Pauline Hanson: The Truth*.

I have read and used verifiable quotes and information from hundreds of newspaper articles, blogs, transcripts, TV appearances, videos and other source material, plus Hansard and other official records.

Pauline's words are quoted as she said them at the time. They speak for themselves.

# PROLOGUE

PAULINE HANSON looked like she'd been slapped with something wet and smelly from the old days, when she ran a fish and chippery. It was the night of 25 November 2017, and the Queensland state election results were slow-dripping onto TV screens as the state's Electoral Commission toilers counted votes in the 93 seats up for grabs.

As in the Western Australian election, held eight months previously, Hanson had boasted of unprecedented support for her party, which would 'send shockwaves across the country'. She had anticipated something similar to the 1998 Queensland state election, when her fledgling party had scooped eleven seats and bagged nearly 23 per cent of the primary vote. 'This is going to be the real beginning and resurgence of One Nation,' she hyperventilated to the press agency, AAP.

But now the One Nation seat tally started its slow march across the screen, and the wet fish started flapping her way. By the close of counting, beaming Queensland Premier Annastacia Palaszczuk looked to have a better-than-good chance of winning the election for Labor in her own right. The Liberal National Party's candidates, who up until then had been high with hope, were plummeting to earth like parachutists who'd forgotten to pull the cord; their party heavyweights and vanquished MPs were reeling like drunks on and off TV screens. One Nation was squatting in the naughty corner with its most likely outcome being one modest seat.

One Nation's parliamentary leader, Steve Dickson, who had defected to the party from the LNP during the outgoing parliament, had been kicked to the kerb in his Sunshine Coast seat of Buderim. Unenlightened voters had also rejected Malcolm Roberts, the mercurial oddball who had announced his state candidature in a joint press conference with a teary Hanson the previous month.

Roberts, a former One Nation senator who had once signed a letter to Julia Gillard as 'Malcolm-Ieuan: Roberts, the living soul' had unsuccessfully contested the seat of Ipswich, the location of Hanson's former takeaway. That shop is still in the battering and frying trade; but now, with exquisite irony, given her well-known views on Asian immigration, it is run by a Vietnamese family.

\* \* \*

Surrounded by sobbing supporters at a victory-turned-wake party held in the garage of Steve Dickson's pad in the modest Sunshine Coast town of Buderim, Hanson began blame shifting.

'It was a scare campaign that the Labor Party did!' she frothed. 'Saying that a vote for the LNP is a vote for One Nation, people were confused about it! Overall I think we've run a very strong campaign. We are polling in the mid to high 20s, some in the 30 per cent. I'm very pleased with that result. When you look at even the Greens vote, it's gone down.'

On Channel Nine's *60 Minutes* the following night, Hanson said she was hearing 'from some of our people' that 'there's about ten seats that we possibly have got a chance of picking up. So the counting is not over until the last vote is counted. Both the major political parties will be actually shaking in their boots.' They weren't; they had in their ranks experienced election scrutineers and Labor people had been punching the air with victory well before counting closed.

When the Queensland Electoral Commission finally announced the result late on Friday, 8 December, despite a historically low primary vote Palaszczuk had snagged majority government by three seats, scooping 48. The LNP had tanked to 39 seats, its primary support just 33.69 per cent. Leader Tim Nicholls swiftly announced he'd trudge the well-worn Walk of Shame to the Opposition backbench.

One Nation had a lonely single representative: Stephen Andrew, in the seat of Mirani. The Greens matched that single figure tally, but had nevertheless polled well. Labor-friendly Independent Sally Bolton had won in Noosa, and the rebel Bob Katter's Australian Party had been returned with a healthy three reps.

But did it really go all that wrong for One Nation? If you believe much of the media wash-up: yep, a shocker. If you look at the statistical and seat breakdown, not at all.

Given the shambolic way it operates, One Nation was immensely successful. It secured the third-highest primary vote of all parties, despite contesting only two-thirds, or 61 of 93 seats. Its state-wide primary vote was 13.7 per cent, based on all votes in all seats, but it contested only 65 per cent of the seats. In reality, its primary vote averaged 20 per cent-plus in the seats it contested.

In its non-city heartland, its primary vote zenith was 34.4 per cent. Its candidates ran second in primary votes in 23 of the 61 seats. The steady march away from establishment parties at a state and federal level was also evident in the poor showing of the big parties: combined, Labor and the LNP pulled in their lowest vote in decades—just 69.4 per cent. Given One Nation's faction-riddled, directionless, cult-like way of operating, the result was remarkable.

* * *

Hanson and Dickson erred on many fronts during the campaign, none so silly as their constant over-egging of the party's chances, reflecting Hanson's inflated sense of her own importance.

But Hanson seems perennially incapable of learning from past mistakes, doggedly determined to follow her own flawed instincts and the dictates of whichever young male political handbag is cleaved to her side at the time. Hanson is nothing if not consistent in her need to have a ruthless male political operative close by as she autocratically controls the ebb and flow of her party.

She rejoined One Nation in 2013. She'd had a merry time for a decade as a celebrity and a professional candidate running for state and federal elections. Time for the vanquished leader to return to the mother ship.

She wasted no time rebranding with her own name the party that had stoically soldiered on without her for more than a decade. Brandishing the sword as its new leader in 2014, by 2015 'Pauline Hanson's One Nation' had risen from the ashes of defeat. It was run, again, as her kingdom.

Welcome to the nightmare, comrades.

But it may have escaped the notice of those party members who returned her as leader that Hanson's conceit had been growing for decades. No matter to her that she'd been rejected more than a handful of times in two decades-worth of state and federal election tilts until her Senate win in 2016, a success she owed more than anything else to the lower quota required because it was a double dissolution election. Her motivating force has always been her strong belief that she has been repeatedly cheated in the past, and she wants her slice of fame back. One Nation was the only vehicle left available to her after so many rejections.

But the reality is that One Nation will never be what its founder wants it to be—the ultimate kingmaker, with her its queen—as long as it remains a homage to the woman it is named after.

Office-bearers, long-time members, candidates, inner circles come and go on Hanson's say-so. She is still as uncompromising and tough as she ever was—demanding absolute loyalty. She picks and kicks candidates, supporters and friends at whim. She is the party's guiding star, its hot centre and the rot at its core.

When she nimbly steered her way back into Canberra's House on the Hill at the 2016 federal election, some of her former state Queensland MPs had a few words of sage advice that sounded remarkably like sentiments uttered by others that she's been ignoring for years.

'Communicate, communicate, communicate,' was the blunt offering via the ABC from Dorothy Pratt, a long-standing MP who started her days in One Nation and ended them as an Independent. Hanson needed to 'start trusting people a little more', advised Jeff Knuth, who remained as a One Nation MP for less than a year before joining a few breakaway parties.

From David Dalgliesh, another defector: 'We all have time for Pauline, it's Pauline that needs to find time for us. We were a by-product.' And short and sweet words from another One Nation-turned-Independent MP, Ken Turner: 'Pauline Hanson's communication was no good.'

Hanson may not have changed much, but the Queensland and federal electoral terrain had moved on apace since One Nation's salad days in 1998.

\* \* \*

When she first blazed her unique trail into the House of Representatives in 1996 and turbo-charged eleven candidates into the Queensland Parliament two years later, Hanson was like the nudist who accidentally wandered into an Eastern Suburbs high tea party. She shocked and rocked an establishment that was dominated by the two major parties. Her virulent racism was bluntly expressed; her flag-waving, simplistic Australians-first rhetoric gained her instant stardom in depressed and disgruntled electoral pockets.

Nowadays, even though she would hate to be considered such, the one-time very short-lived federal Liberal Party candidate is a recognised political figure leading a recognised political party. Close to mainstream even. She does deals. She cosies up—too closely for some of her supporters—to the Liberals, an affinity and affection she can't seem to shake.

She can't get away with what she used to get away with. She claims her voice is being stifled or the left-wing media is out to get her when journalists or her political colleagues demand accountability for her stunts and statements. She's pressed for evidence-based answers, apart from the free kicks she's given when she bats her eyelids at Paul Murray or Andrew Bolt on Sky News, or whinnies to Alan Jones or Ray Hadley in cranky-man radio-land.

And where she used to be a relatively uncontested player in a wide open paddock, the minority space is now crowded. On the right flank there's Cory Bernardi's Conservatives, the Jacqui Lambie Network, Family First, Katter's Australian Party. In the centre sits the Nick Xenophon Team, or what's left of it; the organised force of the Greens dominates on the left. That's a smorgasbord of choice for voters, and it's highly competitive.

Nevertheless, the 2017 Queensland election showed that One Nation's strength continues to lie in regional and remote Australia, where it consistently pulled between 20 and 30 per cent. In many of those outer seats, the vote was closer to 30 per cent—that's nearly one-third of voters in non-metropolitan Queensland who wanted Pauline and her merry band rather than any other party or grouping.

It's a case of déjà vu all over again. It's a remarkable feat for Hanson to have two separate political careers, two decades apart. Queensland, as it has been for so many other political parties over the decades, is the state that's keeping her alive. But it could just as easily be the state that kills her off. It's all up to her.

What motivates the political creature that is Pauline Hanson? Where does such a consuming, winner-takes-all personal ambition come from?

# Chapter 1
# AMBITIOUS YOUNG PAULINE

LIKE MANY POLITICIANS who believe they are destined for greatness, the fiery redhead has always seen herself as one of the brightest matches in the box, rarely with fault. Her telling of her life reflects this: there has seldom been a sin or error for which she needed to take responsibility; a relationship breakdown that wasn't caused by the other party; a political blunder she couldn't sheet home to someone else; a child who she let down through her own doing.

Her life has been blighted by people who have wronged her, told fibs about her, hurt her, been disloyal to her, misrepresented or misquoted her, disappointed or betrayed her.

Her fondness for alternative facts started early. Why was she, the fifth of seven children born to Hannorah and Jack Seccombe, called Pauline? As she tells it in her 2007 autobiography, *Untamed and Unashamed*, she was a little tacker enjoying the backyard swing one night when she asked her mother: 'Where did you get my name Pauline from?'

'I read it in a book, and I wanted to call you Pauline,' her mother replied.

Young Pauline: 'What book, Mum?'

Mum: 'I can't remember. It was one I was reading when I was expecting you.'

Mum's memories are summarily dismissed. Pauline tells her readers: 'Sometimes I've wondered if it was from the movie, *The Perils of Pauline*.' It's unknown which particular movie the memoirist is fantasising about. But the most famous cinematic Pauline was the heroine of the popular 1914 American melodramatic serial *The Perils of Pauline*, in which the central character is always in a distressed state, set upon and menaced by a dishonourable array of villains, including American Indians. No cliff-hanger endings for these episodes; the resourceful Pauline always extracted herself from life-threatening danger, or had a burly bloke whisk in and save her.

Life, mused Irish satirist Oscar Wilde, ultimately imitates art. Real-life Pauline has been strapped to the railway tracks many times, but she always breaks free. In 1969, at the gentle age of fifteen, the then Pauline Seccombe met her first husband, Walter Zagorski, and married him a year later when she found she was pregnant. Since then, she has slayed the dragon of economic adversity, defeated political bastardry and deflected the slings and arrows of treasonous good-for-nothing partners and duplicitous friends.

Her romantic history is a chronicle of impetuous, passionate, headlong liaisons followed sooner rather than later by abrupt, poisonously bitter endings—a characteristic mirrored throughout her life in her platonic friendships and commercial and political relationships.

She appears to have had a happy early life among her siblings. Her hard-working parents owned a takeaway café at Woolloon-gabba and, by her accounts over the years, were a steady and calming influence. In particular her mother, known as Norah, was a powerful role model with her strong-minded and hard-headed approach to work and child-rearing.

Norah was a touch scary. Even John Pasquarelli—the first in a long line of Hanson's dominating and highly influential male parliamentary staffers—kept his distance from the feisty mother. Mrs Seccombe didn't think much of Pasquarelli either, but wouldn't say why. 'I think I blotted my copybook for not asking [her] permission to call her by her Christian name,' he later sheepishly said. Her third youngest child adopted the same stern approach to the decorum of titles, and would brook no disrespect. She retained the title of 'Mrs' long after her marriages had detonated.

Norah was clearly an inspiration to her youngest daughter, who has cherry-picked her way through life with a gut-feeling approach, uncluttered by the fripperies of evidence or objective fact. The redoubtable Mrs Seccombe was similar, holding narrow views of the Asian race that clearly appealed to her young daughter and were stored in her memory vault for future use.

In a video filmed in the 1990s and aired on Channel Nine's *60 Minutes,* Nora dished out some advice over tea and scones with a few of her children: 'I was always taught the yellow race will rule the world. And if we don't do something now, I'm afraid, yes, the yellow race *will* rule the world.'

Apart from the odd racist attitude, Mr and Mrs Seccombe taught their daughter the benefits of hard work and thriftiness. In *Untamed and Unashamed*, Pauline recalls sometimes walking the five kilometres home from school to save the five-cent tram fare. This was another behavioural pattern that would endure through her professional life: a keen eye for the bottom line that would boost, but also blight, both her personal and professional life at various junctures.

In one of the accounts of her life, an ambitious young Pauline was committed to a business path in life by the time she'd finished Year Eight at school. She wanted to take her parents' lead: at their urging, she'd worked part-time in their café from a young age and was schooled by them in the value of hard work and 'getting ahead'.

She spurned her school principal's advice that she should progress to Year Ten and take the Academic course—advice, she reminisced proudly in her autobiography, that was based on her excellent academic achievement of topping her class over 40 other students. Instead, in Year Nine she opted for the Commercial course.

But her memories of her strong academic abilities don't sit easily with the recollections of Pasquarelli. In his modestly titled 1998 book about his volatile days with the first-time MP, *The Pauline Hanson Story by the Man Who Knows*, Pasquarelli recalled that she wouldn't read briefs, wasn't intellectually curious, had no real interest in the job of MP, and was staggeringly uninformed about Australian history, world events and basic knowledge. David Oldfield, who replaced Pasquarelli, echoed those thoughts. He has kept up a running commentary for decades on Hanson's intellectual and academic shortcomings.

Pasquarelli recounts a time Hanson angrily swept briefing notes off her desk when he ticked her off for not doing any parliamentary work. 'I can't retain, I can't retain!' she yelled. When he first read her hasty attempt at her 1996 maiden speech, he was taken aback: 'She was running at about ten to fifteen mistakes per A4 page and she could not construct sentences properly. Leaving school far too early had cost her dearly.'

Her attention span was, however, excellent when it came to anything to do with herself. After she delivered her rabble-rousing maiden speech in parliament—Pasquarelli claims most of the credit for its construction, ideas and source material—she would lock herself in her office and spend hours, sometimes days, reading and re-reading her fan mail. She sometimes took these letters home with her as bedtime reading.

Undertaking the Commercial course in Year Nine had been a wise choice, she concluded later when assembling her life's facts for her autobiography. Indeed, she judged it as 'the most influential decision' she ever made, because it set her up to pursue her ambition as a businesswoman.

Another day, and it's another ambition: in January 1999 she told *Woman's Day* one of her life's goals was to be a model. She might even start up her own clothes label. 'A lot of women are fed up with these dull, boring colours which seem to be in the shops,' the self-described expert seamstress said. Politics never figured in the script.

\*    \*    \*

The young Pauline, despite leaving school abruptly and being a teenage mum, had big dreams and always leapt starry-eyed into every one of her life's rich episodes. Seventeen, married, with a young bub and working part-time, life couldn't get much better! Especially when you had an older husband who loved you.

Years later, Walter would say he only married Pauline under extreme pressure from her parents; that 'she wasn't a person I was in love with. The only reason I got married was because it was the right thing to do, but I went through living hell because of that woman,' he told the *Good Weekend*'s profile writer, David Leser, in 1996.

The stars had also dimmed pretty quickly for Pauline. The young wife began to conclude only a few years into the marriage that Walter was not living up to her expectations of a husband who could share her sales and entrepreneurial aspirations.

Her parents, with whom the couple lived when she was pregnant, had been generous to the newlyweds, who were made partners in the Seccombes' business of making and selling pre-cut, uncooked chips—the first in Brisbane to tap into this new market. However, the 'business didn't succeed because Walter was not putting enough effort into it', Pauline stated later.

Her patient parents, by this stage living on the Gold Coast, fronted with another opportunity: they set up an adjoining shop to a café they owned as a commercial games room with pinball and pool tables. Alas. 'Again,' Pauline stated in her memoir, 'it was not successful. Walter was just not business-minded.'

The young wife meanwhile was working part-time at the café and baby Tony would often go to her parents at the Gold Coast 'to give me a break'. This pattern—of leaving her children for long periods with extended family—was established early, while their mother set about making money and fulfilling her dreams.

By 1977 and with another son, Steven, born in February 1975, the marriage to Walter was over. Her version of those times is muddy; both parties at various times accused each other of infidelity—Walter never accepted Steven was his son—and both have very different recollections of the decline in their relationship. Asked about his former wife when she first entered parliament, Walter's derisive reply to journalists was that she was 'only ever interested in a Mercedes sports car'.

The new MP fiercely denied this. 'My priorities and responsibilities were to my children and their wellbeing,' she states in her memoir. This would become her standard avowal, repeated over the next few decades when accusations of her abandonment and neglect of her children—sometimes levelled at her by those children themselves—were aired.

Pauline moved on quick smart. In November 1978, two months after meeting plumber Mark Hanson when waitressing at the Penthouse Nightclub in Surfers Paradise, she picked up sticks and moved her young family to his home in Ipswich, the future centre of her political universe. She helped him establish Hanson's Plumbing Service, learned the tricks of the trade, made sure 'his washing and ironing was always ready for him, and meals cooked' and, in her eyes, was the commercial powerhouse and emotional bedrock of the household.

The happy couple married in May 1980 when Pauline was unexpectedly again pregnant, with third son Adam. When she bolted into parliament and before she slapped Mark Hanson with a Supreme Court writ to stop him talking, her former husband would say he didn't want to marry her but felt he had to because she was pregnant. 'I'm an old-fashioned bloke with strong family values, and my only option was to stick by her and marry her,' he told *New Idea* in 1998.

Pauline's account is different: she was the one who didn't have time for another pregnancy, but Mark was thrilled to ribbons and he proposed. Off they waltzed, hand-in-hand, with her making another doomed attempt at nuptial bliss.

The couple snapped up a budget-tour package and honeymooned in Asia, where she'd never visited except, perhaps, in her mind through her mother's warnings. As if written in the stars, it wasn't an appealing experience for the well-brought-up Mrs Hanson, who was revolted by the spitting in Manila's streets and outraged by the 'sleazy male-filled' bars in Thailand.

At one of many doorstops following her flammable 1996 maiden speech, in which she claimed Asians were swamping Australia, journalists queried if she'd ever been to Asia. Yes, she replied, thin upper lip curling.

And would she ever go back? No!

Why? 'Because I don't like it.'

This would become a constant pattern in her personal and professional life: a refusal to yield to any other world view or opinion than

15

her own, even when she was faced with persuasive facts or where her views were based on only the most fleeting of experiences.

By 1985, with daughter Lee now added to the mix, the Hanson marriage was lurching. She accused Mark of drunkenness and violence. By this stage Tony, Pauline's first-born son to Walter, had been despatched to live with his grandmother, Dachau concentration camp survivor Lydia Zagorski.

Mrs Zagorski was gracious enough to take in her grandson, despite still nursing deep hurt that her former daughter-in-law and only son had somehow forgotten to invite her to their shotgun wedding. It was Walter's fault apparently; nothing to do with Pauline: 'In all the excitement, Walter did not make arrangements for his mother to attend,' she fails to properly explain in her autobiography.

Despite the couple's personal issues, Hanson Plumbing boomed. In Pauline's telling, this was mainly due to her slick entrepreneurial and business smarts. She had also invested in residential properties: remarkably, by the time the marriage imploded, the couple had squirrelled away four properties. She claimed these were bought from rental income, her housekeeping budgeting skills, child endowment and maintaining the properties herself, 'with some help from Mark', she added dismissively in her book.

She point-blank refused to respond to well-sourced claims made to *Good Weekend* by family members that she had not passed on the child endowment payments to her mother-in-law for son Tony's care. 'I'm not going to answer that,' she snapped at Leser.

Once the turbulent relationship started breaking down, the family dynamics—which often included Mark's daughter, Amanda, from a previous relationship—were punctuated by violent arguments. Late one night, after the warring couple had gone hammer and tongs at each other, Pauline grabbed her youngest child, Lee, intending to flee and leave the others in the care of someone she believed was a violent drunk. 'I thought it best to leave the other children there for the night and pick them up in the morning,' she states without further explanation in her memoir.

When Mark grabbed Lee from her arms, Pauline fled on foot without any of the children. As she tells it, he left them at home and followed her in the car, yelling out the window that he would drive into the river unless she returned home. She returned.

She claims that on another occasion he came to bed, woke her and said he was going to hang himself. 'I just looked at him then rolled over and went back to sleep,' she states matter-of-factly. She was a heroic, hard-working, dedicated mother and devoted wife, who had no responsibility for the deterioration of her husband's behaviour.

The stormy marriage inevitably reached its natural conclusion; it crashed and burned in late January 1987. Pauline's second husband echoed the tormented sentiment of her first: he wished he had never met her. 'She's embarrassed the Hanson name and the goodwill of the Hanson family . . . I don't think she knows what love is,' he told *New Idea*. 'She doesn't have a heart that can love. I wonder sometimes what I ever saw in her. I never thought a woman could be so overbearing. She didn't compromise on anything. It was her way or nothing.'

When it came to divvying up the assets with Mark, Hanson's version is that she was left with little. However, she scored the investment properties and she managed to buy a timber house for herself and the children.

\* \* \*

Pauline moved on quickly from the busted relationship with Mark and formed a new one with Morrie Marsden, whose uncle owned Marsden's Seafoods, which would soon enough become world famous for its next owner. Just ten months later, by November 1987, she was busy battering and frying in her own shop and enjoying her new relationship.

Her children again inched their way down her priorities ladder: a young woman named Barbara moved in with the family so Hanson could work long hours six, sometimes seven, days a week. If she got home by 8 p.m., she'd bring the children something to eat from the shop. When Barbara moved out a few years later, young Steven was moved on—to her parents on the Gold Coast.

Marsden helped her in the shop after finishing his day job by doubling up as her mop-and-clean man. He also stepped into a fatherly role with the children, even though he and Pauline maintained separate residences.

Marsden supported her financially and morally, and would also help mentor her political career through all her ups and downs until after she won the 1996 seat. He was the most enduring of all Hanson's adult male relationships; he stuck like glue in one capacity or another for years, and could be regarded as the most important in framing and advancing her political career, at the same time keeping her steady and focused on her business.

He was a shy and loyal man who was deeply affected by the treatment she ultimately dished out to him. Pasquarelli in *The Pauline Hanson Story by the Man Who Knows* painted a picture of a decent and honest bloke who was utterly out of his depth with the object of his affections: 'Morrie is a real Ipswich boy—part of the local furniture—and he has no pretensions,' he wrote. 'He goes to the races and plays the pokies at the local Brothers' Club. He is a typical Queenslander—open, truthful and without real malice, and therefore totally unsuited to playing the grubby and deceitful game of politics.

'Plagued by the onset of panic attacks during his bumpy relationship with Pauline and with a pathological fear of flying, he told me she had "cost me ten years of my life".'

In late 1990 Marsden was given the boot from the Hanson bed. In the space of a rapid heartbeat she'd moved on to Rick Gluyas, an Ipswich councillor who would ignite her interest in politics. By January 1991, the happy couple had bought 150 acres (60 hectares) together outside Ipswich. She claimed she paid the deposit and all the repayments, but included him on the title deeds. Ever-loyal Morrie remained in her orbit, shifting from bed-mate to just-mate.

Ipswichians must have dearly loved her takeaway burgers and fry-ups because, within a year, she'd built a shiny new expensive home on the property derisively nicknamed her 'convention centre' by her soon-to-be-ex partner Gluyas. She also still had the family home in town. But before she and Gluyas could get around to saying 'let's shack up together', they were rocking to that old familiar song about sweet love turning bad. Less than three years after their impetuous coupling, the flares had well and truly gone up.

A bitter Hanson made a pay-out to Gluyas, complaining—as she had done with Mark—that he didn't deserve what she paid him, but he 'had me in a bind' and she had had no choice than to shell out to him a 'considerable sum of money be believed he was owed'. Her friend Morrie was there with a consoling shoulder. But he, too, would ultimately walk the well-worn path of hurt and abandonment experienced by other partners. Hanson is nothing if not consistent when she's had enough.

On the 1996 election night, Marsden—her campaign manager, as he had been before—hosted the vote-counting-turned-victory party. The victor didn't thank her helpers, or invite them to stand with her for the assembled media throng. 'Her almost silent, unidentified "thank you" to Morrie Marsden on the other side of the room could have been directed to a picture on the wall,' Pasquarelli recalled. 'Marsden told one of Pauline's workers from the fish and chips chop that he felt Pauline's win marked the absolute end of his relationship with her. He was right.'

But before all that, with two husbands and one de facto partner behind her, and guided by the steadying influence of loyal friend Morrie, she was about to launch into the fractious, double-dealing, tempestuous world of Australian politics. Her life to date had set her up nicely for it.

\* \* \*

Over the years Hanson has been at pains to keep the collapse of her marriages out of the public eye, either by threatening to sue her former husbands or adopting the position that it is below her dignity to talk about such personal matters.

Yet Hanson has been the one who turned her gaudy romantic life into tabloid fodder when it suited her, at times shocking and puzzling her ditched partners. It was critical for her to maintain her profile during the dry years—well, *decades*—between her parliamentary stints, and she simply loved those glossies. She was Pauline, the star of her own long-running soap opera, just as she'd imagined when she was a kid.

Everything was breathlessly chronicled, from her love affairs to her TV appearances and her political adventures. But, most of all, it was her love affairs that kept her readers enthralled. She was always unlucky in love—a damsel pining for a good old-fashioned man who wouldn't desert her when times got tough.

In January 2005 Pauline introduced us to her new bloke, 47-year-old Irishman, Seamus Doheny, through the pages of the *Women's Weekly*. She backed up in July with a gushing ode to the Irishman in *Woman's Day*. She couldn't be happier!

But the nimble-footed Celt disappeared as quickly as a pint of Guinness on a warm Dublin day, and in August 2007 we read in

*Woman's Day* about her love for country crooner Chris Callaghan. Exactly two years later she informed us through tears in the same women's mag that she was 'totally devastated' after he recently walked out on her, just six weeks after proposing.

But wait! She had a unique solution, which handily was already in the planning stages with Channel Seven. According to the sympathetic *Woman's Day* scribe, the dejected dumpee, while 'staring sadly into the log fire, holding back the tears', spruiked the exciting news that she might very soon star in her own find-a-hubby reality show, modelled on *Farmer Wants a Wife*.

Carelessly someone, possibly with red hair, forgot to tell the rural yodeller that their affair was kaput and his now ex might soon be on the small screen on the prowl for someone else to sing sweet nothings in her ear. 'It's a shock. I haven't heard it from her,' Callaghan spluttered when informed by the *Northern Territory News* that his presence on her Queensland country estate was no longer an option. 'I would have expected an email . . .' They were having issues, he explained, but working through them. 'Pauline was getting over the [Queensland state] election loss and deciding whether to stay in politics.'

Perhaps it was those wretched nude photos. Allegedly of Hanson, they had been splashed all over the front page of the Sydney *Sunday Telegraph* the previous March, five months before the loved-up couple split; or one left the other wailing; or the other left and lied about it; or . . . regardless of what story to believe, this had at the time been a red-hot yarn.

The happy snapper was one Jack Johnson, at the time of publication enjoying a stint in one of Her Majesty's finest for crimes that weren't disclosed in the media. He claimed he had had a raunchy romp with Hanson at a Coffs Harbour motel in 1975, when she was still married to Zagorski.

While addressing only the provenance of the photos and not the circumstances of the alleged romp, Hanson sued the paper, which ultimately apologised to her and claimed it had been conned by Jackson, who subsequently retreated to his narrow, single bunk after conceding he could have been wrong. But Hanson continued to bleat about it. And bleat, and bleat, at the same time as weeping about the awful things the media did to her. In October, she was still moaning about her pain and hurt, telling *Woman's Day*: 'I've lost trust in everyone!'

\* \* \*

After all the excitement of 2009, the publicity trash tabloid trail soon went eerily cold. This phenomenon coincided with Hanson looking to re-emerge as a credible political voice through paid stints on TV.

However, on 23 June 2016, when running for the Senate, she reprised her tales of adversity, recounting the alleged domestic abuse at Mark's hands. Since the publication of her autobiography and up to then, she had not bothered to include this as part of her life's narrative, despite all the showy pieces in women's magazines and the ample opportunity to curry sympathy with the growing number of single mothers and abused women who could have been a powerful political bloc.

With trembling voice, she tearily told one of her media friends, Paul Murray—a paid-up member of Sky's night-time stable of right-wing ranters—the tale of the night her husband had threatened to drive into the river. She pledged that, as a senator, she would work with communities to find out why domestic violence was on the rise. 'We need to stand up and fight against domestic violence, by all means,' she said reasonably. As a single mother who claimed to have experienced abuse, the odds were good she'd stand up for women in similar circumstances.

She disavowed that notion when speaking to Australian Regional Media's Newsdesk at an event in Brisbane: 'We need a full overview of the child support system and the family law courts to find the answers [because] you know some [women] are going out there and claiming domestic violence because they're told "I don't like the colour of your dress". They are making frivolous complaints and it's time that our court system [is looked at] . . . '

This twice-divorced single mother of four—who claimed that she had received little or no financial support from her husbands, suffered domestic violence and mental abuse, and had had to scratch and scrimp for her family, for her future and even, presumably, for her four investment properties—had no truck with single mothers like herself. She was not like them; they did not rise above it all, as she has managed to do.

In the Hanson view of their worlds, these women get themselves pregnant to earn government benefits; they rip off former partners through inflated child support payments, in order to live cushy lives with new beaux; and they use their kids as pawns in custody battles. In a One Nation-ruled Australia, welfare benefits would be denied to single mothers after their first child; all parents, regardless of circumstance or disposition, would automatically get joint custody; and abusers would have access to kids, even if authorities deemed the children at risk, and even if a court had issued a protection order.

It is an unusual position for a woman whose two marriages were both shotgun and who was paid some child support by her second husband, even though he had periods off work due to ongoing back problems. Mark Hanson complained bitterly that she allowed him no say in his children's upbringing. Pasquarelli also notes in his book that Hanson has never admitted or denied that she received government benefits when the relationships with her children's fathers broke down.

# Chapter 2
# A FIRST TASTE OF POLITICS

HANSON WAS A product of her times. Ignorance was bliss in the Queensland of National Party leader Joh Bjelke-Petersen; he had no truck with lefties, libertarians, upholders of democracy, Aborigines, feminists or anyone who stood against his oppressive soft dictatorship.

Until his government descended into an apocalyptic mess of corruption and cronyism in 1987, Bjelke-Petersen ran Queensland for nearly two decades as a personal fiefdom. Morally, there was no high horse he refused to mount while denying basic human and legal rights to many of his state's constituents with a cheery 'don't you worry about that!'

One of those constituent groups was Aboriginal Australians. Bjelke-Petersen was a racist. He steered his state defiantly against a growing national tide of soul-searching about the shameful historic treatment of Indigenous Australians, which culminated in the overwhelming passing of a national referendum in 1967 that granted them equal citizenship rights.

That historic event occurred one year before the peanut farmer from Kingaroy became Queensland Premier. He'd been the state's Aboriginal Affairs Minister before that, chirpily continuing a repressive regime that had been in place since the late 1800s. As Premier, he maintained the raft of ancient legislative control measures, collectively known as the 'Black Acts', that kept Aboriginal people as little more than natives to be controlled and assimilated, and permitted their lands to be exploited. He remained deaf to the increasingly vocal, horrified criticism of these repressive laws, including by the United Nations. An impressionable young Pauline was just fourteen at the time.

Racism towards Aboriginal Australians was a way of life for many Queenslanders. It suited them, and it suited their Premier and his land-owning mates and the multinational companies baying for a slice of Queensland's rich natural resources, particularly in far north Queensland where most of the state's Indigenous population lived.

The Premier's attitude to the growing land rights movement in the 1970s was to label it a 'Soviet takeover plot' because 'Aboriginal land would be used as bases for assaults by foreign forces on Australia'. He ordered the removal of church workers from Aboriginal communities in far north Queensland in the 1960s and 70s when these good folk of God gave support to their flock's growing agitation for land rights. He doubled down by proclaiming the disputed areas as Crown land to prevent Aboriginal ownership.

One of the great founders of the land rights movement, Cape York's John Koowarta, was blocked by Bjelke-Petersen from buying his traditional lands. When he won a landmark Supreme Court case, the Premier cunningly thwarted his victory by declaring the land a national park. Aboriginal people shouldn't own land, he fumed. The future Member for Oxley would in time become a feisty opponent of native title.

One of Joh's most notorious henchmen was Pat Killoran, the coddled and protected head of the Department of Aboriginal Affairs for the entire duration of Joh's premiership. Killoran oversaw the mass removal of Aboriginal and mixed race children from their families.

One of Killoran's most notorious actions was to order a police raid on the Cape York township of Mapoon. Like a colonial overlord, he watched on through binoculars from the deck of a government ship docked nearby while family homes were burned to the ground. The distraught townsfolk—men, women and children—were forcibly relocated 200 kilometres away. To round out his savagery, he garnisheed the slave wages of the workers of the Mapoon community to recompense the government for the cost of their 'relocation'.

Who cared? So what? The government had important business to conduct: the multinational miner Comalco wanted the bauxite reserves near the land. This was just the way things were at that time.

As Pauline skipped into her twenties and then thirties in staunchly white outer-metropolitan Queensland, Joh's regime endured and the Premier became more defiant in standing up for white rights. To him, the Whitlam Government's 1975 Racial Discrimination Act was abominable social engineering. His government repelled federal legislation to protect sacred Aboriginal and Torres Strait Islander sites because it would 'freeze development'. He vigorously agreed with the inflammatory declaration by the president of the Victorian RSL, Bruce Ruxton, that South African anti-apartheid hero, Archbishop Desmond Tutu, was a witchdoctor.

The pompously titled and these days little-known publication, *Pauline Hanson: The Truth*, echoed Joh Bjelke-Petersen's virulent racism. This 1997 collection of thoughts and speeches by Hanson stated that unnamed 1930s academics had 'discovered' that nineteenth-century Aborigines were cannibals. 'They killed and ate their own women and children and occasionally their men,' the book stated. 'The older women were often killed for eating purposes, like livestock.'

Europeans had to 'appropriate' Australia because Indigenous people couldn't defend the land, the book declared. Presumably because they were too busy chowing down on their old folk or eating Chinese newcomers, which the book suggests the human-eating natives found pretty damned tasty.

'Striped with white and yellow war paint', Aboriginal cannibals would attack Chinese immigrants while 'screeching like demons from the deepest hell'. To the cannibal blacks the new chum Chinese were manna from heaven. Hundreds of them were 'ambushed, captured, and eaten at leisure.'

These scribblings, copyrighted to Pauline Hanson and with her beaming face on the cover, also included pearls about a future Australia being run by President Poona Li Hung, a part-cyborg lesbian of Chinese and Indian descent; and about gun control supporters being 'sexually retarded'.

No need rushing out to buy this valuable collection of whimsy. It's a relic of the past, no longer available. Some years after its publication, Hanson disavowed knowledge of its contents and authorship, despite having urged devotees at a small 1997 event to buy her 'very informative book'. She later claimed she had no idea who was responsible for it, but understood it to be 'four authors'. A George J. Merritt is noted on official records as either the compiler or a co-author, but this mysterious genius has no electronic footprint.

Uninformed views about Aboriginal people and their history were as much a part of white Queensland life as a sunburned nose. Government policies that entrenched Aboriginal dispossession and poverty were sewn into the seams of the state by many decades of conservative state governments, culminating in the granddaddy of them all, the Bjelke-Petersen-led regime from 1968–87. Many Queenslanders didn't understand rising Aboriginal militancy about their peoples' continuing humiliation and degradation. If they did, they chose to ignore it.

But Hanson willingly incorporated ignorance and intolerance into her growing history, her learned truth. As she was to find out to her delight when she rocketed into the national consciousness, she wasn't alone. Many Aussies were more than happy to accept blessed witlessness as a way of life that needed protecting. There was no reason to change, and every reason to be resentful of a group of people who seemed to get benefits others couldn't.

Ipswich was mainly a white battlers' town, a long way from becoming a melting pot of diversity. It was a small town orbiting on the outskirts of big country town Brisbane; and it was suffering the dislocation blues from the decline of traditional pursuits. Miners, tradies, a smattering of small business owners and low-income government salary slaves from the railways and RAAF base populated its heart.

Friction in the town between the small Aboriginal population and whites wasn't a major problem, more like a constant mosquito buzz on a hot Queensland night. But if there was any vandalism or a petty crime was committed, it was the fault of one of those jobless, idle, taxpayer-subsidised blackfellas.

Despite Joh's strongest attempts to stem any influences from the outside world, modern thinking—about race, segregation and the poverty and dislocation wrought by dispossession and successive governments' abject failure to improve, in particular, the health and education of Indigenous people—was beginning to penetrate the consciousness and conscience of many Queenslanders. Ipswich was no different.

But Hanson liked Ipswich the way it was. She was comfortably at home as a commercial success story in a small, white-dominated Queensland orbit, where hard work and free enterprise rewarded people like her. Where everything was in its place, and everyone was at the right end of the queue, just as they deserved.

\* \* \*

Political upheavals, happenstance and perhaps a dash of personal competitiveness drove Hanson's arrival at Ipswich Council chambers in 1994. Labor had descended into internecine brawling: ultimately the comrades had frogmarched one of their own, Mayor Dave Underwood, from office in 1993 because of his autocratic style and treatment of unionised workers.

The council elections in March 1994 were ripe for a clean sweep to remove the old Labor guard, and voters were happy to enthusiastically answer the call. One Labor councillor and ten Independents, including Pauline, replaced the ten Labor councillors and one Independent who had made up the previous council.

Hanson has said that her then-partner, mayoral associate Rick Gluyas, had switched her on to politics; he had asked her to join him on an Independent ticket. By the time the election rolled around, however, Pauline and Rick were in an off-again phase in their on-off relationship. Nonetheless, as Hanson tells it, she was already committed to and focused on running for council, so she ran as a 'true Independent', supported by the campaigning skills of the ever-faithful Morrie Marsden.

Pasquarelli, a good friend and confidante of Marsden's, recalls it differently: 'It was as if her only motive for standing for council was simply that the man she had been living with intended trying his hand, and she didn't want to be left out of the process,' he wrote in *The Pauline Hanson Story by the Man Who Knows*. 'There appears to have been no pressing local issues that may have prompted Pauline Hanson to put up her hand—no obvious stirring of political ambition.'

She was, by all accounts, a workaholic loner; she had no involvement with community organisations, no political affiliations, little social life and none of the usual neighbourhood bonds forged by raising a family locally. She acknowledged such in *Untamed and Unashamed*. Only months before jumping the shark into council politics, she declared her priority was 'running my business and rearing my children as a single parent'. With the help of her parents, former in-laws and live-in help, that is.

Her council stint was short-lived. Just a year after her victory, new elections were held and she lost her spot. The new poll was held because, she claimed in her book: 'the last thing the State [Labor] Government wanted was to have a group of Independent councillors running Ipswich Council for the next three years'.

The Labor Government under Wayne Goss 'decided to redistribute the boundaries of Ipswich, Brisbane City and Boonah shires to regain their control over Ipswich Council', she maintained. 'It was in Labor's interests to regain control of Ipswich Council, and another election was called for March 1995 . . . boundary changes were used as the reason for holding a fresh election.'

The longest-serving councillor on Ipswich Council, well-liked local larrikin Labor identity Paul Tully, served on council with Hanson back in the day. He knows Ipswich and its political ancestry like his palm-lines. He lived the stories. He's Ipswich's town crier, and the equivalent of a local government extreme marathon runner: he holds the record for the longest-serving councillor in Queensland, still going strong in 2018 after first being elected to Ipswich Council 39 years before, in 1979.

Tully's a bloke who talks as fast as a threshing machine, so the silence on the phone after putting Hanson's conspiracy theory to him is noticeable. 'That's simply not right,' he says after a few seconds. 'It is just not true what she says. The government had a well-known program of amalgamations across Queensland, it was happening everywhere.'

He sketches out the background, how important the amalgamation was to Ipswich's future. 'Up until 1995, Ipswich was a city of twelve square kilometres—it was very small. It wasn't growing, and unemployment rates were high. The economy was relatively stagnant. In 1995 it amalgamated with Moreton Shire Council, so we immediately went to 130,000 square kilometres and the rest is history—the economy is booming, unemployment is down. Our population will double within the next 20 years, so the amalgamation helped the economy of the city change dramatically.'

Hanson's version—that she was dudded by political forces working against her—is now a very familiar Hanson whinge. In this, her first taste of politics, she didn't let the opportunity slip by. The denizens of Ipswich, if they had had their ears cocked on election night when the news rolled into the Hanson lounge room that the inexperienced, unknown new councillor had lost by 132 primary votes, may well have heard the shrill refrain 'I was robbed!'

'I had no chance with the boundary changes to my electorate and the boundary changes I had done with nearly all the candidates putting me last on their how-to-vote cards,' she complained incoherently in her autobiography. 'Many successful candidates stood as Independents, despite their association with the Labor Party, and some were the previously elected councillors under the Labor banner. I should have woken up then to the devious and dirty game of politics!'

She claimed she achieved much in her first political outing. We don't know doing what, as she was coy about ticking off her achievements. But her short-lived stint on the council was apparently very successful indeed. 'I managed to gain several improvements for my electorate,' she wrote in her book, mislabelling the area she represented—in local government councillors do not have electorates, they are known as *divisions*.

She 'gained the trust of a lot of the administrative staff and council workers,' she decided, without expanding on how. 'It was to me they brought issues that needed to be raised in Council,' although we aren't informed what those issues were. 'It allowed me to question and call for accountability on behalf of the people of Ipswich,' she rounded out, without giving us examples of when and how she did that.

Tully doesn't think any of this is true. He recalls her being like any other newbie councillor, asking questions and generally lying low. 'She had no profile on the council. None whatsoever,' he says bluntly.

There were a few episodes he remembers clearly, though, because they were unusual. One was her attendance at a selection committee for a new staffer. Hanson asked the woman how she intended to work full-time, considering she had children. 'The interview had to be terminated,' says Tully. 'She had no idea about what questions could be lawfully asked. It was bizarre, given her own personal situation too.'

Hanson didn't like spending money, whether it was hers or anyone else's. She didn't speak up on much, but on a couple of items with dollars attached she was vocal. She spoke strongly against financial support of 'about $20,000, I think', Tully says, for the Ipswich Rugby League Club. 'She thought it was too much.'

Another beef was the proposed modernisation of the Ipswich Library, championed by other members of the council as a balm to the commercial deterioration of Ipswich. Forward-thinking councillors proposed a spanking new addition to the modest town library, including a Global Info Links program, which would see the library become the first in Queensland to jump aboard the internet-propelled information superhighway.

Hanson vigorously opposed spending the money and the modernisation program, which would have included free dial-up internet access for local schools. She liked things the way they were, and she joined with a few other councillors to make opposition to the revamp of the library their main re-election platform.

It didn't matter to this opposition group that the contract had already been awarded, and building had commenced. No dummies, the building company worked hard to get as much built as it could, even as the anti-modernisation cabal intensified their campaigning. This utterly infuriated Hanson—they were being outwitted!

To this day, Tully is still flabbergasted by a question she asked one day in committee about the building activity: 'I couldn't believe this—she asked if the workers could be fined for working too fast.' The library revamp went ahead. In a short time it helped save the battered town and was lauded as a proud achievement for the state of Queensland; it helped put Ipswich on the national map.

At one time during the year, councillors tootled off on a junket—what in polite company is known as a 'planning retreat'. The venue was a sprawling rural property outside Ipswich called Old Hidden Vale where, much to Hanson's delight, they offered horse riding.

When it came time to check out, she was asked by the receptionist to pay for the soft drink she had consumed from her mini-bar. With a line of councillors behind her with their ears cupped, her trademark high voice lifted a note or two. She hadn't had a soft drink, she proclaimed vehemently.

Perhaps, it was suggested to her politely, a guest of hers had.

Hanson, much to the amusement of her fellow councillors, exploded. 'I do not have to disclose who was in my room!' She didn't pay for the drink.

\* \* \*

The year on council gave Pauline her first taste of the 'backstabbing, egos and hidden agendas of politics' and 'the start of the experience of political manipulation I was to encounter during the whole time I was involved in the political scene', she sighed in her book. Clearly this was an appealing combo as, her appetite whetted, she set her sights higher.

As Pasquarelli remembers it, she wanted a shot at the local state seat but Marsden, a prominent town identity with fabulous grassroots connections, advised her to focus instead on the federal seat of Oxley. He believed that Labor's traditional hold on Ipswich and its hinterland was weakening, and she'd be in with a shot. 'His advice to Pauline . . . was extraordinary and prophetic.'

Pasquarelli—like many others near, dear and actively participating in her life—clearly has a faulty memory. It turns out that it was her astute political antenna that was responsible for the path she chose to take: 'I had discussed my plans of running for politics with Morrie who suggested state politics, but I was not interested. I had my mind set on the federal arena,' she wrote in *Untamed and Unashamed*. Morrie, it seems, was only ever 'moral support' in her well-planned journey to political infamy.

Setting out along this track, she addressed Liberal Party branch members in early July 1995 and told them she wasn't a party member, had no political experience, but wanted to be their candidate; they should look no further, given her success as a small business owner in the area.

There was a motion for them to curtail their normal pre-selection procedures, such as advertising for candidates in the local papers, but this was put and lost. Because of 'the women', she said later. She'd won the blokes over, but the women annoyingly wanted to do it properly. Pauline was indignant: 'I couldn't believe what I was hearing!' she spluttered.

Undaunted, the following month she became a paid-up party member and in November she won pre-selection in a canter over two other candidates. She was a tough hard-working female, a single mother, and presented as a battler despite her status as a well-off small businesswoman with property. 'She was a good bit of gear at the beginning of the race,' local party leader Steve Wilson quaintly told the *Good Weekend*'s David Leser in 1998.

But, a few weeks later, Pauline burst into notoriety on an Aboriginal issue. She penned a letter to the local rag, *The Queensland Times*, objecting to federal Minister for Aboriginal and Torres Strait Islander Affairs Robert Tickner's concern about black deaths in custody. Her letter read:

Black deaths in custody seem to be Robert Tickner's latest outcry. Pity that as much media coverage or political grandstanding is not shown for white deaths in custody. As for Mr Tickner's statement that Aborigines should not go to jail because apparently it is not working: imagine what type of country this would be to live in if Aborigines didn't go to jail for their crimes. One of these men was serving a 12-year sentence, and it wasn't just for a speeding fine.

Can you imagine then if we had equality, then we would have no prisoners at all. The indigenous people of this country are as much responsible for their actions as any other colour or race in this country. The problem is that politicians in all their profound wisdom have and are causing a racism problem.

I would be the first to admit that, not many years ago the Aborigines were treated wrongly but in trying to correct this they have gone too far. I don't feel responsible for the treatment of Aboriginal people in the past because I had no say but my concern is now and for the future. How can we expect this race to help themselves when governments shower them with money, facilities and opportunities that only these people can obtain no matter how minute the indigenous blood is that flows through their veins and that is what is causing racism.

Councillor Tully hit the roof. A dab hand at media engagement, he wrote to the Liberal Party and to Prime Minister John Howard; he also excited the interest of Brisbane's *Courier-Mail*, which in turn contacted Liberal Party headquarters for a comment.

State Director Jim Barron hauled Hanson in and told her to do the party dance by running any such material in future under the noses of HQ. She grudgingly agreed; but, in doing so, she showed that even as a political novice her approach was to dispense with teamwork. This was a trait she would carry with her throughout her political career, along the way fracturing her party, her friendships and her parliamentary teams. She told Barron: 'When I win the seat, then I will have my say.'

When the *Courier-Mail* told her the Liberal Party had apologised for the letter and asked if she too would apologise, she snapped: 'No, I will not.' She said later: 'I was not impressed with having the Liberal Party apologising on my behalf. I owed no one an apology for speaking the truth.' It was, she said, her first encounter with what she labelled 'political correctness', even though it was neither more nor less than what was expected of any candidate for a major political party.

Being a straight-shooting, I-did-it-my-way style of politician was a characteristic she particularly admired in Joh. It was a model she adopted. She loved that her state's long-serving patriarch hated political correctness and called it as he saw it. He lived his authentic truth, no matter how fact-challenged that truth was. Many years later, when visiting a fading Lady Flo Bjelke-Petersen in a nursing home, Hanson purred: 'You're on [our] minds . . . Queenslanders will never forget the name of Bjelke-Petersen.' About Joh's destructive run for federal parliament in the 1980s, she sniffed: 'Of course, they didn't want to see him in Canberra because he speaks his mind.'

But she was no Joh, and the disendorsement train was on the tracks. On John Howard's insistence, on the night of 14 February 1996 the backroom boys cut her loose after she'd had another media crack at the 'indigenous issue'. She claimed it was because Aboriginal groups had threatened to protest outside her shop.

It was only sixteen days until the election. She thumbed her noses at the party and adopted Morrie's advice to stand as an Independent. The following morning, when she arrived for work at her shop, she was met by a throng of media, the likes of which she could only have dreamed about when she was an invisible party-hack candidate.

In her memoir she displays a curious mixture of boasting, loathing and spotlight-loving as she marvels at this exhilarating turn of events: 'They were like vultures hovering to sensationalise a story. I was the most political incorrect candidate they had come across and I was standing in the election.' Her love/hate relationship with the media had started, and she didn't half mind it at all.

A few weeks later, she won the seat of Oxley with a kick-arse 19.3 per cent swing. While some credit can go to confusion about just who she was representing—she remained the Liberal candidate on the how-to-vote ticket, and the Liberals didn't run a replacement candidate—her critical views on Aborigines' access to government-subsidised programs and services struck a chord with outer Queensland suburbanites only just emerging from a Joh-programmed fog.

Says Tully: 'My feeling about her is she galvanised a lot of unknown and rarely heard-of fringe groups, like the Citizens' Electoral Council, who put out newsletters and that sort of shit, and she tapped into all those fringe groups and racist people. She had the benefit of major media interest at the time, the national swing against the Labor Party, the unpopularity of [sitting Labor MP] Les Scott, and she was still on the ticket as a Liberal candidate.

'As well, the anti-Labor sentiment was still reverberating in Ipswich because of the turmoil around the Underwood sacking. She had many things going for her.'

The bitter irony for those who, wittingly or not, gave her a political voice must surely be that her platform was based on nothing more than the whingeing she heard from customers and at the fish markets. The truth she so righteously claimed about Aboriginal issues was her truth; she had never researched Aboriginal matters, government funding on programs, black deaths in custody or historical Indigenous disadvantage.

She wrote her letter to the paper and entered the political and media fray 'armed only with the determination that I was right and justified in what I was saying', she admitted in her book.

She had 'no documentation, no statistics, and no research'. She was equipped only 'with the knowledge from talking to countless other Australians over the years, people who were also fed up with the whole Aboriginal issue and the waste of taxpayers' dollars'.

A little bit of knowledge is a dangerous thing. But it can take you places.

# Chapter 3

# 'JUST ATTACK THE BLACKS OR THE ASIANS'

QUEENSLAND IS THE natural birthing site for political fringe-dwellers with an uncanny knack of becoming national disruptors. Aside from Hanson and One Nation, there have been the League of Rights, Citizens Electoral Council, Confederate Action Party and Palmer United Party; all of these have either emanated from, or found their strongest base in, the Sunshine State. Madcap political loners who carved their names in history for all the wrong reasons—think Albert Field, Vince Gair, Mal Colston—emerged from the sunny north.

To understand why Pauline burst from the pack, why the peanut farmer survived for so long, and why federal political strategists tremble at the thought of Queensland voters requires a psychedelic trip into the many pulsing arteries of the Queensland heart.

Of all our states, Queensland is the most varied: an extraordinary smorgasbord of people, temperaments and demographics. Australia's second largest state is nearly five times the size of Japan, seven times the size of Great Britain, two and a half times the size of Texas, and hosts a gloriously diverse scattering of cities, towns

41

and communities best described as clusters of people rather than a fused society.

Some pockets are among the most progressive in Australia; others prefer to remain frozen in a time and era of their choosing. It is more regional than metropolitan—more than half its nearly five million population live outside the capital, Australia's only state to have that population mix. That vast regional sweep embraces a great diversity of regional communities. It's a demographic Russian doll.

The two land rights giants, John Koowarta and Eddie Mabo, who ushered in the native title era, were proud far north Queenslanders. Their communities were among those that suffered the greatest losses and deprivations prior to and during Joh's regime; and their people would be sent packing back to their disadvantaged, wretched past if Ms Hanson had her way. Even today, representatives of Queensland's Indigenous peoples continue to be the standard-bearers in the never-ending quest to forge better black and white relations in our country.

In spite of the spirited attempts by greedy white-shoe developers, colourful business types and assorted shysters during the Joh era to rip the rich heart out of the Sunshine State, Queensland has remarkably and consistently proved to be the economic engine room of the country. It's been bested on economic growth figures only seven times since the mid-1980s, according to the Queensland statistician.

But remnants of Joh's era still linger: doing business with Queensland is murderous for non-Queenslanders in the summer months as it clings stoically to Eastern Standard Time, and the doors of many shops remain bolted on Sundays—a relic of Joh's edict that the Sabbath should remain reserved for family fun and church.

From the hippies, retirees and alternative life-stylers clustered on the southern border in the Tweed area to the remote Aboriginal, mining and wild-north outback communities at the tip of Cape York, if you can read Queensland right then (apart from being a sociological genius) you can gauge the mood of just about any community in Australia.

But there's loyalty, and then there's perceived disloyalty to the Queensland way. Even though in 1922 it was the first Australian state by a country mile to abolish the death penalty, when it comes to political crimes Queenslanders from its townships to its cities scream for the hangman to perform a good-ole town square hanging.

Unlike those in New South Wales, voters in Queensland swing hard from one side to the other, like dancers cavorting in unison this way or that around the maypole. It's why figuring out what Queenslanders want and how they're shifting electorally is a political party's greatest challenge. But it offers the greatest reward: if a party wins over Queensland voters, a federal win becomes a hell of a lot easier.

Queensland started off as a 'natural Labor' state. The party was born there, following the prolonged shearers' strikes in 1891, and eight years later its voters propelled into office the world's first Labor Government, led by Anderson Dawson. But when, in 1975, the country tossed out Gough Whitlam it was Queensland voters who led the revolt, leaving Labor with one paltry seat there. And yet it was Queensland voters who propelled Bob Hawke into an unexpected fourth term in 1990 when, for the first time in four decades, Labor's share of the Queensland vote eclipsed its share of the overall national vote.

It took John Howard nearly a decade to claw back from his bruising confrontation with the best Queensland could throw at him: the bonkers 1987 Joh-For-Canberra push. This rebel movement derailed Howard's ambition to become PM at the 1987 election; it led to a split in the federal Coalition that kept Labor in power for another decade; and helped cost him the Liberal leadership in 1989.

Queenslanders started turning against Paul Keating in 1993 and then led the national charge in 1996 to dump his government on its arse. The bared teeth of Queensland voters were on full display: Labor lost eleven of its thirteen seats in that state, its representation plunging to a humiliating rump of just two out of a possible 26 seats.

Then along happened the northern man of the moment, Kevin ('I'm from Queensland and I'm here to help') Rudd, who at the 2007 election restored Labor's vote, confidence, seat tally and place on the government benches. For only the third time in 50 years, Labor recorded a majority of the two-party preferred vote in Queensland, and its seat tally soared by nine—from a miserable six to fifteen out of 29 electorates. Queensland won that election for Rudd, the fourth Queenslander ever to make it to The Lodge.

Only three years later, its pissed-off electors swung heavily against the Gillard Government. It wasn't just that she'd deposed their man—after all, loyalty can only go so far. The opinion polls had been showing for some time that Queensland, of all the states, was the most dissatisfied with the Rudd Government's performance and, even when Rudd deposed his deposer, those disloyal Queenslanders didn't return to the Kev cult at the 2013 election in the slavish manner he had dreamed of. He did narrow the yawning gap that had opened up in 2010 and so saved some of the state's seats; but Queenslanders don't stick like glue if it ain't right, and they didn't give him back the keys to The Lodge.

\* \* \*

The 1996 federal election that introduced Pauline to the world was one of Labor's most humiliating national collapses. At 36 per cent, its primary vote was its lowest since 1934. The 29-seat swing against it was the second-largest federal defeat ever, and the Liberals alone, *sans* Nationals, could have formed majority government with their 75-seat Lower House tally. John Howard swaggered into office with a 45-seat majority—the second largest in our history, surpassed only by Malcolm Fraser's massacre of Whitlam in 1975.

But it wasn't just a passionate craving to kick Labor to the kerb at play. Alarm at globalisation was starting to rumble like a dieter's tummy in Queensland's outer-suburban belly. The effects of Keating's 1991 'recession we had to have' were still being felt with lethal force in industries and households. Pissed-off, turned-off voters were coalescing as a lethal threat against the old parties; they were willing and determined to whack big-party politicians who they perceived as acting out of self-interest, rather than in their interests.

Federal parliamentary researchers, Drs Mark Rodriguez and Scott Brenton, tracked the phenomenon of the breakdown in voter loyalty to the major parties. Unsurprisingly, this was in lockstep with the rise of the polished professional pollie and the blooming of judgmental journalism. In a 2010 paper they noted that in each decade from the 1950s to the 1980s, first preference votes cast for the major parties in the House of Representatives averaged around 92 per cent. In 1987, the major parties attracted a total of 91.8 per cent of the first preference vote; but this dropped sharply to 82.6 per cent in 1990. From thereon in, the major party share plummeted progressively through the floor. Hanson had been sitting in the sweet spot to pick up this disaffected vote.

The media didn't see her coming until she landed with a thud. There'd been some coverage of her expulsion from the Liberal Party and her subsequent comments, but she wasn't really on the national media radar. The Canberra political media was becoming a beast force-fed by the major parties as the era of slick, highly controlled election campaigning accelerated. The campaigns run by both major party leaders were inane magical mystery tours of made-for-TV stunts in cities and at destinations the travelling media weren't informed about until the last minute. They were like SWAT exercises without any pressing threat.

As well, newsrooms started shrinking as traditional media wheezed under the pressure of escalating costs and dwindling consumers for their products. In bygone years media outlets would have had an army of journalists on the road during campaigns, following the leaders and gathering colour pieces. But in 1996, many seasoned political journalists opted to stay in Canberra or at their media organisation's headquarters, coordinating coverage so as to save money and time. In so doing, they were no longer taking the pulse of the electorate. Comment pieces were based on perception rather than knowledge, and much news coverage was guided by opinion polls.

\* \* \*

But in Queensland, Hanson's ballsy middle finger salute to the Liberal powerbrokers who had tried to muzzle her had given her a media leg-up that other candidates would have sold their beloved grannies for. She particularly appealed to voters who were reacting hostilely to the emerging breed of career politician, who didn't speak their language or empathise with their worries.

But there's Ipswich, and then there's Canberra. When she landed awkwardly in the national capital, a place she'd never before visited and knew little about, other politicians welcomed her warily. Some had already publicly rebuked her; others shrugged their shoulders; a few saluted her as an ordinary woman with life experience, who was standing up for the little person and fighting the scourge of political correctness.

MPs knew she had a beef against government-subsidised assistance to Aborigines. Apart from the infamous letter that had led to her Liberal Party expulsion and subsequent election, she'd chucked petrol on the embers just 24 hours after polling day via an incendiary interview with Christopher Dore of *The Australian*. She told him she would be fighting for 'the white community, the immigrants, Italians, Greeks, whoever, it really doesn't matter— anyone apart from the Aboriginals and Torres Strait Islanders'; this sparked another media firestorm and a long-running complaint to the Human Rights Commission, which was eventually dismissed.

That was the sum total of her fellow parliamentarians' knowledge of the new MP for Oxley. She was a drop-in, a small-town wannabe with narrow views who'd lucked her way into the House on the Hill, but who would as quickly wander back to the boondocks dragging a bruised ego.

Very few—except for Nationals Senator Ron Boswell, who'd previously donned armour against the League of Rights in Queensland in the 1980s and suspected Hanson could stir up similarly destructive, but more far-reaching, anger—had any real clue about what was to come. Mainstream politicians were just starting to be infected with tin-ear-itis.

\* \* \*

Hanson's first office appointment was John Pasquarelli, nicknamed 'Kojak' for his bald-headed, imposing presence similar to the title character in the TV series played by Telly Savalas. Pasquarelli had been a member of the PNG Government, a crocodile hunter, an opal miner, a gun-toting punter and a political junkie who could turn a decent colourful phrase.

He was a gun for hire. He'd worked for maverick Queensland Nationals Senator John Stone, and had been up to this time on the staff of the mercurial Independent MP for Kalgoorlie, Graeme Campbell, who had been booted from the ALP in 1995 for consistently breaching Labor policy with inflammatory statements against immigration. When accused of being politically correct for forcing Campbell's expulsion, Keating had retorted in typical style that, of course, it was the correct political thing to do. He was proved to be right in 1998, when Campbell lost his seat.

Having previously delivered rabble-rousing addresses to Australians Against Further Immigration and the far-right League of Rights, Campbell initially got along famously with Hanson. Campbell was an admirer of hers straight off the bat: he could see a damsel in distress. Clearly she needed the towering Kojak to knock a few heads together. 'I saw the dingo-like attack from the media,' he explained helpfully to the *Australian Financial Review*. 'I thought, hell, this girl needs help.' Ever the politician, Campbell also thought she would be a like-minded soul to second his motions. It could have been a marriage made in heaven; but it ended up like so many other of Hanson's relationships, in the ashes of acrimony.

Another office appointment was Barbara Hazelton, a former Liberal Party staffer who would start off as a staunch Hanson loyalist and defender. Pauline once described Barbara as her best friend; but she would ultimately end up on the lengthy list of Ms Hanson's spurned and discarded.

The new member for Oxley wasn't particularly taken with the big bloke Campbell sent her way to help. Looks and appearance mattered. As she nastily pointed out in her scribblings: 'A big man in stature, 1.8 metres tall with a shaved head and, I must say, a big nose. He is what I would call a man's man, definitely not a pretty boy.'

In the echo chamber that reflects the history of Hanson's relationships, she and Pasquarelli would have a spectacular falling-out less than a year into his tenure, resulting in his removal under escort from Parliament House. But before that predictable end, he would shape the MP for Oxley. Pauline has always downplayed his immense contribution to her initial nation-shaking success; she has cultivated a lifelong habit of being determinedly constrained about recognising those who nurture and support her.

\* \* \*

Those of us in the federal parliamentary press gallery at the time recall the energy, dynamism and prowess Pasquarelli brought to his new role. The material he strode around the gallery distributing always carried his large paw prints: her written words echoed his phrasing and inflammatory rhetoric.

He was the type of political operator people outside the bubble—and many within—frown on. He was free of conscience about cause and effect; he gave the impression that the noble calling of civic service was a quaint and faintly ridiculous notion. Pasquarelli simply loved the game. But he knew how to research, and the importance of gathering facts and supporting documentation to give substance to Hanson's narrowcast thought bubbles.

He introduced her to the words and thinking of prominent former politicians and academics that would shape her: historian Professor Geoffrey Blainey's 1980s criticisms of the perils of immigration, particularly Asian; and the delightful bon mots of the fiery National Civic Council and Democratic Labour Party firebrand

Bob Santamaria, whom she credits with inspiring her to write her own maiden speech.

Pasquarelli took her to one of Santamaria's meetings on the night of 28 August. 'As he spoke, nothing could distract me from what he was saying,' she said later. 'I was in awe, and truly impressed with his knowledge and common sense, and found I could do nothing but agree with him.'

Pasquarelli also led her to the work of former Labor leader and White Australia policy supporter Arthur Calwell, and various statements on immigration by Bill Hayden, Andrew Peacock, John Howard and others. He was the political Henry Higgins to a naive Eliza Doolittle. He knew that the fire in her belly and her beliefs were shared by many in the depressed and uncertain pockets of Australia, where she had spent her early years; he knew how to tap into that mood for political gain.

Former Senator Ron Boswell, the longest-serving Nationals senator who positioned himself as the frontline Coalition defender against her, recalls Pasquarelli coming to meet him in Sydney one day. 'He said to me: "Just get out there and attack people. You can get on board, too." He wanted me on board with his thinking. He kept saying: "You know, you should tap into this. Just attack the blacks or the Asians."

'But I said: "You can't just go out and say things, there are consequences. You can't just tell people what you think they want to hear." It was pure populism. He directed her that way, and I think she gets directed by people like him.'

\* \* \*

Her maiden speech was six months in the making. By 10 September 1996, the day the terrified new MP for Oxley was finally ready to deliver it after postponing it three times, Pasquarelli had redrafted the speech four or five times. Another short-lived staffer, Brett Heffernan, had sourced the Asian immigration figures from the Australian Bureau of Statistics on Pasquarelli's instructions, and he takes credit for the immortal phrase about the high level of Asian migration. Pasquarelli says he wrote in black pen at the bottom of the page of statistics: 'If we keep this up, we will be swamped.'

Hanson's telling is that the figures were from the Santamaria rally. Alight with ideas, she'd started handwriting her speech the morning after the 28 August meeting—including the figures which she'd not written down at the time—and gave it to Pasquarelli to 'tidy up'. Only two people know who led who to write what would go down in history as one of the most explosive maiden speeches given in the House of Representatives chamber.

Wearing a neat, black pleated dress with gold buttons she'd bought especially for the occasion, Hanson entered the House of Representatives chamber late on 10 September 1996. Morrie Marsden and Barbara Hazelton were in the public gallery. Only a sprinkling of MPs remained in the chamber. Labor had decided to boycott her speech in protest at her comments about Aborigines. A few Liberals and a healthy quota of Nationals hung around. Her new BFF, Graeme Campbell, sat by her side and, out of loyalty to the small club of outsiders, the two other Independents, Peter Andren and Allan Rocher, kept close.

At 5.15 p.m. following a vanilla contribution from the new MP for North Sydney, Joe Hockey, she got the nod from Deputy Speaker, Nationals MP Garry Nehl. Although her voice had been tidied up by five hours of public speaking training, it still quavered with fright. She rose to her feet and dropped the mother of all bombs.

The Australia that Hanson/Pasquarelli wanted should be fortressed against multiculturalism, Asians, interference by the

United Nations. It was isolationism writ large, scripted for an audience of frightened and disenchanted Aussies pining for the safety of an uncomplicated yesteryear they remembered wistfully, where neighbours had easy-to-pronounce names and jobs were plentiful.

But first, those underclass Aborigines, who really aren't. 'Along with millions of Australians, I am fed up to the back teeth with the inequalities that are being promoted by the government and paid for by the taxpayer under the assumption that Aboriginals are the most disadvantaged people in Australia . . . this nation is being divided into black and white, and the current system encourages this. I am fed up with being told "This is our land". Well, where the hell do I go? I was born here, and so were my parents and children.'

The Aboriginal and Torres Strait Islander Commission (ATSIC) was a 'failed, hypocritical and discriminatory' body. Native title and compensation to Aboriginal people for land was a lawyer's con. Child support and the Family Law Act were social engineering failures. The government's sale of Telstra and Qantas were policies clearly devised by economists who she wouldn't let handle her grocery shopping.

Snuck into the middle was the attack on immigration and multiculturalism. Clearly borrowing from Professor Blainey's bomb-chucking Rotary Club speech in Warrnambool in 1984, she stated: 'I and most Australians want our immigration policy radically reviewed and that of multiculturalism abolished. I believe we are in danger of being swamped by Asians. Between 1984 and 1985, 40 percent of all migrants coming into this country were of Asian origin. They have their own culture and religion, form ghettos and do not assimilate.

'Of course, I will be called racist but, if I can invite whom I want into my home, then I should have the right to have a say in who comes into my country.' Five years later, John Howard would borrow the sentiment for his 2001 election campaign slogan: 'We will decide who comes to this country, and the circumstances in which they come.'

The firestorm over Hanson's Asian immigration comments obscured what was just as strident a condemnation of migration from other countries. Without explicitly saying so, Hanson emphatically put the case for a return to the White Australia policy, dumped less than two decades before her election.

The tidal wave of attention to the Asian angle swallowed attention to these words: 'Japan, India, Burma, Ceylon and every new African nation are fiercely anti-white and anti-one another,' she said, quoting Arthur Calwell. 'Do we want or need any of these people here? I am one red-blooded Australian who says no and who speaks for 90% of Australians. I have no hesitation in echoing the words of Arthur Calwell.'

Her other panaceas for Australia's woes have receded into the obscurity of history. They included compulsory national service (Pasquarelli and Hanson's mother, Norah, would both claim credit for that policy), an end to foreign aid and reducing business tax to single figures. She would later refine the latter into a daft, roundly ridiculed flat 2 per cent tax rate policy, which still sat as policy in the One Nation platform up until the 2016 federal election. The hands of time move on, but many of Hanson's policies proudly stay put.

Before she was done, a flag-waving flourish was in order. 'I consider myself just an ordinary Australian who wants to keep this great country strong and independent, and my greatest desire is to see all Australians treat each other as equals, as we travel together towards the new century,' she concluded, after outlining ways that white Australians could remain more equal than anyone else in the land of opportunity.

*Hear, hear!* cheered the disconsolate in neglected suburbs, jamming parliament's switchboard and flooding her electorate and parliamentary office with letters of support. The media flared up like rockets in only one of two directions: for or agin. The shock jocks in the capital cities turned her into a celebrity, either through philosophical affinity or a drive for ratings.

\* \* \*

There were glaring errors of fact in her speech, including the all-important percentage of Asian-born Australians, and she immediately acknowledged she was wrong. But the attention she created in the media was like a feeding frenzy in a fish pond: intense, lightning quick and over in a flash.

In the outside world, however, it was a different matter. She had lit a fuse with a very long wick. She became an overnight sensation, with everyone claiming a piece of her. Thousands wanted to donate to her, and did: cheques flooded into her electorate office. Bags of fan mail, running at six sacks a day at its height, kept Australia's posties working overtime.

The astute politicians saw the danger quickly. Kim Beazley, who had become Labor leader following Paul Keating's post-election resignation in March, called his troops in to discuss her. 'I said to the Whip: when she comes into the chamber and speaks, there will only ever be two people in the chamber—the duty shadow minister, and the Whip. And we stuck to that,' he reflects. 'But the Nationals would always go in. We knew we needed to send a clear message to our supporters, because some of our supporters were sympathetic.'

Beazley—who his many supporters believe was the best Prime Minister Australia Never Had, and who was mowed down in 2006 by Kevin Rudd's ambitions—was alarmed at the strength of support for Hanson's views among Labor's traditional base, and startled that the sympathetic Nationals couldn't see she competed against them for votes. He urged them to follow Labor's lead and vacate the chamber when she spoke.

'I said to the Nationals, "If you support her, if you go in there, then you're going to find a lot of your supporters will think that's ok." I told them: "She's eating your lunch, not the Liberals. She's strong in the bush, in your areas." A lot hadn't thought that through. I think they thought erroneously that if they went in there to show support, it would help them. Ronny Boswell understood that if you fed this woman, she'd eat you alive.'

Ronny Boswell did indeed understand it well. The former small business owner, who ultimately served 31 years in the Upper House and was respected and endeared across the political ravine, had a good nose for Queenslanders' whims and peculiarities. No stranger to tackling the extremes that lurked in the hinterlands of his state, he was a strong Christian, family-values man who believed in the goodness of Australians and in our future as an egalitarian, compassionate and fair country.

Boswell was horrified at what Hanson had ignited, and privately aghast at the way Howard tiptoed around her. The importance of converting the PM to his way of thinking and combatting her influence became his twin goals. He noted as such when he gave his valedictory speech on 17 June 2014.

'Politics is an honourable calling, but will remain so only if politicians have the courage of their convictions,' he told a packed chamber. 'In 1988, I tackled the League of Rights, a far right-wing, anti-Semitic organisation I saw as trying to exert influence over the churches and other areas of society. For me, this was a defining moment: to be taken seriously, you have to stand for something. In the fight of my life, against Pauline Hanson, I risked everything to stand up against her aggressive, narrow view of Australia. Defeating Pauline Hanson and One Nation . . . has been my greatest political achievement.'

Winning over the new PM would take a bit more than Boswell's influence. Howard had flirted with the notion of reducing Asian immigration in 1988, just as quickly retreating after his party and large sections of the media slapped him around. He was unsure how to respond to Hanson. He had sympathy for her views and knew she had tapped a possibly powerful voter vein. So he pirouetted around her, musing out loud about how she 'made sense' on some issues; and how refreshing it was that 'political correctness' had been untethered from a shackled society and people like Hanson could openly express themselves.

In 1988 Boswell had made a memorable speech to the Senate, in which he exposed the way in which the tentacles of the League of Rights in Queensland were reaching into the churches and regional and remote communities. At that time his high voltage agitation against them—even personally distributing anti-League literature in churches—had been effective in puncturing their tyres before they'd gained too much traction. But the well-funded League and other similar fringe groups lingered, like cockroaches after a nuclear storm, waiting to re-emerge.

Inadvertent or not, Hanson's raw, rough brand of populist Australia-first rhetoric would provide a powerful vehicle for the League's views. Beazley also noted strong sympathy for her among Labor's traditional blue-collar constituency. Both he and Boswell knew she had the potential to be more destructive than anything the League and its ilk could ever hope to muster: after all, she was an elected member of parliament with a national platform. And once the media cottoned on to the extraordinary impact in the electorate of her maiden speech, she was trailed like a Hollywood celebrity almost 24/7. High-profile supporters, such as influential businessman and Liberal Party donor John Elliott, added to the growing list of public figures prepared to out themselves as Hanson supporters.

But to Boswell she was someone whose simplistic, unaccountable ideology and destructive anti-Asian views would prove divisive for the Australia he knew, particularly his constituency—small business owners, farmers, fishers, average working-class families and those struggling to have a decent crack at a good life.

He was a lone voice in his party for some months. As his long-time researcher Joanne Newbery recalls: 'We had a big problem in that most people in the Liberal Party wanted to attack her, and in the Nationals we wanted to get into bed with her. Ron had to walk this tightrope. It was very stressful. Everything had to be judged very carefully—the tone, the words, so we couldn't be accused of attacking her personally.'

Lone warriors on the conservative side, Boswell and his staff threw themselves into their task with gusto. Every time Pauline popped her head up, they whacked her with facts. Every time she made a call for something she couldn't deliver on, they called her out.

Newbery was responsible for drawing up a list of all the groups on dangerous fringes of the far-right that they believed supported Hanson financially and morally; they tracked the extreme policies from which she and her staff cherry-picked. Newbery kept a meticulous chart on a large white bed sheet, which she and Boswell added to in bold black pen the more they researched. In the centre was Hanson. Their task was given a boost when another of Pauline's short-stay staffers, Jeff Babb, claimed at the tail end of 1996 that 'League of Rights style groups' had 'established footholds in her support organisations'.

From the get-go, Hanson was off and running around the country basking in her popularity and gathering support. Pasquarelli pushed her in front of crowds from the east to the west coast. In Queensland alone, more than a dozen support groups emerged in the last quarter of 1996. Gold Coast businessman Bruce Whiteside, with whom Hanson would naturally go on to have a spectacular falling-out, led the charge.

A phenomenon had been born. It was a remarkable trajectory for a nobody from Queensland who had, without warning, lit a simple but powerful anti-immigration, anti-Asian fuse that few MPs saw coming.

But was she—is she—for real, or a clever political invention with the sole goal of political infamy?

\* \* \*

In his 1998 book about his fraught nine months in her employ, Pasquarelli revealed that Hanson was not particularly opposed to Asian immigration after all. Indeed, she didn't much care if Asians outnumbered Anglo-Australians. There was one particular moment when this became crystal clear to him.

It was December 1996. Hanson was making some last-minute changes to a speech to parliament on immigration that Pasquarelli had written for her. Another staffer was typing her amendments into the prepared speech and Pasquarelli was proofing it. 'I was scrolling line by line when, suddenly, some words caught my eye,' he wrote in *The Pauline Hanson Story by the Man Who Knows*. 'Like a scud missile, seconds before obliterating its target, the words leapt out of the computer screen and my eyes were riveted on them. I couldn't believe what I was seeing.'

The words she had inserted read: 'I wouldn't mind if there were more Asians in Australia than Anglo-European Australians, as long as they [the Asians] spoke English.'

Pasquarelli gagged. 'In one simple sentence, Pauline Hanson was poised to commit political hari-kari. In one sentence she had just become a fervent preacher for the Asianisation of Australia. In one sentence she had jettisoned overboard her policies on multiculturalism and immigration. In one fell sentence, she had totally and utterly repudiated her "swamped by Asians" statement, converting Asianisation into a desirable goal . . .'

When Pasquarelli remonstrated with her, he says she didn't respond or seem to understand why she couldn't say it. However, he got his way and her words were deleted; the softer, multicultural, Asian-friendly Pauline disappeared before she showed that face to the public, never to be seen again.

The episode rattled him. 'Had Pauline's twenty-two word political suicide note been a Freudian slip that exposed what she really thought? Was I really the sinister puppeteer depicted by the media who, in the end, had pulled the strings just too hard? We will never really know.'

Pasquarelli wouldn't be around long enough to find out. Their relationship crashed on 9 December 1996, just nine months after he'd arrived in her office as her first in a long line of puppet masters. The usual fireworks of accusations and counter-accusations of disloyalty and duplicity were hurled between the pair, resulting in the comic-book spectacle of the fierce giant of a man being marched out of parliament by a couple of faux coppers who usually do little more than check the legitimacy of entry passes.

What Pasquarelli didn't know was that David Oldfield, who would go on to form One Nation the following April with Pauline and David Ettridge, was waiting in the wings to take his place. He'd been there in the shadows since the evening of Hanson's maiden speech.

That night Hanson had kicked on after dinner with Barbara Hazelton to La Grange bar in upmarket Manuka (Morrie had bowed out early). This was the place for politicians, staffers and journalists to see and be seen—drink in hand, fake smile on face. Even then, Hanson had an eye for the theatre of politics.

When a drunken Liberal staffer began haranguing her as 'white trash' and 'a slut', Oldfield intervened. By his own account, he cast himself as the rescuer of a damsel in distress, defending her honour. But it would be some months before he officially stepped into Pasquarelli's over-large shoes. The interim Svengali would be the experienced political operator, David Thomas, who would last only months and would quickly become very loud and vocal in his condemnation of Hanson's character flaws.

In the meantime, while still working in Liberal MP Tony Abbott's office, David Oldfield was pulling her strings from the sidelines. Much later, after he became yet another addition to her ever-growing caryard of relationship wreckages, Hanson would say she rued the day she ever laid eyes on Oldfield. The feeling was murderously mutual.

## Chapter 4
# THE BIRTH OF ONE NATION

KISSING A NAZI SKINHEAD at a public rally isn't a picture opportunity many Australian politicians would leap at. Babies are generally viewed as more appealing than bald-headed thugs. But such was Hanson's hubris and soaring popularity that, as she launched herself into a national White Australia-inspired tour following her maiden speech, she had no qualms smooching and saluting for the cameras whoever she wished, whenever she wished.

Trailed by a caravan of drooling media eager to chronicle her every utterance, she was bulletproof—the super-star of her own reality show. The sack loads of fan mail that swamped her office and kept her, in Pasquarelli's words, 'wasting hours of valuable time that should have been spent working on the job of being an effective politician' were starting to turn her head. She was hypnotised by her fans.

'I tried to impress on her that reading the letters served no meaningful purpose—after going through the first hundred or so, the basic message of support was coming through loud and clear,' he said later. She ignored him. She was, he reflected, 'starting to like being a star'.

No matter that she was supposed to be representing the good people of Oxley in the people's palace in Canberra, not bouncing around the country on the taxpayer's dollar feeding her fans and raising her profile for the next phase of her voyage into infamy. No matter that in the aftermath of her volatile maiden speech the Australian Human Rights Commission received a record number of complaints of violence and racial hatred against Asians and Aborigines. She took no responsibility for what she had unleashed, nor did she attempt to assuage its violent outcome.

The adulation must have been dizzying; she was mobbed wherever she went. She exuded super-star. But was she thinking of expanding her efforts? Not at all. She told the *Gold Coast Bulletin* on 26 September 1996 she had no intention of capitalising on her overnight stardom by forming a political party. She would run again for Oxley as an Independent. People were 'fed up' with (political) parties, she stated.

Six weeks after her maiden speech, on 30 October, federal parliament sprung into half-hearted action to try and contain the Hanson national contagion. It passed a limp motion reaffirming a number of important commitments: equality for all Australians, a non-discriminatory immigration policy, the process of reconciliation with Aboriginal and Torres Strait Islanders and a culturally diverse nation. It concluded with the grand but hollow gesture of condemning racial tolerance 'as incompatible with the kind of society we are and want to be'.

A reluctant Howard, intent on harnessing for himself and his government some of that good old-fashioned Hanson electoral magic, moved and spoke first to the motion. It was a classy performance of double-speak, spruiking restrainedly the virtues of a tolerant society while bemoaning political correctness and the tendency of hand wringers towards a 'black armband' view of the sins of our past.

He damned with faint praise some of the most significant milestones in Australia's historical progression from racist backwater colony to sophisticated, relatively harmonious polyglot society:

The abolition of the White Australia Policy in 1966 under the Liberal prime ministership of Harold Holt represented a very significant cultural and attitudinal change on the part of the Australian people. I accept that it was supported at the time by people across the political spectrum. I also accept that it was not at that time greeted with universal acclaim but I believe it gradually won very strong acceptance . . .

We can within our ranks have legitimate debate about the size of our immigration program. There is a different attitude towards immigration now than there was in the 1950s and 1960s. All of us, whatever our political views, should take account of that. You cannot isolate the sense of insecurity and anxiety that people at a time of relatively high unemployment feel from considerations of levels of immigration . . .

This motion also says something about our attitude towards the Aboriginal and Torres Strait Islander people of Australia, the original Australians and first inhabitants of this continent of ours, however one would wish to describe it. There will continue to be debate and there will continue to be sharp differences of opinion between the government and the Australian Labor Party about the appropriate policies to respond to Aboriginal and Torres Strait Islander people . . .

I think there has been a wholly disproportionate reaction by too many people in too many areas of Australian society to one particular speech. I find it rather interesting that I pick up the newspapers, I watch the television, I listen to the radio and I hear constant talk about the deeply divisive debate on immigration which is going on within the Australian community . . .

A few weeks ago I made a speech to the Queensland division of the Liberal Party, which subsequently attracted some attention. I do not recant, retract or take away one syllable of what I said during that speech. I might be permitted to say something to the House about that speech. I remind the House that, having said that I believed we had entered an era of clear and more open debate in the Australian community, I supported the right of Australians to participate in a vigorous fashion in open political debate.

I then went on to say that freedom of speech carries with it a responsibility on all of those who exercise that freedom to do so in a tolerant and moderate fashion and to not convert the newfound freedom, if I may put it that way, into a vehicle for using needlessly insensitive and intolerant language . . .

Howard didn't utter the word 'multicultural' once. He didn't mention Hanson's name. There was no passionate tub-thumping, no vigorous advocacy for Australians who had been targeted and abused because of Hanson and her supporters who were seeping into the nation's psyche and terrifying many overseas-born lovers of their new country.

The intent of much of what the Prime Minister said was not audible to the human ear, but then again the 'mainstream' of Howard's imagination—middle-class white Australians—wasn't the target audience.

The Prime Minister started sending people to sleep at 3.06 p.m. and concluded twenty minutes later. And did Pauline care? Hell, no. She and Kojak had taken to the skies at 2.30 p.m. to gladhand and be adored by the fruit and vege stallholders at the Footscray Market in Melbourne the following morning. This was a far more rewarding way to fill in her time than turning up for the job that taxpayers paid her handsomely to perform.

The tokenistic motion in parliament indicated that most MPs were like pet pooches relaxing on the verandah the way they treated the Hanson phenomenon: one eye closed, the other only lazily alert to possible danger. That would change within days.

On Melbourne Cup Day, November 1996, the *Bulletin* magazine carried an explosive poll conducted by Morgan Research showing Hanson's support was in the stratosphere. As the National Affairs writer at the time for the magazine (which until the 1950s proudly carried the cover slogan 'Australia for the White Man'), I wrote the accompanying story.

A few weeks earlier our editorial team had sat around pondering how best to tap into what Hanson had kindled in the electorate. To us the extraordinary polling figures that rolled in from Morgan posed a bold question: What if she led her own party and ran candidates for the Senate?

My article started: 'A Pauline Hanson-led Party that fielded candidates for the Senate would command 18% of the national vote and sweep the Australian Democrats aside to decisively hold the balance of power in the upper house, according to an exclusive *Bulletin* Morgan poll conducted last week.' She would win seven seats in any half-Senate election, and up to twelve in a double dissolution election, in both cases delivering to her party the balance of power. Not bad.

Hanson's divisive policy positions were popular: 66 per cent of respondents agreed with her call to stop immigration, and 51 per cent agreed that Aborigines received funding and opportunities not available to other Australians. The fact that she had majority support for those positions among both Coalition and Labor voters would have made both Howard and Beazley wince. They both knew it, of course, but now it was as easy to see as a bare baby's bum on a crowded bus.

The Morgan/*Bulletin* press release issued the day before publication, in order to generate publicity and increase readership, contained in the headline the words 'The Pauline Hanson Movement'.

Pasquarelli and Hanson leapt on the figures like thoroughbreds lunging to the line to clinch the million-dollar Melbourne Cup. Pasquarelli gave his boss two options: thank her supporters across Australia for the overwhelming endorsement, but announce she was restricting herself to the people of Oxley; or convert the support into a political organisation with the aim of winning the Senate seats the poll predicted.

No contest, really. Seizing the Senate was a worthy goal. The day after publication, Pasquarelli obtained registration forms from the Australian Electoral Commission and prepared to make her a political rival to the big guns. The Democrats and Greens would look at the support for her newfound party with awe.

And he didn't even have to crack a frown to come up with a catchy name. Our magazine had given it to him, he claimed with glee in *The Pauline Hanson Story by the Man Who Knows*: 'The Morgan organisation's press release for its poll, published in the *Bulletin*, referred to the "Pauline Hanson Movement". There it was plain and simple—just Pauline's name and no mention of that dreaded word "Party".'

The organisation would have members, but no formal branch structure. Pasquarelli says he advised her to set up the Pauline Hanson Movement Trust Fund, and to organise its financial affairs properly. The pair hit on Australia Day 1997 as the formal launch. But, before he could yell 'Eureka flag!', Pasquarelli was shoved out the door.

Within months David Oldfield, the Tony Abbott staffer who'd brandished his sword in defence of the damsel at La Grange and who'd been plotting with Pauline behind Abbott and Pasquarelli's backs ever since, would officially become her new controller. In reality he'd been by her side—and, she would publicly claim later, in her bed—plotting and scheming ever since he played Sir Galahad at the political junkies' bar. Oldfield has strenuously denied that he had an affair with Pauline.

\* \* \*

Oldfield is best known these days as one half of the most disliked couple on reality TV. Like his former red-headed political boss, he gravitated to loud public displays on TV and radio after he disappeared from political life, which was to include a post-Pauline eight-year gig in the New South Wales Upper House, where he did little and impressed no one. Next came stints as an obnoxious shock jock on commercial Sydney radio—gigs usually reserved for loudmouths who don't have the guts to try for a political career—and a few inglorious political commentary gigs. Then he finally flicked the switch to low-rent vaudeville.

One of his 2018 outings was to happily humiliate himself on Channel Ten's *I'm a Celebrity, Get Me Out of Here* alongside his wife Lisa, who had already made a bad name by playing herself as a foul-mouthed uber-bitch on the trashy *Real Housewives of Sydney*. The sophistication of the pair's public image is best summed up in a naked head-and-shoulders picture she posted to Instagram in 2017 with the classy caption: 'Gave the old bloke a sympathy shag . . . to be fair, I haven't eaten in a week . . . and just wanted something warm inside me.'

The *I'm a Celebrity* series relies on flying a cast of ageing fourth-rate nobodies into a 'jungle' in Kruger National Park, South Africa. Here they obediently interact like sociological studies in a human zoo. They eat grubs and do other silly stunts 24/7 under a glare of brightly lit cameras in a made-for-TV campsite, dining on miserable rations of jungle food. To this unappealing mix starving drop-ins are added, kitted out in different matching outfits, jauntily tied at the throat with a kerchief or a glaringly obvious African-themed beads-and-seeds necklace. Must have a helluva wardrobe department hiding in that rugged, scary jungle. The only redeemable feature of the show is the winner takes home $100,000 for his or her chosen charity.

Given its lowball approach, it was a damn good effort for the Oldfields in their first full belligerent hour of presence as campsite 'intruders', whatever that means (don't they just walk on set from their dressing rooms?), to send the already lackadaisical ratings through the floor. Their debut episode recorded 489,000 viewers and was the first time the viewership for any episode had dipped below the mid-500,000s in any of the three seasons of the show aired to that time.

It was worth watching, with one eye closed and a hand cupped over the other, to get a glimpse of the bloke who helped mangle the One Nation experiment and propel Pauline Hanson to number one spot on the ledger of political notoriety. Seen scheming with his Mrs in a secret huddle outside camp, mysteriously captured on multiple cameras and with sound so clear you'd swear they were wearing mics on their Tarzan and Jane clobber, they were plotting ways to get under the skin of their 'snowflake, social justice warrior' campmates.

But it was just a game of exploitation and one-upmanship, wasn't it? Come to think of it, hadn't David always played the winner-takes-all game?

When Oldfield and Hanson created their political double act, they were plotting to win the electoral lottery. Hanson had always had her sights set high—the very highest. The prime ministership was a dream, had always been a dream—once, she'd naively asked Pasquarelli if an Independent could become PM.

The thing about games, though, is they can go badly wrong, have unintended consequences. All this, and more, awaited the cosily small cast of Hanson's very first celebrity show as they schemed to set up One Nation.

\*   \*   \*

Five weeks after her maiden speech and a week before Pasquarelli and Hanson's lightbulb moment on Melbourne Cup Day, a Gold Coast bloke called Bruce Whiteside launched a network of supporters for the flame-haired Queensland Independent. The 64-year-old New Zealander had been politically active on the glitter strip for years objecting to what he perceived as a foreign buy-up of Australian interests, and had developed skills as a grassroots networker. He was passionately proud of the country he adopted as home in the late 1970s, and wasn't hesitant about letting his views be known publicly.

Whiteside set about establishing the infrastructure for an energetic advocacy group. To bolster Hanson's profile, he printed off T-shirts, flyers and car bumper stickers proclaiming 'I'm a Pauline Hanson Supporter'. The Pauline Hanson Support Movement (PHSM) was launched on 28 October 1996, with membership cards issued at $5 a pop. Pasquarelli knew a support movement was in the making; he'd noted Whiteside's efforts even before the official launch. Protective of his own power and position, the big man watched the pensioner on the Gold Coast warily.

The *Gold Coast Bulletin* attended the launch at the Albert Waterways Community Centre. An impressive 850 people swarmed in, and 125 immediately signed up as supporters. National media picked up the yarn; the movement took off like 'a bull', Whiteside would later recall in an unpublished book he wrote about his troubled time trying to support the woman he thought was speaking for average Aussies like him.

Whiteside applied for incorporation of the Movement. In the interim, he and a handful of others ran it as if it was incorporated. Minutes, notes, resolutions and independent financial records were established and kept. He claims he sought Hanson's permission to use her name by phone in November 1996, and she had no objection. When the Office of Corporate Affairs tried to confirm that agreement with her office, the fun began.

'From time to time we approached the Ipswich office and we were always told the same thing,' wrote Whiteside. '"Pauline's workload was so heavy that it had simply been overlooked." However, it appeared that Hanson was so emotionally infatuated with David Oldfield that she abdicated the essence of loyalty that she so stridently demanded of everyone else.

'John Pasquarelli had prevented Hanson's name from being used because he believed unscrupulous operators would exploit it. Later he admitted as much, but Hanson never took advice from Pasquarelli anyway. The real obstruction was coming from the unknown David Oldfield, of whom Pasquarelli was blissfully unaware.'

In mid-November Hanson and her secretary, Barbara Hazelton, travelled to Whiteside's home in the Gold Coast suburb of Miami to meet him, his wife Iris and supporters. It would be the first of a few trips Hanson and her new female bestie made to Miami as the Movement took off across the country.

The Movement's Gold Coast based committee built the national support base over the next few months, appointing recruiters in most states and working around the clock. They sent out thousands of letters in response to inquiries, with Hanson's maiden speech attached. The work was done by a core group of three or four, and a dozen or so other enthusiastic volunteers who were steadily building an influential national supporter network.

The committee funded the Movement. As the demand for leaflets, bumper stickers, membership tickets, T-shirts and other paraphernalia escalated, so too did the costs. A PHSM newspaper was in the pipeline, with the first edition forecast at a 10,000-copy print run. People were generous with their donations of both time and money.

'Hanson's attitude to those who worked their fingers to the bone—and there was a whole legion of them—was that "they did not have to do it",' Whiteside wrote.

On Hanson's request, in early February Whiteside and twenty of the core PHSM Gold Coast headquarters volunteers put on a dinner for David Ettridge, a smooth-talking bloke who'd suddenly bobbed up as a behind-the-scenes adviser. He'd yet to be paraded on any public stage; he was still a shadow behind the set.

Halfway through the evening, Ettridge dropped a bombshell. Pauline was going to launch her own party, called One Nation. Whiteside recalled him saying: 'There is only one person in charge from now on, and that is myself. This is the way it has to be.

We do not and cannot succeed with an independent organisation. It has to be understood that all of you will take your orders from me. When I say all, I mean from Pauline down. Pauline will be marketed; she will be sold as a commercial product.'

Ettridge explained that One Nation would be orchestrated by a shadowy figure codenamed 'Mr X' and the headquarters would be moved to Manly in Sydney. It was all very cloak-and-dagger and pompously conspiratorial.

Mr X would later be revealed as Oldfield, but at this time he was still drawing a salary as an adviser to Tony Abbott. Given Oldfield's future Instagram notoriety, it seems apt that One Nation's first office digs in Manly—established by Oldfield and conveniently around the corner from Abbott's electoral office—was situated above a sleazy adult sex shop.

On the night this future scenario was foreshadowed, Whiteside exploded and called Ettridge a conman, screaming at him that the Movement couldn't be owned, couldn't be controlled. It was separate, independent.

At the time, there were 6000 paid-up members of the Pauline Hanson Support Movement, with 39 branches across the country, $12,000 in the special PHSM bank account and hundreds of inquiries a week pouring in to its headquarters at Whiteside's private residence in the beachside suburb of Miami.

It was influential, growing and valuable to someone with the intention to launch a new national party. But Whiteside and his committee were, at that stage, wearing rose-coloured goggles.

In a phone call in mid-February designed to soothe Whiteside's fears, Ettridge asked him for a list of the names of supporters, allegedly to give Pauline some idea of the size of her support. Whiteside initially refused; but then he relented and on 18 February, temporarily mollified and wanting to be cooperative, he sent a floppy disc with 539 names on it to Ettridge at the Manly address. The list didn't include any interstate members and was received on Thursday the 20th.

Three days later, Ettridge, Hanson and Oldfield met at Sydney Airport and drew up a document about the formation of 'Pauline Hanson's One Nation'. All three signed it—curiously, on 28 April. Whiteside provides a copy of the document in his unpublished book. It appointed Hanson as founder and first president; Oldfield as national campaign director; and Ettridge as national director. The document included the following as part of Ettridge's duties: 'Manage the support group, arrange full accountability for each branch and the transition of support movement members to party members.' This was despite Whiteside's strong objection to Hanson and Ettridge attempting to hijack the Movement for a party political purpose.

By 6 March Whiteside, his mental health suffering after battling with both Ettridge and key members of his committee, attended his last PHSM meeting. A day later Hanson signed the incorporation papers for the Movement, months on from when Whiteside first received her verbal agreement to use her name.

Within weeks Hanson and Ettridge had forced the resignation of most of the old committee members and called for nominations for executive positions for the new body, which carried the same name as that founded by Whiteside but now with an 'Incorporated' attached. Hanson became President; Ettridge and former PHSM executive member, Paul Trewartha, became joint Vice-Presidents. One Nation was registered as a political party with the Australian Electoral Commission just one week after the incorporation of the Movement.

A Gold Coast branch of the new association was established, and was immediately ordered to organise the 11 April launch in Ipswich of Pauline Hanson's One Nation, using funds in the old Movement's kitty. Even though Whiteside had washed his hands of the new outfit, his wife Iris remained deeply involved and planning meetings for the launch were still held at the Whiteside home.

One night, at the height of this feverish planning activity, Iris took a distressing phone call from Barbara Hazelton. She was told that under no circumstances would Pauline countenance her husband attending the launch.

Whiteside had cultivated media contacts over the previous months. Insulted by his exclusion, he promptly gave an interview to Greg Roberts of *The Sydney Morning Herald*, who blew the whistle on the planning for the launch. Whiteside told Roberts: 'The support movement has been hijacked by a politician and parasitic hangers-on and that makes me extremely angry. To mention the words "political party" will be absolutely fatal to the support she has been getting.' Whiteside described Hanson as delusional.

Animus towards Whiteside exploded. He was ostracised and stories questioning his mental stability spread through the media and the networks like black ink on a white carpet. The committee was ordered to isolate and abandon him. Ettridge wrote him an eviscerating letter that included the line: 'If you have any dignity, you will now withdraw and have nothing more to do with our organisation and we will have nothing more to do with you.' Where the formal date usually sits on the top right-hand corner, Ettridge had typed: 'April Fool's Day 1997'.

The committee terminated Whiteside's membership by letter dated 3 April, effective from 17 April. The dates bookended the launch of Hanson's sparkling new political entity, built on the sweat, tears and loyalty of the Pauline Hanson Support Movement.

Whiteside, like so many who would come after him, was a crushed man. The brutal political machine that was Pauline Hanson Inc. had mowed him down. He was the first, but would by no means be the last.

Much later, after she too had been despatched to the vast wilderness where Hanson's ex-friends were rapidly piling up like stenching bodies on a battlefield, Barbara Hazelton would publicly decry the skulduggery that Hanson, Ettridge and Oldfield perpetrated on the loyalists who created the Movement.

*     *     *

While a brace of police kept a weather eye on hundreds of noisy protestors, Pauline Hanson's One Nation was launched on 11 April 1997 before 400 ticketed fans at Ipswich Town Hall. Membership tickets of the old Movement were still handed out to new recruits.

The Hanson at the launch was not the Hanson of the federal election or of her first tentative months in parliament. She had been primped, prepped and made marketable by a slick professional. Her polished language was markedly different to the raw emotion of the Pasquarelli/Hanson maiden speech.

It had none of the rambling passion of the letter she wrote to the newspaper that precipitated her disendorsement from the Liberal Party, or her simple but strong stump speeches delivered to throngs of devotees after her maiden speech. Consecutive sentences using the skilled political speechwriter's trick of repetition anchored the presentation.

> We, all of us here tonight, and millions of people across Australia, can celebrate at last there is the chance for change.
>
> The chance to finally rid ourselves of the inequity that has grown from years of political correctness . . .

The chance to stand against those who have betrayed our country, and would destroy our identity by forcing upon us the cultures of others . . .

The chance to turn this country around, revitalise our industry, restore our ANZAC spirit and our national pride . . .

The chance to make sure the Australia we have known, loved and fought to preserve will be inherited intact, by our children, and the generations that follow them.

There were the stirring calls to arms in short, sharp sentences laced with adrenaline-pumping rhetoric that would have made Churchill proud for its fight-'em-on-the-beaches language:

Tonight we start to push back.

It's a mammoth task that lies ahead, but we cannot step lightly, even though we tread where our enemies are waiting.

We must be resolute and unflinching.

We must not be slowed by the many obstacles that will be thrown in our path.

Ladies and gentlemen, who of you will not join this fight? Who of you would not stand up for your country?

In the crowd was a bespectacled, suited bloke, standing out among the retirees and blue-collar workers like a blackfella at a Cronulla Beach Australia Day bash. It was David Oldfield, who would later take credit for every word she uttered that night. Indeed, he would take credit for all Hanson's thoughts, words, the party, the product. He had as much arrogance as the whole Australian cricket team, but ultimately as much stupidity as Stephen Smith in the March 2018 Third Test against South Africa.

Hanson gushed with thanks to her parents and Ettridge. But the hard workers of the Pauline Hanson Support Movement didn't rate a mention, even though they were sitting in the hall, had been the worker ants for the event and had built the foundation that birthed the party.

Bruce Whiteside later wrote:

> The very least that Hanson could have done was personally thank them. She didn't, and that in my view negates any claims of integrity and principle that she might lay claim to. Class always shines through. This night it was nowhere to be seen. I know that the team here was deeply slighted, but what none of them knew was that they had served their purpose.
>
> One Nation had been launched on the back of the people's movement. It had cost Hanson nothing, had provided a platform, a membership and most of all the financial funds to put in place the mechanisms for the printing of money, purportedly to build a political party.

But even though he had been royally done over by Hanson and her new henchmen, Whiteside was still unwilling to hold her as accountable as she should have been. 'Ettridge and Oldfield have known exactly what they have been doing, from day one and the interests of Pauline Hanson was [sic] not it.' He added darkly: 'Hanson and I were simply used by predatory forces. In a word we were naive in the ways of political bastardry . . .'

Hanson, Pasquarelli, Ettridge and Oldfield would go on to paint a very different picture of those days, despite the documented evidence presented by Whiteside in his unpublished book. They portrayed Whiteside in a variety of ways: either as a star-struck follower of Hanson; as someone she had instructed to establish a support group and who subsequently got too big for his boots; as a limelight-seeker who used Hanson to push his own pet beefs about foreign acquisitions in Australia; or as a media groupie who loved to see his name up in lights.

Registration of Pauline Hanson's One Nation as a political party under the *Commonwealth Electoral Act 1918* was effected on 27 June 1997. While it looked at the time as if its future was as bright as a brilliant Queensland sunrise, like asbestos in the walls it would only be when the House of Hanson collapsed that the deadliness of its materials would be noticed.

\* \* \*

David Oldfield officially resigned from Tony Abbott's staff to become Hanson's new political adviser on 20 April, telling his boss he was going to 'a job in marketing'. At least that part was true. Ettridge waved goodbye to World Vision as its fundraiser on 1 April, and officially took up with Hanson 24 hours later. Both men, while employed full-time by their previous bosses, had worked tirelessly for Hanson. As far as the best of political double-dealing goes, it was world's best practice.

David Thomas, who had been the stop-gap adviser after Pasquarelli, was shoved out the door and vacated the senior adviser's chair for Oldfield. But Thomas was no pushover, and no intellectual slouch. He'd worked for the batty, but politically bright, MP for Kennedy, Bob Katter, and also been a staffer for Liberal MP Warren Entsch. He'd go on to continue to work as a skilled strategist in state and federal politics and in private consultancies long after Pauline bit the dust the first time around, showing that the people she discarded were generally a lot better and more organised at politics than she was.

While Thomas had been hired as a seat-warmer until Oldfield got there, at the time he hadn't known the name of the person whose seat he was warming. He had been aware that Hanson had

had daily contact with someone known only as 'David O'. But when Thomas read in the *Sun-Herald* on Sunday, 11 May that David O was David Oldfield (not a particularly clever camouflage), and that he had been working for, and on the payroll of, Abbott until two days prior to the story breaking, Thomas was horrified and decided against staying on her staff in any capacity.

Furious, he decided to draw up a detailed statement about his three months working with Hanson. Better still, he made Abbott's year by contacting him and offering it to him.

Thomas meticulously itemised in his statement the grip Oldfield had on Hanson, and Oldfield's abuse of his taxpayer-funded staff position, to which Hanson had been a willing party. In one of his first points, Thomas noted that Hanson had advised him that he would only occupy the senior adviser's role from 6 February until the end of April, when another person would take the position. He could then take up a lower-paid job on her staff if he wished: 'It was made perfectly clear to me that negotiations with this (to me) unknown person were already complete at the time of my negotiations with Ms Hanson,' he stated, directly contradicting what Hanson would later claim.

'I found it totally abhorrent that a staff member of an MP would abuse his situation by not only working for another MP, but be totally instrumental in the setting up of another political party while on that MP's payroll,' he stated.

Hanson isn't one to be walked out on. She jumped in and terminated Thomas' services on Wednesday, 14 May, before he could quit. But the skilled political operative, who had taken the canny step of making a written statement to another cunning political operative, a former journalist to boot, had the final word.

Dot point 7: 'From the time of my appointment on February 6, 1977, virtually everything that I did for Ms Hanson as regards media was first checked with her by phone with "David O". There were regular daily conversations with him by Ms Hanson and there was no doubt in my mind that she rarely made a single move without first checking it with him.'

Dot point 18: 'There is no doubt in my mind that Pauline Hanson's One Nation Party is the total creation of David Oldfield; that he was intimately involved in all aspects of its setting up; that he has deceived his previous employer for at least the past three months and most likely longer; and that it is the intention of Ms Hanson and Mr Oldfield that he be used to continue the development of One Nation while on the Commonwealth payroll.'

For good measure, as Thomas took his leave, he told journalists that One Nation was 'a party founded on deceit', and described Hanson to Pasquarelli as being 'dead from the neck up'.

Tony Abbott is slow to anger, but he was fit to spit because of Oldfield's actions and aghast when he realised the extent of the duplicity of his former staffer. Nor is Abbott one who takes easily to being dudded, as can be attested from his consistent stabs at Malcolm Turnbull's integrity and leadership after being tipped out of the prime ministerial chair in 2015.

Within weeks, Abbott had launched a bitter attack on Oldfield in parliament, accusing him of deception, disloyalty and treachery. Within months the Commonwealth had requested Oldfield cough up more than $870 on calls made to Hanson on the mobile phone provided under the terms of his employment with Abbott.

\* \* \*

Back in December, Pasquarelli had also noted Oldfield's mobile phone calls to Hanson, which revealed an astonishing reliance on the brash young operator from Sydney's northern beaches. On the day Pasquarelli was booted, for instance, thirteen calls bounced between Oldfield's mobile and Hanson's various numbers. A few hours after the longest of those (for 21 minutes), she summoned Pasquarelli to her office and sacked him and, for good measure, researcher Jeff Babb as well.

'Why are you sacking us?' an astonished Pasquarelli had asked. 'I'm not telling you,' she snapped, just before one walloper and one fake walloper arrived to evict them from the office. By the time Pasquarelli reached an exit, a camera crew had miraculously materialised and a journalist was peppering him with questions about why he had been sacked. Was it, as Hanson said, that she held 'fears for her life'? Had he threatened her? Characteristically, Pasquarelli roared at the questions, took his leave, and launched an action against Hanson for unfair dismissal, which he would later win.

Hanson and Oldfield played politics hard. She was the darling of the deserted and desolate, and everyone would believe whatever version of events she'd tell them. Oldfield was the new marketing mastermind, and he had it all in hand. Within a nanosecond of taking up his now official duties, his arrogance and hubris were cranked to full throttle. Media wags took to calling him 'the Proxy for Oxley', so fond was he of bobbing up on camera to speak on Hanson's behalf.

In the same way that the deadly pair had set about destroying Pasquarelli's reputation, for no good reason except a need to exert total control, Oldfield rang Whiteside a month after taking up his new role.

'You were never going to be allowed to stay in the Pauline Hanson Support Movement,' Oldfield spat down the phone at the startled pensioner. 'You would have only stood in the way of our agenda. We are going to destroy you.' They followed through. Whitehouse has endured years of verbal attack, but has never stopped highlighting the injustices of that time.

The woman who called for honest accountability in politics—who had railed at her party's launch that 'all Australians must be told the truth, we must not be afraid of the truth' and that 'lies are so deeply rooted in the Australian political culture that even the politicians cannot tell the difference any more'—had shed her principles like a snake skin.

Tony Abbott watched, and noted. The hit to Oldfield over his mobile phone charges was just an appetiser. Abbott is to political revenge what a gourmand is to a chef-hatted meal. He appreciates the quality, the lingering taste. But revenge is a dish best served cold, and the angry MP had a feast in store for his former staffer and Ms Hanson. Like fatted lambs to the slaughter, they were delightfully unaware.

# Chapter 5
# TAKING ON ONE NATION

JOHN HOWARD AND those in his team who were ideologically aligned with the Hanson message suddenly awoke from their slumber. Pauline had almost overnight morphed from a low-flying oddity who'd stumbled from Queensland to Canberra into an admired leader of a popular political party that could imperil their futures. What the? Branches of One Nation were flourishing across the country. From Queanbeyan and Canberra to Perth, Adelaide, Darwin and Katherine, they'd sprung up like prickly bindii weeds.

Within months of the formation of One Nation 200 national branches were humming along, their members drawn from many different walks of life. There were people disenfranchised by the policies of the big parties, or just angry with life; there were small-town retirees and single-issue obsessives, plus outright racists, far-right nutters and professional ratbags. It was going to be a challenge to corral them into a cohesive and influential political movement, given that the party was largely a policy-free zone and its leader was motivated as much by personal ambition as civic duty.

The inaugural meetings were often ugly affairs. Groups for and agin One Nation clashed outside the venues, the numbers often running into the hundreds. At the opening of the Dandenong branch in Victoria, the chanting crowds outside ran into the thousands. Anarchists and extremists on both the left and right of the argument used these branch launches as excuses to hurl invective, fear and missiles.

Local police in defensive lines and on horseback clocked up healthy overtime tabs marshalling the mobs. Marches in the major capital cities against Hanson drew crowds in the tens of thousands. The country was on fire.

Hanson became the politician whose security protection and monitoring outstripped any other in Australia, including the Prime Minister. Bulletproof glass was installed in the reception area of her Ipswich electoral office. She had a security detail trailing her around the clock, at work and play.

When One Nation was launched, it was barely a year since John Howard, the former suburban lawyer who had spent a decade trying to become PM, had finally triumphed. He had begun his term with few cares in the world, except for massaging a tight Senate and managing a party room that was bloated with egos after the Coalition's big electoral win. But now the PM was facing turmoil in the streets, and turmoil in the Coalition. Life just wasn't fair sometimes.

It was not until after the launch of Pauline's party, and thirteen months after he became PM, that Howard emerged from under the table. But even then, instead of confronting her head on, he set about walking on both sides of the street. As a lawyer back in the day, he'd mastered the art of nuancing an argument; lawyers are good at making statements that leave wriggle-room for interpretation.

Since he overtly revealed his hand in 1988 with his unsubtle call to cut Asian immigration, Howard had lowered his volume to a whisper on race, multicultural and equality issues. But his views remained, as was clear from the soft dog-whistle of his 1996 election campaign slogan—'For All of Us'—to his refusal to acknowledge past injustices to Aboriginal people through the camouflage of his avowed distaste for a warts-and-all view of Australia's bigoted history.

Talking in code was a trick he'd also learned during his time on the inter-change bench between 1989, when he lost the Liberal leadership, and 1995 when he reclaimed it. One of the reasons for his 1989 downfall had been the rupture he created between his party's left and right flanks by his talk of slowing the pace of Asian immigration and his questioning of the policy of multiculturalism.

How much smarter to welcome Hanson's racist and factually incorrect views as opening up a healthy new era of free speech, of throwing off the shackles of political correctness. In so doing, the PM managed an extraordinary feat: he licensed racial bigotry at the same time as giving its advocates the right to claim victimhood over those who, particularly in Indigenous Australia, had been the real victims of egregious injustice.

Saying it was healthy to have a 'debate' about contentious issues was a patent falsehood. He was a PM standing mutely by while one side was allowed free rein to air ill-informed views without correction or recourse. The encouragement of 'free speech' gave Hanson license to try to turn back the clock and resurrect a time— not too long before in Queensland—when our Indigenes had far fewer rights and privileges than even the most disadvantaged non-indigene enjoyed.

As Hanson ran around the country decrying Aboriginal people as lazy, as welfare bludgers and so on, Howard remained at

Kirribilli House—the official prime ministerial Lodge in Canberra didn't suit his family's lifestyle—watching the yachts sail under the Harbour Bridge.

He didn't initially repudiate repugnant comments by one of his own, Western Australian Senator Ross Lightfoot, a former weekend soldier, mounted policeman and pastoralist who was about to luck his way into the Senate through a vacancy created by the untimely death of John Panizza. Before taking up his undeserved spot, Lightfoot made headlines with disparaging remarks about the intellect and capacity of Aboriginal people.

Howard remained deaf and dumb, brushing off media questions about his senator-elect. But when Lightfoot coughed up again, in a speech to the Senate in May 1997, referring to Aborigines being 'at the bottom colour of the civilisation spectrum', Howard forced him to issue a tepid correction in the manner that politicians apologise when they don't want to.

It wasn't sincere. At the time, Howard was under pressure for his failure to respond to the Stolen Generations report, and for criticising Aboriginal leaders for having the temerity to oppose his Wik ten-point plan, which stripped away Indigenous rights.

The free speech fig leaf also gave the PM free rein to remain silent as Hanson tried to noisily exhume the buried White Australia policy. It allowed him to stay mute as she blame-shifted Australia's social and economic dislocation to immigrants, particularly of the Yellow Peril variety, and to the policy of multiculturalism which had, by the by, brought to our shores the parents of her first husband Walter Zagorski, fleeing the terrors of Nazism.

Hanson too was part of Australia's rich multicultural mix, being of English and Irish stock. But they were white and here first, as she made plain in her maiden and other speeches. And they had had to tame the natives anyway, as she stated in *The Truth*, the book she would later disown. So really, Anglo-Celts like her and her family didn't count as part of Australia's multicultural mix— they stood above it.

*    *    *

Five weeks after Hanson launched her party, the federal parliament again had a crack at asserting its collective integrity. This time, fuelled by political vulnerability and, for some, genuine concern about where Australia was heading, MPs lined up and spoke with passion and conviction. The man who led this charge was Ron Boswell, who had played an important role in having the Coalition introduce to the parliament the previous October the tepid motion reaffirming its commitment to racial equality.

Boswell was truly motivated. He'd worked hard to shift Howard to his thinking and to discredit Hanson in his party's electoral heartland, where she was inflicting deep gashes.

Much had changed from October, when Howard half-heartedly moved the motion on racial tolerance but tiptoed around the substantive issues. Since then, he'd endured months of horse-whipping for his passive stand on Hanson from sections of the domestic and international communities and media, and from people within his own party.

Howard, now energised into action by Hanson's growing popu-larity, was politically savvy enough to know that every time she was personally attacked, her poll numbers shot up. Boswell had advised him that the most effective tack would be to discredit her policies and bigotry, which in turn would discredit the politician and persuade the audience. Go for it, Howard told Boswell. Just keep me at arm's length, and don't get personal.

Boswell now had allies across the parties, and in both chambers. The Labor and Coalition whips in the Senate caucused before his speech and—something that happened only rarely—they agreed to give Boswell the latitude to speak for as long as he wanted. For nearly 40 minutes—double the maximum allowance for a Matter of Public Importance speech, with extensions of time granted throughout—he strung together her appalling descriptions of various groups of people, particularly Aborigines and Asians (drug pushers, disease carriers, job-stealers, ghetto-formers); he quoted her speeches and press releases back at her; he exposed the extremist sources from which her world view was plucked and her dismissive attitude to her job as a parliamentarian.

Ms Hanson is no downunder Evita. What can she offer? Platitudes—plenty of them—but they do not get the job done. Does she have the ear of ministers or a voice behind the cabinet door? No. Does she have some way of influencing government decisions? No. The truth is that Pauline Hanson can do nothing . . .

Her strategy is to evade the truth by reducing current affairs into catch phrases that demand no brain power and no energy to digest. This is to let down and fail her supporters because it denies them understanding of reality—a reality that is full of complexities, trauma and variables beyond anyone's control . . .

The people of Australia deserve the whole truth, not a self-serving, rose-coloured glasses vision. Anyone in this place could grab headlines by coming out with unrealistic, populist statements. What judgment prevents us? It is the judgment that says you will not be taken seriously in the long run. The judgment that says a platitude is no answer to the complex problems of today's changing world and, most importantly, the judgment that says it is wrong to escape responsibility by attaching blame to scapegoats, easily identified because they look or act differently . . .

I also urge the nation's media, from the large city dailies to the small-town weeklies, to prosecute the truth with regard to Ms Hanson and her extremist associates. Morally, socially and economically, Australia cannot afford Ms Hanson. It is not serving the truth to report Ms Hanson's platitudes without her prejudices or to report one-line policy statements without reporting on their consequences . . .

He concluded:

While she provides a temporary emotional outlet for fear and uncertainty, her solutions would only entrench trauma, insecurity and division. What sort of Australia do we want? One where Australians shout at other Australians across police barricades, where hearts that should beat as one in facing the challenges of our future instead beat to the drums of division? No, for in that conflict, we are all losers.

\* \* \*

But what would entice wavering conservative voters, those who were contemplating defection to Hanson, to stay loyal? Howard decided he needed to deal with the High Court decision of December 1996 in the Wik Case, which pronounced native title was not necessarily extinguished by the granting of a pastoral lease and that the two could legally coexist.

This was a priority. Indeed, the Howard Cabinet had already foreseen the outcome of this case, and had unsuccessfully tried to amend the 1993 Native Title Act before the judgment was handed down. But the Senate had refused to play ball.

The ruling had sent a rocket of fear through a swathe of regional and remote seats in Hanson's Queensland, where the Coalition had enjoyed a massive election-winning resurgence only six months before the ruling. Queensland was Howard's electoral bedrock; he and Nationals leader Tim Fischer needed to protect it.

The PM set about attempting to water down the provisions of Keating's 1993 Native Title Act so as to ensure pastoralists and white landholders remained happy with their lot. The blackfellas didn't have the same voting numbers in Queensland as they did, after all.

Black negotiating committees did their darnedest, but Howard was on a mission. He sounded perfectly reasonable, in a very lawyerly way, when he stated on the ABC's *7.30 Report* in mid-1997: 'What has happened with Native Title is that the pendulum has swung too far in one direction, particularly after the Wik decision. What I have done with this legislation is bring it back to the middle.'

But wait! Fear needed to have its run in the park. Pointing at a map, he declared: 'The Labor Party and the Democrats are effectively saying that the Aboriginal people of Australia should have the potential right of veto over further development of 78 per cent of the land mass of Australia.'

This was a nonsense. The court had found that, depending on the type of pastoral lease, native title could coexist; but where there was a conflict of rights, the rights under the pastoral lease extinguished remaining native title rights.

Howard's blustering also neatly obscured certain inconvenient historical facts. Back in the early days, pastoral leases were granted to white squatters who were marching across the land grabbing whatever they liked, regardless of the Aboriginal people peaceably living their lives on those lands. Pastoral leases had been a way of accommodating the squatters while keeping the vast plains as Crown land.

But Howard was out to prosecute a case on behalf of the landowners, who almost to a person were non-Indigenous. Parliament was the theatre of choice for this lawyer, who had never tested his abilities to persuade and argue in a high-powered courtroom. In the court of public opinion, this was going to be a big one. And Queensland was at stake—Joh and Pauline's Queensland could lose him the next election.

As the countdown to the Queensland and federal elections neared and after more than a year of argy-bargy, Howard would finally get a lot of what he wanted in 1998 with his ten-point plan that restricted native title: it broadened the power of governments to extinguish native title; it introduced restrictive measures to make the initiation of claims burdensome; and it removed rights to urban claims.

The Keating Government's 1993 Act had offered the handshake of reconciliation—it had been a collective parliamentary and legislative nod to address historical inequities. But Howard's plan was a direct act of defiance against this spirit of goodwill—it unashamedly withdrew any attempt to right past wrongs.

To get his ten-point plan through the parliament in 1998, Howard threatened minor party senators that, if they did not pass the legislation, he would conduct a race-focused double dissolution election. Brian Harradine, the quiet, deadly, Catholic Independent Senator for Tasmania, helped force through the final amended package, guided by prominent Catholic priest Father Frank Brennan.

Years later, in a 2011 article he wrote for *The Sydney Morning Herald,* working-class-born, Catholic social justice advocate, Paul Keating, was still upset at Brennan's intervention: '. . . As a Catholic, let me say, wherever you witness the zealotry of professional Catholics in respect of indigenous issues, invariably you find indigenous interests subordinated to their personal notions of justice and equity: because unlike the rest of us, they enjoy some kind of divine guidance. And so it was with the Wik amendments.'

Brennan sees it very differently. Following Brian Harradine's death in April 2014, he wrote in an article for the Catholic *Eureka Street* magazine that the late senator had rescued Howard's original 'lamentable' package. After One Nation's astonishing 1998 Queensland win, when Howard was vulnerable, he had picked his time to force through 'improvements', Brennan maintained. History has many lenses.

\*　\*　\*

Another item on the agenda to appease the Hansonites was the Aboriginal and Torres Strait Islander Commission (ATSIC), which figured high on Hanson's whinge list.

Howard had already hacked into its operating budget in his first budget, four months before Hanson's maiden speech. Over subsequent years he shackled it with a string of paternalistic controls until it was finally abolished in March 2005. It wouldn't take that long, though, to cut the guts out of Aboriginal welfare programs and the ABSTUDY education funding program. He did that within the first few years.

Those politically correct do-gooders at the Human Rights Commission were in for a dose of castor oil, too: forty per cent of its budget was carved out over Howard's first two budgets. Overseas aid to struggling countries, another of Hanson's beefs, similarly took a hammering over the course of Howard's first term.

But it was immigration policy that copped the greatest reinvention.

The minister responsible, the pale, po-faced Philip Ruddock from Sydney's leafy Upper North Shore, had started out on the Liberal Party's left. This had meant that any big ambitions he entertained would be constrained by a low factional ceiling, particularly during John Howard's first spell as Leader of the Opposition.

(Ruddock was only brought in from the cold and made a shadow minister when Andrew Peacock took over from Howard.)

Ruddock ended his parliamentary life in his party's right reaches, but it must have been a harrowing journey for this lifelong member of Amnesty International. When Hansonism was running riot, he cut the migration program, particularly family migration. After Hanson's maiden speech, the migration intake tapered from 88,000 to 77,000 through to the 1998 budget. After Hanson immolated later that year, the immigration intake bounced back.

The pressure would have been intense on Ruddock, who had years before stuck to his human rights principles by crossing the floor to support a Hawke Government motion rejecting discrimination on the grounds of race in Australia's immigration policy.

Before the politics of race spooked the Cabinet, Ruddock had remained loyal to his beliefs, condemning Hanson's demands that refugees only be given a temporary stay in Australia. She wanted them forced back to where they came from the moment a Canberra bureaucrat decided they were no longer in danger in their former homeland. It was 'highly unconscionable in a way that most thinking people would clearly reject', Ruddock had stoutly proclaimed. Temporary entry would make recipients 'anxious, uncertain', and would deny them the breathing space to 'address the torture and trauma they had suffered', he said.

Within a year Ruddock had flipped—or had his mind changed for him. The government introduced three-year temporary protection visas for boat-arriving refugees—making recipients anxious, uncertain, and denying them the breathing space to address the torture and trauma they'd suffered.

Howard was laying the foundations for building a world according to Hanson. By then, One Nation was a diabolical threat. Its membership numbers were leaked to the media, and revealed a 25,000-strong army in 250 branches across Australia. Dennis Atkins of Brisbane's *Courier-Mail* reported there were at least 10,000 members in New South Wales, with membership running into the thousands in other states and an undisclosed membership figure in Queensland, which dwarfed everywhere else.

The resounding response to Pauline's clarion call from pissed-off Aussies had been relayed to Howard by anxious regional Coalition MPs. If that hadn't scared the pants off the PM, surely these numbers did. After 50 years in operation, the Liberals had only 80,000 members in 2000 branches. Hanson had pulled in a quarter of those figures in less than a year.

Time for the gloves to come off.

\* \* \*

Hanson and her two lieutenants ran One Nation like a secret cult; this was reflected in the complicated two-entity structure that was One Nation Inc. The interconnected bodies were like two family hotel rooms linked by one door that only opened from one side.

The parent company of Pauline Hanson's One Nation was incorporated with only three family members—directors Hanson, Oldfield and Ettridge—plus a few other members. Rank-and-file members joined Pauline Hanson's One Nation (Membership) Incorporated and it had three tiers—the management committee, managed by the troika; an ordinary committee; and affiliated members.

The management committee controlled everything—finances, membership, terminations, policies, the whole box and dice. One Nation's original constitution stated that management committee meetings were only to be attended by members of the management committee—and ordinary members as agreed to by a majority of members of the management committee. Monty Python couldn't have dreamed it up. Hanson described the set-up as 'bulletproof'; critics slammed it as undemocratic.

Ettridge told Melbourne's *Herald-Sun* in July 1998 that the structure was to prevent the registered party being attacked by 'wreckers' and 'white-ants'. He justified the structure to the ABC's *Four Corners* program as being designed so that if the party was attacked by people seeking to destroy it, it could 'drop its tail as a skunk does, so that if one part of our organisation is contaminated . . . we could discard it and the party itself would remain intact'.

It wasn't just the structure that raised eyebrows. Despite the secrecy, One Nation and its leadership attracted zealous supporters and enemies in equal measure.

Some former supporters were later to beam themselves out of the compound and become whistle-blowers. They reported extraordinary demands from the leadership, like the absurdly undemocratic requirement that new members sign undated resignation forms that could be dated and used later to oust a member deemed sinful. The leadership also maintained a hit list of *persona non grata* former members, whom current members were forbidden from contacting. Ettridge's detailed list of 'white-ants' was notorious; it was the ultimate shaming label that he used with impunity.

It was all a bit creepy—a whiff of Scientology and a tad Jonestown-ish. It did nothing to retain the loyalty for the long haul of the genuine Hanson supporters, who put a high value on independence and freedom of thought and expression—a bit like Hanson espoused, but didn't practise. But those deep flaws and fault lines would only be revealed in dribs and drabs later on, after the dust had settled on the remains of what was one of the boldest political experiments in modern Australian politics.

After the success of the One Nation launch and with nothing to lose, Hanson and her two-man band were politicians in a hurry. This politburo justified the way they ran their party as necessary for discipline and to prevent hostile take-overs. They had no time to waste.

With that mindset and with Hansonism storming the political barricades, they looked in the short term to the sunny horizon of the Queensland state poll looming in June 1998. A party needed to be registered in that state to run candidates, so in October 1997 the leadership applied to register the Queensland support group as 'Pauline Hanson's One Nation' on the basis that it had more than 500 Queensland members. Registration was effected in December, and the trio set sail for the June poll.

\* \* \*

The history books need a lot of thumbing through to find a result more stunning than One Nation's performance at that 13 June election. Across the country, Coalition leaders and supporters awoke to a living nightmare: One Nation had captured a uniform 22.68 per cent of the state-wide primary vote and won eleven of the 79 seats it contested, out of a total possible 89. The Coalition's Premier, Rob Borbidge, had suffered a devastating defeat.

Almost overnight, One Nation leapt to become the most important political force in Queensland; if not by numbers of seats, then by the sheer force of the disruption and chaos it unleashed on the major parties.

The fledgling party outpolled each of the Coalition parties: the Liberals attracted only a shade over 16 per cent of the primary vote, the Nationals 15.2 per cent. One Nation's parliamentary representation outflanked the Liberals, which couldn't even muster double figure representation, winning just nine seats. Borbidge had held out against preferencing One Nation, but he had been overruled by the Coalition's organisational wing. His government paid a mighty price for that decision.

The Liberals were caned in city seats for the preferencing deal. Six of its seats went to Labor, which took the high ground and placed the Hanson party last on its how-to-vote cards. But Labor didn't get off scot-free, even though it won government. One Nation's support base was in all sorts of places, from the vast paddocks to the 'burbs, leaching support from traditional Labor voters.

Nevertheless, One Nation's support remained predominantly regional, showcased with deadly potency in the rolled-gold former Nationals seat of Barambah, centred on the town of Kingaroy. This was deep, pulsing Joh Bjelke-Petersen country. One Nation's Dorothy Pratt won the previously safe Nationals seat in a canter with a leg in the air, polling 43.5 per cent of the primary vote.

Pratt's win was One Nation's most stellar performance. It was aided by the quality of its candidate. Pratt ultimately jumped ship from One Nation in 2001, but she was such an effective local representative that she remained in parliament as an Independent until she stood down in 2012.

One Nation won Burdekin (33.1 per cent of the primary vote), Caboolture (30 per cent), Hervey Bay (around 40 per cent), Ipswich West (38.6 per cent), Lockyer (39.2 per cent), Maryborough (42.6 per cent), Mulgrave (31 per cent), Tablelands (42 per cent), Thuringowa (34.9 per cent) and Whitsunday (30.7 per cent). Six were Labor-held in outer metropolitan or urban/rural fringe districts. Five had been Nationals' rural seats. The renegade party just fell short in other seats.

The result was nothing short of a stunning, humiliating rout for the ruling conservatives, the most forceful up-yours ever inflicted by Australian voters on a government via a minor party vote. One Nation had arrived with a deafening roar.

\*    \*    \*

When opinion polls during the Queensland campaign started to reveal the staggering support One Nation might attract, Howard tried to give his best shot at taking her on. In a lawyerly way.

In a radio interview with the ABC's Fran Kelly on 3 June, he was critical of the One Nation leader, something he had spent fifteen months avoiding. The previous night Hanson had proclaimed that Indigenous Australians and the United Nations were plotting to establish taxpayer-funded Australian states. Well, of course—didn't everyone know that?

'I've got to say it is not only an inaccurate, dishonest speech, but it verges on the deranged in various places,' Howard tut-tutted to Kelly. 'I said all along that whenever she says something that is wrong or against the interests of Australia, I will attack it.'

No, he hadn't said that all along. And no, he hadn't attacked 'it'. He had stood by for endless months while Hanson made insulting, inflammatory and ill-informed comments that dramatically hurt Australia's interests. His silence had been a top-hat doff to the interests of 'free speech'.

So was she a racist, Kelly inquired? Even then, as the walls were closing in, with weeks to go to a poll that he knew could be diabolical, Howard couldn't quite bring himself to slam her. 'Well, I've said, I mean, she is fanning racist sentiment . . . now, let's not sort of, I mean . . . I think we agree that a racist, strictly speaking, is somebody who believes one race is superior to another. But by using this sort of language she is, I believe, appealing to racist sentiment.' There you have it: we now knew when a racist was not a racist. It was a definition for the ages, or maybe for a legal dictionary.

During the previous month the PM's deputy, Peter Costello, had told the ABC bluntly—no ifs, no buts—that One Nation would be placed firmly at the bottom of how-to-vote cards in his

Victorian seat of Higgins in the federal election that would be called not long after the Queensland poll. In response, Howard, in his address to his party room on the morning of the May budget, warned his MPs against following any such heretical course of action.

However, it's amazing what a good night's rest after a bad election result can do for a bloke. At the end of June, Howard, possibly restless after a few disturbed dreams about the Queensland result, and tossing and turning over when to hold the federal poll, awoke from his harbourside slumber to declare that he'd experienced an epiphany. By George, he'd put One Nation last in his seat of Bennelong at the upcoming federal election! In a nanosecond, this also became the official position of both Coalition partners. Until the next time, that is.

Howard minister, Tony Abbott, had also uncoiled and was preparing to strike. Writing in *The Australian* on 19 June, he stated that: 'The Hanson phenomenon could destroy the Howard Government and give responsible conservatives a bad name.' Super deduction after more than a year of inertia from the Prime Minister, and the Queensland slaughter.

A few weeks later, on 2 July, Abbott told parliament that One Nation was 'not a validly registered political party', but 'a couple of political and financial brigands trying to hoodwink decent patriotic Australians'. He said it was a business, not a political party.

At the same time, somewhere behind the political curtains, the ambitious Abbott, along with former Liberal MP Peter Coleman and former Labor minister John Wheeldon, established a body called Australians for Honest Politics. Given the organisation was, by Coleman's later public admission, 'oblique' rather than transparent, the title must have been a pub joke devised at midnight after the trio had had too many beers and tequila chasers.

The aim of the Honest Politics group was to de-register One Nation. Political heavy-hitters, such as Paul Everingham, the Liberal Party's Queensland president, and Nationals' leader Tim Fischer, joined with others to try to make contact with disgruntled One Nation members—those who hadn't fallen foul of the dictatorship and been shipped to a faraway gulag.

One such was former One Nation candidate Terry Sharples, who initiated legal proceedings in July to de-register the party in Queensland. He argued that One Nation's registration had been induced by 'fraud and misrepresentation' because the members relied upon for registration were from the supporter list. Sharples was under the clear impression that Abbott had agreed to cover his costs, or at the very least ensure he wasn't out of pocket if he spent his own dough on proceedings. That financial assistance didn't materialise, and Sharples would later be bankrupted.

It took more than a year, but Queensland Supreme Court Justice Roslyn Atkinson decreed that the party members were not, in fact, members because 'those who controlled Pauline Hanson's One Nation Ltd' intended to restrict membership of the party to only Hanson, Ettridge, Oldfield and other elected members of parliament. All other members were deemed to be part of the second entity created by Hanson and her two cohorts.

The troika's autocratic zeal for control had worked against them. But that was just the beginning. The legal system wasn't done with two of the trio just yet.

\* \* \*

After the June state elections, a strange rump of eleven unknowns landed in the Queensland Parliament. They had no staff, no local branch infrastructure to support them and no political strategists other than the control freaks in Hanson's Canberra/Manly outfit.

They had few policies, zilch experience in politics and little affinity with each other. They were probably as shocked as anyone else to end up in Brisbane's parliament, and the cracks started appearing almost immediately.

As this slow train crash beetled along its inevitable track, Hanson herself had an important decision to make. A federal election had been called for October but, in the most recent redistribution, her Ipswich support base was located half in Oxley, her current seat, and half in the newly created seat of Blair. In the end she opted to run for Blair. This was against the advice offered to her by John Pasquarelli, that she should run for the Senate.

In her announcement about her election intentions, she slapped down those who'd dared advise her against such a next move. She had always been the one with the right political instincts: 'Despite considerable gratuitous advice that I had to stand for the Senate, this was not really an option for me as I believe the first rule of leadership is to lead by example and therefore never to ask someone to do what you won't do yourself,' she explained at her press conference. 'I could not reasonably expect candidates all over Australia to stand in the lower house without facing that fight myself.

'Further to this, for One Nation to truly succeed in returning Australia to its people, it is necessary for us to have a presence in the lower house—we must not be another obstructionist Senate block like the Democrats and the Greens.' In the future just such an obstructionist role became her goal; but for now she was prepared to roll the dice for the Lower House, in the full belief she would triumph.

But this was not 1996. The major parties had toughened up during the two tumultuous years she'd been in the big house on Canberra's Capital Hill. The major party politicians had strengthened and hardened their arguments against her. Howard had moved decisively along the path of plucking her policies, and the Nationals were alive in the regions repelling the threat. And this time around, she was not included in any preference deals.

The only free speech allowed during the election campaign was anti-Hanson. The worm turns in strange ways, and Hanson was now in a deep hole, equipped only with a clutch of hard-nosed but inexperienced advisers and a burning ambition. It was crazy-brave stuff, regardless of what lens you peer at Hanson through.

The dawn rose kindly on Howard on election day, 3 October. He'd neatly sidestepped making race and immigration an issue by introducing the GST policy, which dominated the campaign. His government squeaked back over the line with one of those quirks that our electoral map sometimes tosses up: with only 49.02 per cent of the two-party preferred vote, the Coalition nevertheless clinched more seats than Kim Beazley's Labor, which won 50.98 per cent of the popular vote.

In his victory speech, Howard gave a monstrously hypocritical pledge to 'very genuinely' commit to 'the cause of true reconciliation with the aboriginal people by the centenary of federation'. Nationals leader Tim Fischer crowed his party had 'stood up and repulsed this full frontal assault from One Nation . . . this is one of the finest hours for the National Party . . .'

Beazley, emboldened by his pyrrhic victory, pointedly pledged to help with healing the nation: 'We must, as a people, constantly turn to each other and not on each other and against each other. We must, as a people, and I believe we do, operate in a way that gets the very best out of the multicultural and multi-racial society that we are.'

Over at the One Nation watch-house at Ipswich's showground, hundreds of One Nation zealots and an overblown 50-strong media contingent kept company with the blue and yellow balloons and the giant posters of their heroine wrapped in an Australian flag striking her familiarly defiant pose plastered on the walls.

Early counting was promising. But the illusion of triumph, based on an early count, has led many a candidate down the years to a temporary bout of delusion that can make their defeat gut-wrenching and much harder to bear. It's a cruel business.

Pauline had spent the day in a squeeze of cameras and supporters, like a rock star descending on a hick town for a concert. When casting her vote at a local school, she proudly announced that she'd given her preferences to the Liberal candidate. She was very, very confident.

Three hours after the polls closed it had all turned to shit. In stunned silence the assembled throng watched the party's vote collapse. Hanson arrived mid-evening in a twinkling victory ensemble that by 9.30 p.m. was, embarrassingly, out of sync with the result. The hall was awash with tears—many of them hers—and spilled dreams. Her party's overall national vote was an insipid 8 per cent. All it took was a bit of muscle and unity from the major parties—from the Prime Minister, in particular—to snuff out the flame.

Even though Heather Hill had been elected as a One Nation Queensland senator (with 15 per cent of the vote), Hanson had lost her fearless bid for Blair. But her magnetic appeal had been on full display as she pitched for the seat, starkly revealing the cult reality of the One Nation brand. It's all about her; always was, always will be. She pulled in a handsome primary vote of 36 per cent, and secured a respectable 48 per cent of the two-party preferred vote; but she lost to the Liberal candidate, Cameron Thompson, whose primary vote was roughly half of Hanson's. But he had hoovered up the majority of preferences.

The major parties had frozen her out of preferences. It was brutal, uncompromising politics. Despite the predictability of the result—given their tactics—she looked shell-shocked. She promptly banned the media from filming her concession speech, during which she cried and clutched the hands of her children, and afterwards disappeared out a back door.

A month after the federal poll, the Queensland state parliamentary team started cracking like a windscreen that cops a stone and slowly shatters under constant buffeting. Charles Rappolt—a fragile character who resigned from parliament on 4 November, citing political and media pressure—dealt the first blow. He'd been a One Nation representative in the turbulent state parliament for only five months.

No one was to know at the time just how troubled the novice MP was. His first suicide attempt—in Australia and just after he escaped from parliament—failed. He then sued the Queensland Government for turning him, he claimed, into a psychotic manic-depressive. When that lawsuit failed, he fled to New Zealand, and hung himself not long after in his Auckland home.

Another three MPs jumped ship to the crossbenches a few months after Rappolt fled. This was because Hanson, Oldfield and Ettridge had refused their request to stand down from their leadership roles and face democratic elections by the members. A few months later another three tumbled out the door and formed the City Country Alliance; they cited too much control by the two Davids and Hanson.

The spectacular state experiment was all but over.

\*   \*   \*

In political terms, Hanson's transition from queen bee to black widow spider was ferociously short. She now had no seat in parliament and vengeful Liberals and Nationals still in hot pursuit, determined to quash any future threats to their patch. There was a rabble of a team in her home state parliament; and many party members were angry about the party's command-and-control culture.

Back at the ranch, no one would have blamed her if Pauline indulged a little too heavily in her favourite tipple of bourbon, ginger beer and lime, known—seriously—as a Ginger Bitch, which she'd learned to whip up when working at the Penthouse Night-club in Surfers Paradise. What to do with her life? Despite the disappointment, she had cause to be slightly optimistic about her political future. After all, hadn't one million Australians voted for her party? Hadn't they snared one senator, and more than 14 per cent of the Senate vote? By any measure, that's solid support. It wasn't in the DNA of the feisty single mother, with a ferocious appetite for hard work and success, to go away quietly. And she was more than aware of her charismatic appeal.

Despite the blunt political instruments she'd been trained to use by her succession of pitiless henchmen, she was passionate about her beliefs, crudely framed though they may have been. She had tasted the delights of adulation, of opening up fault lines in the country she loved, and she wanted to stay in the game.

If she thought it couldn't get any worse, she was wrong. But what happened in the next part of her eventful life would keep her supporters alive with the hope of her return, and her ambition as bright as it had ever been. There's nothing like defeat and humili-ation to fuel a desire to avenge.

# Chapter 6

# AUSTRALIA'S FIRST POLITICAL PRISONER

WHO DID SHE most admire? Pauline Hanson couldn't give a ready answer when journalist David Leser posed this question for his seminal 1998 *Good Weekend* article about her. Was there any politician, musician, artist—*anyone*—she admired? Nope, she replied. Only her father, she eventually said. When prompted by a staffer about her fondness for the tyrant Joh Bjelke-Petersen, she mused that, yep, he'd be as close to a political hero as she could imagine.

No heroes and few close friends; spurned lovers and husbands; discarded staff and hard-working loyalists: that was Hanson's emotional landscape by the time she faced her Waterloo at the turn of the century.

Those who had walked the perilous path of life with Hanson to that date recounted tales of a contradictory, complex character: a loner, prone to suspicion about everyone's motives; someone quick to friendship, but even speedier to loathsome enmity; a lover and hater in unequal measure who was remarkably confident, yet at the same time acutely vulnerable.

She had become hooked on the limelight, but only on her terms.
She was in a rough, rugged and hardnosed political game; she
played it as hard as any seasoned politician, but was aghast and
cried foul when it didn't swing her way.

While much of the responsibility for her downfall was hers, she
was never at fault. It was the system, political or electoral corruption, other politicians, the Davids, her organisation. Not her.

People were useful, up to the point when they weren't; then
they were adversaries, never to block her sunshine again. 'Pauline
Hanson has always walked away the victor, both emotionally and
financially,' reflected a bruised Pasquarelli after he became one of
the many people she sacked or froze out.

Her once close confidante, Barbara Hazelton, echoed similar
sentiments, as did other former staffers and the scorned and dumped
devotees who started the Pauline Hanson Support Movement.
Oldfield, a goliath in the arena of self-interest, has kept up a running
commentary on the human misery Hanson has inflicted on those
around her over the years.

The people Hanson has been able to keep tight for the long-
term are those who barely know her: her rusted-on voters, who
share a vision of an intrepid Pauline fighting the good fight against
those who would do her ill. But even many of them got the wobbles
when she most needed them, when the Queensland team fell apart
and ugly challenges blighted the horizon.

Oldfield all but deserted Pauline after she lost Blair at the 1998
federal election. He made a beeline for the New South Wales
Parliament and clinched an Upper House seat in the March 1999
election, thanks to an expensive advertising campaign using One
Nation funds. Not long after that, he cemented his spot in Hanson's
mind as one of her many male traitors and black-hearts.

Meanwhile, back on Planet Dirty Politics, Tony Abbott and his cohorts, who'd acted as urgers for some disgruntled One Nation dissidents to legally challenge the registration of the party, tasted the fruits of their labours. In August 1999, Queensland Supreme Court Justice Roslyn Atkinson ruled for plaintiff Terry Sharples in his action against the Queensland Electoral Commissioner's decision to register Pauline Hanson's One Nation.

Atkinson ruled that the decision was 'induced by fraud or misrepresentation' because the people on the membership list were supporters, not members. The founder of the support movement upon which the party had been built against their wishes, Bruce Whiteside, was in court to hear the bitter-sweet verdict. One Nation was ordered to repay $500,000 of public funds. Despite having been showered with millions of dollars in public funding following the Queensland and federal elections—monies that under the contorted One Nation party structure could go only to accounts controlled by Hanson and the Davids—Hanson cried poor and turned to her supporters for financial succour. She also appealed the finding.

In the aftermath, four months later, One Nation in Queensland scampered from the national fold, registering as a separate entity to that controlled by the Davids from Manly. Oldfield caused the split: he'd refused to release control of the Queensland organisation, despite crab-walking away from it following the court decision. The state organisation had 'nothing to do' with him, he harrumphed to the media, while tightening his grip on its books and purse strings.

Across the country, One Nation branches were falling like dominoes. The kangaroo court, presided over by Hanson and the two Davids, was running 24/7. The troika were sacking more people in positions of authority within branches than they were gaining members. The rot was spreading like warm mould from Manly to branches in every state.

One of the party's more astute members was Robyn Spencer, a founder of Australians Against Further Immigration (AAFI); she'd previously come to the attention of Jewish and anti-racist organisations for her close association with the far-right, anti-Semitic, racist League of Rights. She'd addressed many meetings of the League, an organisation that never claimed to be a political party but was known to infiltrate the ranks of other parties in order to gain political influence. Like One Nation, AAFI maintained it was a nationalist organisation that had no truck with racism; yet it drew succour and political inspiration from the divisive League, whose founder, Eric Butler, had spent a lifetime ventilating Jewish world take-over conspiracies.

Ms Spencer and her husband Rodney entered a curious arrangement with Hanson in 1998: they purchased the Victorian franchise to manage One Nation. AAFI Victoria and One Nation Victoria amalgamated, and the Spencers went about building branches. Ms Spencer travelled interstate representing the One Nation brand, taking part in debates and flying the flag for her nationalist party. 'Immigration,' she told a forum in Queensland in the lead-up to the 1998 federal election, 'is not like a tax. You cannot remove its impact three years later. Migrants are here to stay.'

Spencer, a seasoned media performer, was One Nation's #1 Senate candidate in Victoria at the 1998 election; her ticket received 117,000 votes, or 4.1 per cent, which was reasonably respectable. For a party that had just set up shop in the state, it was a solid foundation. Hanson and the Davids should have been thrilled. For whatever reason—perhaps the Spencers were becoming too powerful, Robin in particular—they weren't.

By May 1999 they were on the black list, or rather the infamous Ettridge white-ant list. They were dubbed by head office—in quaintly disturbing cold war language—'traitors to our cause', and their ritual beheading by sacking duly took place.

Hanson personally turned up to carry out the execution, which had been deliberately organised by head office at the remote town of Lake Eppalock, 130 kilometres north of Melbourne. Robyn Spencer won the vote on the floor of the meeting, but Hanson declared she had hundreds of proxies in favour of ousting her. Democracy in action, One Nation style.

Subsequently, branch membership in Victoria plummeted. By late 1999 only three branches remained, down from the previously solid thirty.

\* \* \*

The good times just kept rolling on for the beleaguered party and its cat-fighting leadership. The year 2000 was a busy one for lawyers as a blitz of claims and counter-claims ricocheted between individuals who had once been so close and were now so fiercely divided.

The national executive sacked Oldfield in October 2000 on Hanson's instigation, after a comical episode when Hanson stormed the Manly office looking for documents and bank records after Oldfield barred her entry. He told the ABC: 'We were locked out because Pauline Hanson arrived with a locksmith to try and change the locks and so in the midst of that she caused herself to be locked up inside . . . she locked herself in, sort of—it was a bit like the Alamo. I think she thinks she's a Texan.'

For her part, Hanson claimed she wanted the bank records and other office documents for 'transparency and accountability'. All trust between the pair had evaporated.

It was kindergarten stuff from a leadership that had descended into name-calling and threats. Two weeks after being booted from the party he had helped create, Oldfield faxed Hanson a sinister letter, stating in part: 'You are clearly incapable of halting your run of destructive, dishonest and despicable behaviour. Hence, in the interests of the issues One Nation represents and the people who support us, you leave me no choice but to slow you down.'

The New South Wales party followed the pattern already established in Queensland and Victoria, imploding in a mess of court actions, expulsions and desertions. Oldfield ultimately set up 'One Nation NSW', taking advantage of the chaos shuddering through the party and the once-united leadership. He first registered 'Pauline Hanson's One Nation' in New South Wales without her approval; but she appealed against the registration and had it cancelled so he struck like a cat at a bird to quickly register the shorter title, which lacked her name and also her imprimatur.

Oldfield isn't a person to attract admirers. A lot of colourful insults have been hurled his way, all water off a slick duck's back. Former Hanson secretary and her one-time BFF, Barbara Hazelton, described him in *The Australian* in tart terms: 'Oldfield is a manipulative, hypnotic, hugely narcissistic individual . . . my biggest single worry about Oldfield is that he holds the ordinary people who support Pauline in contempt.'

Oldfield's passing swipe on the way out was no less bitter: 'Bear in mind that since, you know, Pauline said a few things in Ipswich in the middle of 1996, everything including her maiden speech and every word of any consequence that she's said since, has actually been written for her.'

Hanson herself has often rued the day she met him, and across the country he's earned a string of humiliating epithets. He's nothing if not resilient and, as his more recent public appearances attest, he couldn't give a stuff what anyone thinks. He's remained in the baffled public gaze for two decades, and that for him seems to be all that matters. He has more in common with Hanson than both of them would care to admit.

*   *   *

The pull and power of the political limelight isn't a drug that many politicians like to forgo. Hanson was no different. She inhaled a second wind in 2001 as a series of elections across Australia gave her and her careworn party the possibility of entry back to centre stage.

First up was a state election in Western Australia in early February. One Nation polled a respectable 10 per cent of the vote—30 per cent in some rural seats. Its decision to preference anyone except sitting MPs dealt the conservative government led by Richard Court a career-ending blow. It failed to win any seats, but that didn't matter: Western Australia counted for little in the larger scheme of things for Hanson. She had her sights set on bigger national goals: the general election was just around the corner.

To hit her main target, Hanson was now adding the political potency of her sexual allure to her kit of campaigning tools. She revamped her image in a multi-pronged strategy to catwalk her way back to stardom—or maybe it was as much about being the centre of attention. Whatever her motive, it worked to soften her image and divert focus from the sharp edges of her past pronouncements.

In his book, *The Pauline Hanson Story by the Man Who Knows*, her first henchman, John Pasquarelli, wrote that Hanson attracted marriage proposals from strangers, and ardent admirers fell at her feet. The red hair, shrewd green eyes, hip-swinging swagger and blood-red lipstick, coupled with a brutish aggression weirdly offset by a quivering damsel-in-distress voice, made many blokes weak at the knees.

One former Liberal press secretary tells me her boss was infatuated with Hanson, as were others in the conservative party room.

'It used to make me cringe. We were out there opposing her policies, but some in our party room were drooling over her.' Male colleagues from the press gallery back then say she became more flirtatious the more desperate her position became. Writing in the *Queensland Review* at the time, History Professor Kay Saunders described Hanson's style as 'gaudy, highly sexualised clothes, so full of masculine aggression and coquettish femininity'.

Her appearance at the Western Australian 2001 tally room on the night of 10 February revealed the new Pauline power-dressing strategy. It was a notch up from the frothy get-up she had worn on the night she lost the race for Blair in 1998. For the first time, newspapers concentrated on her wardrobe—a full-length, split skirt was the hero of the ensemble—as much as the result. TV excitedly reported on her clobber, not her clout. It spilled into news spreads for days.

She was morphing into a celebrity candidate using fashion and sex appeal to attract attention. An article in *The Sydney Morning Herald* breathlessly critiqued her tally-room outfit: 'Hanson's frock said it all. The zebra stripes implying wildness and unpredictability combined with the sexual allure of the tropical hibiscus epitomised Pauline's political potency. The packaging, too, was pretty much perfect. The neckline plunged, but not too far. The skirt was decorously long, but frivolous with its spiralling ruffles. She was unencumbered by a Thatcherite handbag, the sandals matched and—let's face it, she has the body to wear such an outfit.'

A week later, at the Queensland state election, the party's vote plummeted by nearly 9 per cent. They won only three seats, which compared unfavourably with their previous eleven-seat haul; but Hanson's outfit again deflected attention from the paucity of the result. She swayed into the tally room in a black see-through ball gown, a sight that must have bulged the eyes of the battlers of Ipswich.

In the middle of this electoral flurry and fashion extravaganza, Hanson barely broke stride in July to attend a committal hearing at Brisbane Magistrate's Court on electoral fraud charges. 'I do believe that this is a political witch-hunt,' she snorted when defiantly pleading not guilty. A court date for the full hearing was not set.

Back then to the business at hand. There she was in a double-page spread in *The Australian Women's Weekly*, with style commentary from earnest designers and fashionistas. Then there came a make-over by Brisbane designer Richard de Chazal: the centrepiece of his collection was a swathe of what appeared to be taffeta with big silver statement buttons topped by a large dead skunk wrapped around her breasts. In the photograph her polished shoulders were unconstrained by clothing.

Fairfax journalist and long-time Hanson admirer, Paul Sheehan, marvelled. 'Pauline Hanson is no longer a Katies conservative. No longer a "Target target". Her clothes generally used to run to cautious, middle-of-the-road and budget-conscious. But on Sunday even the media stopped treating her as the "Roadkill that Will Not Die",' he babbled. 'Bare shoulders was a first, and the media's gushing response—front page across the country—was telling. It marked another milestone. Ms Hanson has now risen to a status beyond politics, certainly beyond policies—she doesn't need them any more—to pure celebrity.'

Next up, a run at the Senate at the November 2001 general election. Her unshakeable belief in her innocence of the charges that had now been laid against her was so strong that she did not give serious consideration to the possibility that, had she won, a criminal conviction could have seen her lugged out of the Big House wearing silver bracelets.

Nationals Senator Ron Boswell was fighting her for the third conservative spot in Queensland. The first two Coalition MPs on the ticket were a shoo-in. For that last vital clutch of conservative votes he needed to attract to get him over the line, he was facing off against a woman he'd fought since 1996. He left no stone unturned.

Some in his ranks were still inclined to preference her, which he freely concedes would have seen her victorious. 'I told them— you preference her, you fight an election without me,' he says. He ran against the fashion-conscious Hanson with the cheeky slogan: 'He's not pretty, but he's pretty effective.' He'd started campaigning almost since the 1998 election result, which had terminated—for the time being—her federal career.

While others on his side of the fence had back-slapped each other in 1998 at their success in sending her back to the 'burbs, Boswell knew then that she hankered to be in politics for the long haul, that one defeat wouldn't quash her ambitions. 'I'd always won from the third position,' he explains. 'I'd been in small business—I understood it. To get there I had to pick up the primary industry vote, the conservative vote, the church vote—right-wing Catholics, Baptists—and small business.'

He won by the skin of his astute political teeth. Hanson received 9.9 per cent of the primary vote; Boswell secured less, 9.1 per cent. But his determination to see the major parties steer preferences away from her clinched his victory. He picked up all the preferences, even Labor's. 'It was really close, I'd been grinding away for three years,' he says. 'Even the Labor guys on the polling booths preferenced me over Hanson.' One Nation's national vote nearly halved, to 5.5 per cent. Not one One Nation candidate would be making their way to Canberra.

The poor showing for the party across the country wasn't just because of a strict no-go approach to preferencing her and her team.

By then, Howard had nicked a lot of her policies, and his blunt mantra that the government alone would decide who and when people came to Australia was a steal from the Hanson pitch. Rather than opt for a message of hope and inclusivity, Howard sought to exploit the mood of grief, suspicion and anger that had washed around the globe like a Mexican wave after the 9/11 attacks in New York.

There've been few in politics able to master such an ideological sleight of hand as Howard's. In a calculated fashion he had managed to mimic a politician whose policies his party opposed at the ballot box while presenting to the electorate an honest, open face of liberalism.

\* \* \*

Hanson may not have noticed, but the three quick election losses showed that the glow was fading on the political stuntwoman. Her party was a rambling, shambolic, riven dog's breakfast and her ego had outgrown her popularity.

Timing in politics is everything. She'd missed the golden window of opportunity the *Bulletin* poll predicted in 1996, when voters gave a booming cheer to the idea of a Hanson Senate ticket and pledged their troth for at least half a dozen seats in a half-Senate election. Strategy and strong policies across a number of portfolios—policies that can be practically, realistically implemented—are a given to succeed in politics.

She and her party had very little of the former, and the latter were sound bites designed to attract attention rather than form policy platforms.

The major parties were always going to combine to thwart her in 2001. They'd done it in 1998, and nothing succeeds like success. For whatever reason, with characteristic optimism and hubris,

Hanson chose to clench her eyes tight against that reality. She was furious that it had happened—again.

She and her party could put the major party candidates last; but when the established parties repaid her in kind, she cried foul. Disgusted at her defeat, Hanson announced she was quitting politics.

\*   \*   \*

All was quiet on the ranch until May 2002, when the law again came a-knocking. Along with Mr White-Ant Ettridge, Hanson was committed to stand trial for fraudulently registering One Nation in Queensland. They pleaded not guilty. Hanson was charged with dishonestly claiming almost $500,000 in electoral reimbursements, and again pleaded not guilty.

Later in the month, she was hit with another charge of siphoning $20,000 out of the fighting fund for her own personal benefit. Her plea: not guilty. It wasn't a great month.

The remaining members of the executive of the party she had helped found didn't think much of these developments, and promptly sacked her. In Hanson's telling, she was 'forced to resign'.

But nothing stops our intrepid heroine, and she decided she wasn't really quitting politics, she was just taking a wee break from Queensland politics. Soon she began setting sail for a parliament again. The next one available was in New South Wales in March 2003, where her frenemy Oldfield had taken up space and oxygen since 1999.

She decamped from Ipswich to the Sutherland Shire's Sylvania Waters, a flashy estate built on reclaimed swampland. It had been the location of a celebrated ABC soapie that carried the name of the area and had proved very popular in England, where the Poms choked with glee over their cod and chips at the posers Down Under.

Sylvania Waters' residents were fiercely proud of their flamboyant suburb, and didn't mind the tag of 'working class made good'. Two years after Hanson moved there, the Shire would also become famous for another unhelpful reason. The Australia Day race riots at one of its famous beaches, Cronulla, became an inglorious international branding exercise for the darkest reaches of the racist Aussie soul after a violent clash between young angry white men and Middle Eastern Australians erupted.

Hanson felt well at home.

'A lot of people from the Shire have come up to me and said: "When are you going back to politics?" There is a lot of support for me here,' she reckoned. 'I have always been passionate about Australians and I don't believe they are being told the truth.' The truth about what, she didn't elaborate. Her party's finances perhaps? Her lack of accountability? Whether One Nation had any real policies?

Oldfield barbed: 'The impression is that Sylvania Waters is where the socially inept ones live after they have made a few bucks.' She had certainly made a few bucks over the years, one way or another.

In the New South Wales state elections of 2003, Hanson stood for the Upper House, the Legislative Council, and she campaigned on law and order. But she forgot to do her homework and she repeatedly failed to answer elementary questions about state policy in this area, or the shortcomings she would aim to remedy. She admitted she did not know the name of the New South Wales Police Commissioner (Ken Moroney) and she had made no attempt to talk to him about her concerns. None of this helped her law and order campaign.

Hanson's enthusiasm for her new stomping ground and the embrace of her supporters weren't matched by votes, and she missed out on joining Oldfield on the crusty New South Wales

Upper House benches. She polled only 1.9 per cent of the vote; but she would have taken some comfort from the fact that she had outpolled her old party, which only managed 1.5 per cent.

\* \* \*

Hanson's resurrection began just a few months later. On 15 July, she fronted court on the fraud charges in the case set down to play out as a thrilling political drama over four weeks. Thirty witnesses traipsed through the court over 23 days.

The jury took a day to decide Hanson and Ettridge were guilty as charged, Your Honour, of dishonestly inducing the Electoral Commissioner of Queensland to register Pauline Hanson's One Nation as a political party. The jury also found Hanson guilty of two more charges, each relating to dishonestly obtaining cheques from the Electoral Commissioner for about $500,000.

Hanson yelled from the dock: 'Rubbish! I'm not guilty, it's a joke!'

Chief Judge Patsy Wolfe of the Queensland District Court sentenced her to three years in the nick. 'It is essential that the electoral process, and the registration of political parties is one of them, is not thwarted or perverted. The crimes you committed affect the confidence of people in the electoral process,' the learned judge scolded.

Hanson stepped out of her glam frocks and smart suits, and swapped them for prison dungarees as she started her stint in Brisbane's Women's Prison at Wacol. A political martyr was born.

Australians love to see ourselves as fighters for the underdog. We will put on a dais anyone we think The System has wronged, and then wrap them in admiration and awe. Coalition supporters veered her way. Bronwyn Bishop led the charge, converting what had been a technical legal argument over electoral law into a courageous battle for freedom of speech and expression. 'Very simply, for the first time in Australia, we now have a political prisoner and I find that totally unacceptable,' she tutted to the ABC.

'What I'm saying is that this is a very bad development in Australia because, for the first time, we are seeing someone who has spoken out . . . This is someone who has been sent to jail because she spoke her views and that is not acceptable in this country.' For good measure, Bishop accused Queensland Premier Peter Beattie of somehow being involved in Pauline's prosecution.

Journalist Alexandra Kirk tried on a number of occasions to point out she was jailed for electoral fraud, not for expressing her views. Ms Bishop scoffed: 'What I'm saying is that in this country to date, Alex, we have not had political prisoners. That's something you'd expect in Zimbabwe, not Australia.'

Even a shameless Tony Abbott, one of the masterminds behind the action that had brought Hanson down, expressed sorrow she'd been flung behind bars. Queensland Premier Peter Beattie stammered apologies and wrung his hands, entreating Queenslanders to refrain from blaming his government for the jailing of this person who had now become a political martyr in the cause of free speech.

Supporters started comparing her to jailed freedom-fighter Nelson Mandela. It looked for all the world like Hanson had returned from the brink of political annihilation, and been reincarnated as a red-headed justice-and-free-speech warrior felled by a compromised political and judicial system.

A small forest of trees lost their lives analysing the arguments for and against Hanson's conviction, and this book does not intend to add to that horticultural misery. There's only two versions: the conspiracy, enthusiastically promoted by Hanson and her attack dogs and milked for years to garner sympathy with her blinkered supporters; or the other.

Eleven weeks after being jailed, Hanson was released after a successful appeal. Queensland's Chief Justice Paul de Jersey delivered the news on behalf of three judges sitting as the Court of Appeal. They found that appeal against the conviction and sentence of both Hanson and Ettridge would be allowed; the conviction and sentences quashed; and a judgment of acquittal be entered instead.

The issue came down to the party membership. The Crown had argued that the pair had knowingly used members of the One Nation Support Movement to register the One Nation political party with the Electoral Commission, but that the two were very separate. The Court of Appeal disagreed with that jury finding.

The finding only confirmed to her steadfast supporters and a new cohort of Hanson converts that she'd been the victim of corrupt politicians and authorities working in cahoots.

Hanson and her supporters had long accused both Abbott and Beattie of helping steer what they claimed was a political witch-hunt through the courts.

The conspiracy theories and accusations of dirty politics and a corrupted judicial system had mushroomed in the suburbs, aided and abetted by the myth-making around Hanson's new status as Australia's first political prisoner. To quell the rising hysteria and in response to the 'lively public debate about the possible involvement of politicians in the litigation, in particular the Honourable Tony Abbott MHR', in November 2003 the Queensland Parliament asked the state Crime and Misconduct Commission to conduct an inquiry into the circumstances surrounding the pair's conviction and jailing.

The CMC examined all relevant police and prosecution files, and considered the record of both the civil and criminal trial and their respective appeals. Its officers conducted interviews with a number of people, including those involved in the criminal investigation and criminal trial. Written submissions were sought from people thought to have relevant information. Many responded. Other submissions were received in response to an advertised call for submissions.

The CMC's subsequent report concluded that 'no misconduct or other impropriety has been shown to have been associated with the conduct of the litigation concerning Ms Hanson and Mr Ettridge, or with the police investigations leading to the prosecution. The Commission also found no evidence of political pressure or other improper influence or impropriety.'

It also noted: 'The Commission found nothing to show a failure to accord due process, in accordance with the rule of law, to Ms Hanson and Mr Ettridge. In particular, the involvement of Tony Abbott in events leading up to the institution of proceedings to de-register the party did not produce or constitute a failure of due process.' Similarly, the CMC found no evidence to support accusations that Beattie had in any way been involved in their prosecution.

\* \* \*

Despite her new persona as a celebrated political martyr, she would have rocks in her head to consider a return to politics, Hanson swore when she was released from jail. A few weeks later she underscored this sentiment by proclaiming she was 'so angry' she felt like 'shaking people' who asked her to stand again.

'I'm sick and tired of seeing people elected to parliament who haven't got the determination or the integrity, and who sell their souls to get their positions. I'm not feeling sorry for myself. I'm just really angry for the system we have . . .'

And in another interview: 'I'm out of it, I'm finished, it's over,' she stated categorically in January 2004, before gargling her throat ahead of an appearance at the Country Music Festival in

Tamworth, where she sang the patriotic 'I Am Australian'—with a young Indigenous singer.

Hanson and ten-year-old Nellie Dargan took to the stage at the Oasis Hotel following performances by a bird whistler and yodeller. Dargan had written to Hanson in jail, laying down a challenge to join her and sing the words of the anthem of equality between all races and peoples of Australia. To her credit, Hanson agreed. The young singer's verdict about her partner's performance after the event: 'She was all right.'

Hanson had arrived at the pub with a TV crew, an odd but increasingly common accessory for her as she went about getting on with her post-jail, allegedly post-politics life. It seemed like a return to the catwalk and stage, to the real theatre of life, offered much more fun to her. Or maybe she could combine these with politics in a neat tandem act!

Eight months later, just three months out from the 9 October federal election and while rehearsing for the Channel Seven shimmy glitzfest, *Dancing with the Stars*, Hanson announced her candidature as an Independent for the Senate via a pre-recorded TV interview sent to media outlets.

Her campaign this time around relied on nothing other than her infamy. Sightings of her on the hustings were as thin on the ground as the policies she released. Media appearances were rare; turning on the waterworks on the Kerri-Anne Kennerley show, while she recalled her experience as a political prisoner, was as good, or bad, as it got.

She did pop her head up to object—as freedom of speech defenders are wont to do—to the lifting of a six-year-old injunction she'd slapped on the playing of a song about her by the drag-queen satirist Pauline Pantsdown (real name, Simon Hunt, and son of a New South Wales judge). In 1998 a ban had been placed on the airing of Pantsdown's song, 'I'm a Backdoor Man'; but now the socialist ABC was petitioning the court to void that ban.

Hanson smelled another conspiracy. It was disgraceful of the public broadcaster, she fumed. 'Why six years later, right in the middle of an election campaign?' she yelped. The song implied she was a prostitute and a transsexual, she said crossly. She would 'hate to think' what the song could do to her chances of winning a Queensland Senate position.

It probably helped her. After all, there weren't many other ways her adoring public would have known she was again running for office, apart from the teary KAK interview and the first episode of *Dancing with the Stars*, which rated very well. By some kind of wonderful happenstance her terpsichorean debut was aired the week before polling day.

Despite her new status as Australia's first political prisoner and the attention that brought, she didn't win a Senate seat. But she won the equivalent of a senior corporate manager's salary for a year by hitting the magic mark of more than 4 per cent of the vote, entitling her to just shy of $200,000 in public funding.

The little person Hanson reckons she represents would have punched the air and shouted 'I've won the lottery!' if they'd received $65,000 a week for three weeks of invisible election campaigning, at the same time being paid by Channel Seven to cha-cha into peoples' lounge rooms glittering like a Christmas tree.

She ran second in the celebrity dance competition to *Home and Away* soapie star Bec Cartwright. The vote musta been rigged! No good complaining, she must have thought. You can't take a feckless reality show-voting public to the authorities. Another injustice would just have to go through to the keeper.

Life was good, though. Hanson had a bit of dough to feed herself and the Arabian horses back at the Queensland ranch, and ponder her next move. Her old party was continuing its free fall into irrelevance without her; in February 2005, Pauline Hanson's One Nation was de-registered.

Politically, all fell quiet for a few years.

# Chapter 7
# A TALE OF SHEER BASTARDRY

THE ELEVATION OF the merciless Queenslander Kevin Rudd to the Labor leadership in 2006 gave Hanson a reason to think the November 2007 federal election might be a winner for her too. Queenslanders rock, right? She reincarnated as a Queensland Senate candidate—the only candidate of the Pauline's United Australia Party—but failed to jitterbug her way back onto voters' dance cards.

Lucky! Despite again running a low-key, no-frills, no-cost campaign, she polled in excess of 4.2 per cent of the vote and the party raked in more than $210,000 in public funding. An unusual transfer of most of the funds from the party to her bank account would later become the subject of a police and Electoral Commission inquiry.

Earlier that year her book, *Untamed and Unashamed*, reportedly ghost-written by former staffer Helen Dodd, had been launched. Many words were spilled in defence of the wrongly imprisoned Ms Hanson. The first chapter—one of many devoted to her savaging at the hands of a suspect legal system and her wretched jailing—was a showpiece of self-obsession and victimisation.

Witnesses against her in the case were liars and perjurers; the evidence was ridiculous. The neutrality of the jury's chosen twelve was in doubt. The media were sensationalist, on a personal vendetta against her and ill-informed. There was 'no doubt' it had been a 'political trial'.

Her voice of victimhood was in full technicolour throttle as Hanson described her feelings as she was being led away from the court to the cells: 'I wanted to scream out, "Leave me alone, you have no idea what they have done to me!"'

But her dogged nemesis, David Oldfield, wasn't fooled: 'She's making a big drive for the dough. It's always about the dough where Pauline is concerned,' was his considered verdict of the motive for the penning of the self-serving memoir.

The timing of her book's publication was certainly very helpful. Or so she had thought before the votes were counted.

\* \* \*

Her unrelenting drive for political relevance and the spotlight continued unabated. Which state map would she stick a pin in next?

Lucky Queensland! Shifting back to state politics, in 2009 she ran as an Independent for the seat of Beaudesert. Dammit, she missed out again. But she received a healthy 21.2 per cent of the vote, and approximately $8000 in public funding. It wasn't the windfall of old; Queensland's public funding laws meant taxpayers' hard-earned were now only paid out to eligible candidates upon provision of campaign receipts.

Being a celebrity political prisoner doesn't mean you eat soup and bread the rest of your life. Hanson has always bristled with anger at suggestions she has benefited from public funding. 'I have not claimed any money personally from any elections,' she is on the record as stating on a number of occasions.

It was at this time that she received a financial top-up from News Corp's Sydney *Sunday Telegraph*, which paid her a handsome confidential figure for publishing those fake nude photos, purportedly of fraudster Jack Johnson and her cavorting in the Coffs Harbour motel room. In unlucky timing for the newspaper—but brilliant for the perpetually victimised candidate—the tabloid had been suckerpunched into publishing the photos the weekend before polling day. That hit on her credibility no doubt enhanced her pay-out.

But she was now sick of rejection. Her failure to capture the hearts of the Beaudesert people meant she was going to throw in the towel. Her political aspirations had been snuffed out, she declared.

She was off to the UK, and would never darken Australia's doors again. She'd had enough. She was angry about Australia and livid at the forces that rose like demons from the dirt to thwart her every move—especially the media. Except for her favourites, including the glossy, *Woman's Day*, which had breathlessly chronicled her romantic ups and downs over the years. She confided to the mag that she wanted peace in her life: 'Sadly, the land of opportunity is no more applicable.'

She was fed up. Really, really fed up. She was going back to the land of some of her forebears—the land of kings and queens—to be a motivational speaker. Off to the grandmother country, whose earliest settler experiences in the wretched Land Down Under, including the taming of the cannibalistic natives, had been lionised in *Pauline Hanson: The Truth*. See ya, lovelies, and thanks for the memories!

But what? Back again so soon? After a few months taking in the sights of Europe and a fleeting visit to the Old Dart, Pauline's thin lips curled. She had been startled to discover that the UK was, in fact, 'overrun with immigrants and refugees'. So back to the colony and another election—this one in March 2011.

The Upper House in New South Wales again beckoned. Nominating just three weeks out from the 26 March poll date, she said she was contesting it because 'it is in the people's interest of NSW to ensure that I am on the floor of NSW'. She 'became emotional' when telling *The Daily Telegraph* that it was her son who convinced her to run because 'the people need you more than I do'. But she hung up on the newspaper's reporter, Andrew Clennell, when he asked whether, you know, she actually lived in the state she wanted to represent. It was later reported that she moved to Nelson Bay, on the central coast.

She nearly got there but no cigar, narrowly missing out on a berth in the Legislative Council by about 1300 votes.

The forces of evil were again out to stop her. She challenged the results in the Supreme Court, maintaining that dodgy Electoral Commission staff had piled 1200 ballot papers marked for her into the blank ballot pile. Her evidence was a flimsy email, allegedly from the Electoral Commission and found later to be patently fraudulent. Case dismissed. She may or may not have known that recent changes to New South Wales public funding laws meant that to receive public funds, eligible candidates—those who met the quota of 4.55 per cent of the vote, after preferences—had to produce receipts.

\* \* \*

No matter where she turned, she found traitors and those determined to keep her down. She was fit to spit after being booted from *Celebrity Apprentice* in November, lashing out at fellow contestants and even at its compere, the mini-Trump who hired and fired, Mark Bouris.

She sprayed about her fellow contestants: 'They haven't been out in the real world. They've never done a bloody job. They've been nurtured and molly-coddled and all the rest of it. For Christ's sake,

I don't know who the hell they think they are but they need to get their hands dirty and get out and do some bloody work. Forget about being up in the bloody clouds.'

'I like fair play,' she fumed in another media interview. 'I've copped it through politics where you think you've got a teammate with you and you haven't. Behind your back they are knifing you. I don't operate like that. Always be up front with people, don't sink the boot in.'

Friends, supporters and romantic interests—who had been flattened over the years by her habit of abruptly turning on them without warning or explanation—could only scratch their heads at this proclamation and go back to picking up the pieces of their lives.

\* \* \*

The siren call of deep political waters again beckoned and the forgiving bosom of One Nation embraced her in 2013. It was her old ally Brian Burston who claims responsibility for her One Nation resurrection. 'Pauline was sitting in our lounge room in the summer of 2013 and I said "Pauline if you ever want to get elected again, you have to get back with One Nation and you must change the name back to Pauline Hanson's One Nation",' he told Fairfax media.

So that's just what she did. She rejoined the party as a humble rank-and-file member in 2013 and, like a pilot in a *Back to the Future* time machine, strapped herself in and retreated to the comfort zone of serial Senate candidate. The target this time was a New South Wales Senate seat in the September 2013 general election. But she was given a massive thumbs-down, the One Nation ticket polling a poor 1.22 per cent.

Not to worry. The Burston blueprint was on track. In November 2014, the national executive anointed her as national leader. She announced her triumphant return on the party's website, stating she would dare to raise issues that were 'politically incorrect': 'Due to public support, I have taken up the role of One Nation leader again. We are here to give Australians a voice in parliament.'

A few old chestnuts were pushed out, with a couple of newies: 'The push for multiculturalism is only segregating us as a nation and not uniting us as Australians with the same values, beliefs and laws . . . Halal is being forced on us by 2 per cent of the population.'

And there'd be no more of those manipulators or control freaks by her side. Indeed, it seemed she wasn't going to listen to anyone, not even from the ranks of the party that had chugged along without her for nearly thirteen years. 'This time I will be in control, no one is going to pull my strings, or tell me what to say,' she said in a TV interview that day.

The grass didn't grow long beneath the flame-haired siren's feet. The newly minted One Nation leader quickly hurtled back to Queensland in another attempt to transcend time and space, this time at the 31 January 2015 Queensland election. Home, sweet home! She was gunning for the seat of Lockyer.

She was standing, she said with her trademark inexplicability, because 'people in this electorate deserve the right to be heard. So therefore I haven't thrown the towel in. If you thought that, well then—go back to Gallipoli. The Australian soldiers fought on those beaches, they didn't turn and run.'

Yet again, her fighting words weren't enough and she lost— although only by a mere 114 votes. She wuz again robbed! As the official One Nation website states: 'Hanson believes it was a corrupt counting system that cost her the seat. Preferences were counted on a notional count and not in accordance with legislation.

'The Queensland Electoral Commission refused a recount, regardless of the difference of only 114 votes between winning and loosing [*sic*]. Legal costs were going to cost in excess of $40,000 to take it to the Court of Disputed Returns. Hanson had to walk away once again from a corrupt voting and counting system.'

Foiled by political and electoral corruption, once again. But she could now smell victory—somewhere, somehow. The second coming was in reach. The forthcoming federal election would be the next cab off the rank, and perhaps here was the opportunity that up until now had been denied her. In July 2015, the transformation of One Nation into Pauline's vehicle was complete when it was rebranded and re-registered as Pauline Hanson's One Nation.

The old saying that if you try, try and try again eventually you'll succeed was in play. The times seemed ripe for her.

She sensed that voters were ready for anyone who could give voice to their anger and isolation; they were poised to kick the hell out of the major parties. They might just give her a time-machine blast all the way back to her glory days in Canberra in the 1990s.

But who could help her revive that symphony and song?

\* \* \*

Pauline may not have won the state election, but the consolation prize wasn't half bad. This was the moment when her next protector and henchman entered from stage right.

James Ashby was a political aspirant with a sordid past in federal politics, a chequered personal and pre-politics professional background, a hot temper and big ambitions. Perfect! Just the man to usher Hanson back from the wilderness into the Canberra corridors of power, even though she had sworn off having anyone by her side that could dilute her control of the party.

Quite how the pair met depends on who's doing the telling. Former One Nation Treasurer Ian Nelson says it was a deliberate act on Ashby's part. He says Ashby had rung with a great offer in the run-up to the 2015 Queensland state election: cheap printing. For a cash-strapped party, it was too good to be true. There was one condition though—he wanted to meet Pauline.

Ashby's recollections don't line up with Nelson's. It was true he'd done some work for One Nation, including shooting video for them, he maintained. In that capacity, he just happened to bump into Hanson on polling day. He told the *Weekend Australian* in July 2015 he'd been drawn to Hanson after she just missed out on winning a seat at the state election. 'I was taking photographs for One Nation on polling day, met Pauline and we began a discussion that now has me working for her,' was his story.

Another of his renditions was that he'd actually met her and been a fan since his blighted time at a Newcastle radio station in the early 2000s. He'd found her 'very frank and up-front', he told the ABC in 2015. 'Maybe because I come from a conservative background myself, I found her intriguing and some of her comments worth listening to,' he explained.

His version for *The Guardian* was that he was really just a saviour, and a reluctant one at that. 'I only became involved in the party through request,' he clarified. 'At that moment I had always indicated I had no interest in returning to politics . . . the party was in need of people to assist, keep it afloat, they were looking for executive members that would help drive the party forward, not backwards, they were looking for some fresh younger blood. My skill set was completely different to everybody else.'

As well, he happened to be a pilot. Luckily, he also happened to be free to fly her around the state following her narrow state loss and while she was eyeing off the 2016 federal election as her next campaigning pit stop.

Within months, Ashby had suggested she might like to avail herself of his other skills. As he explained modestly to the ABC in

June, he had something to offer Hanson beyond transporting her safely to a destination: 'I've learnt a lot over the last couple of years and that experience comes in handy.'

Similarly, in Pauline's characteristic lightning-quick way with relationships, it wasn't long before she was referring to him as her 'adopted son', and he had slipped into the role of being her chief defender, dragon-slayer, manager.

\* \* \*

James Ashby is to controversy what cow dung is to blowflies: he attracts it in swarms. Pauline Hanson's new handler burst into the spotlight after he set off a highly publicised and destructive legal assault on the integrity of Speaker Peter Slipper in 2012.

Ashby's chase of the sad-eyed former Speaker for sexual harassment was an episode that the talented scriptwriters for *West Wing* or *House of Cards* would struggle to beat for sinister undertones, political intrigue, smut and personal tragedy. It was, in Tony Abbott's words, a 'squalid, sordid, miserable period in our national life'—a gallantly big call for a politician whose messy early love life and political trickeries have kept headline writers busy for years.

Ashby cut his political teeth in the fetid depths of the Queensland Liberal National Party where, after the 2007 Ruddslaughter, back- and front-stabbers worked openly to discredit each other. Everywhere the sorcerers of dark political arts were alive with plots. It was a particularly frenetic time for political operatives, and a particularly rotten one for aspiring politicians with pure motives.

By 2010, LNP strategists believed Queensland Labor Premier Anna Bligh's Government was on drunken legs. Branch-stacking within the party had been rampant for a few years; after the 2010 federal election had reduced Labor in Canberra to a one-seat minority government, it reached fever pitch as the party sensed the real possibility of imminent federal and state victories.

In 2007 ambitious former federal minister Mal Brough had lost to Labor his seat of Longman, on the northern fringes of Brisbane, and now he craved a return. He was seen as one of the LNP's smarter stars among a dull lot. He'd been Indigenous Affairs Minister under John Howard, and his ambitions hadn't yet been snuffed out. The former army captain was assertive in pursuit of his goals, highly competitive, and a dab hand at getting his people recruited en masse into branches.

A glimpse into Brough's take-no-prisoners character was his antagonistic performance at a friendly cricket match against the parliamentary press gallery in 2001, during the Howard years. Of all teams to throw a hissy fit in front of, that shouldn't have been it. As Malcolm Farr of News Limited briskly recalled, he was umpiring and Brough was batting. An arrow-straight delivery by the *Australian Financial Review*'s Mark Ludlow hit Brough plum in the pads. Farr slowly raised his finger, giving him out. Brough initially refused to leave the pitch.

When he finally surrendered, 'he threw his bat and pads to the ground and demanded his wife follow him to their car', yelling insults on the way, Farr recalled. He took off in his car 'at great speed', leaving the press gallery team with dropped jaws and hoping that one of their own had tucked a mini-cam with the record button whirring into the kit.

Half an hour later Brough returned to try and make amends, jocularly remarking that 'a bit of aggro' was good for his sex life. Yo, bro.

The seat of Fisher, on the Sunshine Coast, was held by the LNP's ferociously disliked 'Slippery' Peter Slipper—ordained priest in the Anglican Catholic Church, husband, father and subject of tawdry scuttlebutt about his sexual proclivities and love of the high life. Slipper's penchant for fine plonk and fancy outings courtesy of the taxpayer, and whispered secret yearnings that didn't sit well with his loving family image, had long raised eyebrows. He became a prime target for Brough, who declared his intention to run for LNP pre-selection for his seat.

Slipper pined for a ministerial salary. He was consistently one of the highest-spending taxpayer-funded travellers in parliament, even though his career high to date was a low-level parliamentary secretary. His spending habits had ensured that that was his career pinnacle. His overseas 'study' trips were extravagant odysseys, unlike the reports he filed in parliament, which were remarkably bland and insultingly short.

Slipper's Olympian spending of taxpayers' funds gave political journalists easy stories twice yearly when official figures were released. An expenses bill for the six months to the end of 2009 was particularly juicy: the humble backbencher spent an eye-glazing $640,562, easily eclipsing Treasurer Wayne Swan's $491,236 and second only to Kevin Rudd's $1.18 million.

He'd been in the spotlight previously over his spending, and forced to repay $20,000 in entitlements. It had all been a mistake— sloppy paperwork, he maintained. Slipper rather fancied zipping about in cabs, and kept taxi fleets in a number of strange locations working overtime. His pompous eccentricities, lavish spending and tales of personal explorations made him an easy target for malicious media treatment.

His party wasn't a fan either. They labelled him a traitor when he accepted the Labor Government's offer to nominate as Deputy Speaker at the start of the Gillard minority government. His loyalty to the party that had kept pre-selecting him despite his vulnerabilities seemed to have been abandoned when he went up against one of his own and secured this prize gig with Labor's support. He was treacherous, a leech on the taxpayer and an embarrassment to his party, his colleagues muttered.

He confirmed this impression on 24 November 2011, when he became Speaker after Labor's Harry Jenkins announced he was over it and wanted his life back. Slipper's acceptance of the Labor lure to take up the plum post—surely one of the most breathtakingly cynical political offers of recent times—meant the government now had a two-seat majority instead of its previously perilous, one-heart-attack-away one-seat majority. It crushed the Coalition's dreams of forcing the government from office early.

Party frenemies who had previously tolerated him instantly became deeply aggrieved enemies hell-bent on revenge. From that day on, Slipper was a marked man. 'Slimeball', someone spray-painted on his electoral office, one of the nicer descriptions of the turncoat.

The dirty tricks squad immediately sprinted from the back-rooms of the Sunshine State to the offices of key federal LNP players. The stories blackening Slipper started appearing in quickstep time.

Two days after taking up residence in the best suite of offices in Parliament House, tawdry tales that the new Speaker was a star in an alleged video involving a male staffer bobbed up in a number of publications. 'It is understood a video had been made of Mr Slipper and the young staffer lying on a bed hugging,' reported Fairfax.

Anonymous sources used compliant journalists to rehash tales of Lord Slipper living high on the hog on the taxpayer's purse, or to plant fresh ones about unnamed Labor MPs being spooked that more tales of spending splurges could unseat the new Speaker and cause the minority government grief.

Slipper didn't stand a chance.

\* \* \*

Young, fresh-faced, charming and openly gay, Ashby had been a recruit to one of the rapidly swelling LNP branches during the politically torrid noughties.

He'd originally lucked a breakfast shift on Sunshine Coast brekkie radio after only a matter of weeks in community radio. That had been a gift in anyone's book, but he quickly fell out with a manager after a row, and was told to bugger off out of the building and don't forget your hat, thanks.

During his next job, at a Newcastle radio station, a rival broadcaster incurred his wrath. In a career-limiting move, he phoned the bloke and left an abusive and threatening message. 'Next time I see you riding on your fucking bike I'll hit you, you idiot, all over the sloppy road, you dumb prick. If I was your mother I would have drowned you at birth.'

It was a joke! he cried when unsmiling local cops banged on his door after the broadcaster lodged a complaint, saying he feared for his life. The magistrate didn't think it was a laugh, and Ashby copped a charge of using a carriage service to menace, harass or cause offence. He was fined $2000 and slapped with a three-year good behaviour bond.

If he harboured ideas of crawling the ladder to become the next Alan Jones he had parked them at this time, and he drifted around inconsequential regional radio stations for a few years. He had little stability in either his commercial or personal lives. In one endeavour he set up a printing business in Townsville, but that hit the rocks when an internet client went belly-up, owing him thousands.

Ultimately he shuffled back to the comfort of the Sunshine Coast and a job as PR spruiker with the strawberry business, Gowinta Farms, where LNP spotters, always on the hunt for fresh parliamentary talent, had noticed him. So had the local member, Peter Slipper.

The succulent strawberry quickly became one of Slipper's favourite fruits, and he frequented the farm for supplies. Ashby talked video and social media PR with the MP, and encouraged him to do a YouTube video. The Deputy Speaker enthusiastically lauded the subsequent nine views: Ashby had given him 'the best media advice I've ever received!'

Charmed by the charmer, Slipper relentlessly pursued the political novice to work for him in Canberra. Ashby kept refusing.

But just weeks after Slipper became Speaker, Ashby had a sudden change of heart and took up a $155,000-a-year adviser's position. It was 'too good to be true to pass up!', *The Australian*'s Jamie Walker reported Ashby saying. He resigned from the LNP, but his lines of communication with the party remained open.

Inappropriate sexual texts starting pinging from the entranced Slipper's phone to Ashby, who decided they offended him. A mere four months after starting the job, Ashby sued his boss for sexual harassment and discrimination, and doubled down by accusing him of misusing government-provided Cabcharge dockets—an action that would later be dropped.

Among the unwanted sexual advances alleged by Ashby was an accusation that Slipper had asked his staffer to shower with the bathroom door open. Although vehemently denying this, the Speaker stood aside on 22 April pending investigations.

Ashby's acceptance of the job in the first place had raised eyebrows within the party. He was an LNP bloke; any future parliamentary career as a staffer or even an MP relied on support from party heavyweights. He'd been marked for office by party hacks, and he'd also openly talked about one day standing for parliament—even to Slipper, before he'd accepted the job on his staff. Ashby knew the murderous rage Slipper's defection to take the Speakership had sparked among his party comrades, and he'd breezily dismissed them.

There was the other weird bit about it too: Ashby wasn't a shrinking violet. He could be as combative as the next bloke, was quick to anger at a wrong sideways glance and had a history of belligerence in professional relationships.

His early career in the dog-eat-dog world of commercial shock jockery showed he could stand up for himself. Even if he wasn't offended by someone or something, he had showed he could dish it out. By all accounts he was confident, competent, and not someone who'd cower in the corner if someone sexually harassed him.

\* \* \*

By the time Ashby filed his complaint, former LNP colleagues, who he'd mightily pissed off when he'd gone to work for Slipper, were back in the BFF zone. He had drinkies in parliament with Manager of Opposition Business, Chris Pyne; chummed it up with Shadow Attorney-General George Brandis in his office; and even dropped in to see the impeccably politically smart Shadow Foreign Minister, Julie Bishop. Many were on hand to come to the aid and comfort of the allegedly harassed staffer.

Ashby and Brough connected via a network of contacts in the legal and political fraternity; the precise details of that web again depended on who was doing the telling. Within days, News Limited journalist Steve Lewis was also involved. Well before the legal action was filed, the journalist energetically colluded with Ashby in the hunt for one of the biggest political scalps going. Lewis roamed across News Corps' mastheads as one of its favourite political head-kickers, and News' prime target at this time was the Gillard Government.

Lewis broke the story of the sexual harassment lawsuit in *The Daily Telegraph* in a sensational front-page splash on 21 April, the morning after the suit was filed. Slipper hadn't been notified about the action until the last minute, and Lewis did the age-old trick of a journalist ambushing a target: leave it as late as possible to ask for comment.

Slipper, who was in New York on parliamentary business and accompanied by his wife Inge, was about to be blown up by a metaphorical double-decker bus loaded with dynamite by political foes within the LNP, his staffers and a journalist. He had no way of seeing it coming, and it hit him hard.

The ambitious Brough was quickly fingered as being up to his eyeballs in the affair. It was his 'moral obligation', Brough said, to help when the distressed staffer sought him out. 'All I did was to help someone in need,' Brough would later say. 'No more, no less.'

Many others, including Slipper's first wife Lyn, with whom he remained close, saw it in a darker light. She told *The Sun-Herald* that Slipper was doomed from the get-go. 'The moment Peter was elected Speaker we all had the sword of Damocles hanging over our heads, waiting to see what would happen. We knew there would be retribution. Peter stood between Tony Abbott and The Lodge; it was obvious he was fair game. Tony Abbott released the dogs; they were going to come for him, come what may.'

Abbott was a concerned defender of the great institution of parliament. What he plotted and planned behind closed doors was a mismatch for his public utterances. 'I can't underestimate the seriousness of this,' he intoned at a press conference held speedily after the news hit. 'The Speaker is required to maintain parliamentary standards, and yet there are now these extremely serious allegations against the Speaker himself.'

In order to 'maintain the respect and the reputation of the Parliament' and 'preserve the integrity of the government and our institutions', Slipper should be despatched forthwith, harrumphed the bloke who for years had used parliament to misrepresent and abuse political opponents. Abbott is a consistent gold medallist in the Say-One-Thing-Do-Another event.

The eventual roll-call of federal Coalition MPs interlinked with the messy scandal included Brough, Abbott, Pyne, Brandis, Bishop and new Queensland MP Wyatt Roy. But the standout was Brough.

The eccentric billionaire businessman Clive Palmer, at that stage still an LNP bankroller, made a cameo appearance, as did former LNP President Bruce McIver. Expensive lawyers and high-cost media managers allegedly working pro bono were embedded in the action to bring Slipper down.

For a tale of sheer bastardry, naked greed for power, political cunning and reputational slaughter it was hard to beat. And at the heart of it sat James Ashby, Hanson's future trusted aide.

A treasure trove of texts released during the court action lent weight to a conclusion that an Ashby- and LNP-inspired political cell that extended its tentacles into the federal Coalition, backed by the full force of a fiercely anti-Gillard Murdoch empire, had used Slipper to bring down the Labor Government. 'We will get him!' an excited Lewis had texted Ashby.

Texts sent from Ashby to Slipper, containing sexualised banter, suggested a very different story to that of a victimised young staffer. One of them read: 'I'm going to smack u! Arhhhhhhh!' Another: 'Cool. Let's fuck them up the arse instead'; and, coyly: 'You're cruising for a bruising!' One early text among dozens between Ashby and another Slipper staffer, Karen Doane, referred to them preparing their résumés to send to Brough.

Federal Court Justice Steven Rares threw out Ashby's claim as an abuse of process in December 2012. The action was designed 'to expose Mr Slipper to the maximum degree of vilification, opprobrium, sensation and scandal and cause maximum damage to his reputation to the political advantage of the LNP and Mr Brough', he damningly found.

Backed by a phalanx of lawyers, Ashby appealed Rares' finding to the court's Full Bench. In February 2014 it agreed that the action should have been allowed to go to trial.

'I have always believed the original court decision was wrong, unjust and not based on the facts,' a statement released by Ashby's expensive communication consultant, Anthony McLellan, read following the decision. 'This has been a long and tortuous journey, but I am determined not to give up until my claim has been vindicated.'

That determination mysteriously went to water. Ashby abandoned the action in April 2014, just two weeks before proceedings were due to start, claiming in part that it was because the Commonwealth was funding Slipper's defence. Ashby's no-win-no-pay lawyers had reportedly been prepared to continue the fight in view of the excoriating comments of Justice Rares. But it had been too 'intense and emotionally draining', he proclaimed, and the decision by the Full Bench meant he had been vindicated.

Wrong, Slipper and some legal experts responded. The former Speaker said in a statement: 'Any suggestion by Mr Ashby that the Full Court of the Federal Court found that the allegations of harassment had occurred is wholly incorrect. The Full Court decision meant that Mr Ashby could bring his allegations before the court to be tested, something which he has now declined to do. I am pleased to be so completely and publicly vindicated.'

\* \* \*

The miserable end to this desperate tale of political trickery and personal tragedy was almost a footnote. The political and media convoy had swiftly moved on. In July 2014 Slipper faced and was convicted by the ACT Magistrate's Court of thrice misusing Cabcharge vouchers for an amount less than $1000. The convictions weren't related to Ashby's original accusations, but arose out of a subsequent police investigation.

His conviction received scant media coverage, and neither did his successful appeal and quashing of that conviction. He was yesterday's story; justice isn't a great yarn, and anyway journalists are loath to admit when their shark pack attacks bomb. Slipper had lost his job, for a time his marriage and his sanity, and had a spell in a psychiatric hospital. Too bad your time in the limelight was a bummer for you, Pete. We've moved on.

Teflon Tony meanwhile had gone on to become Prime Minister, Christopher Pyne a Cabinet minister and Leader of the House, and George Brandis Attorney-General, later parachuted to High Commissioner to the United Kingdom.

Protesting too much his innocence in any conspiracy, Brough won LNP pre-selection for Slipper's seat, returned to parliament at the 2013 election and started his crawl back up the ladder. He was on his way when newly minted PM Malcolm Turnbull gave him an outer ministry berth as Special Minister of State in his first ministry after ousting Abbott on 15 September 2015.

Brough's world crashed when he was forced just a few months later to stand aside, following revelations police were investigating him for his role in the Ashby Affair. He quit the frontbench in February 2016. His protestations that he had little to do with helping to bring the harassment case to life were disproved. His career was sunk, and the man who had the highest political aspirations disappeared forever from politics at the July election.

Ashby's dreams of running for office, or being a big wheel in politics in another capacity, seemed to be as dead as Slipper's career. His personal reputation was battered, despite the fig leaf victory before the Federal Court Full Bench, and in political circles he was as popular as a snake in a sleeping bag.

The lurid footprints of the Slipper saga would cling to him like dog poo on the soles of his shoe.

But then along came Pauline.

# Chapter 8
# TAKING TO THE SKIES

THEIRS WAS A POLITICAL union made in heaven. Or hell. Take your pick. Both had itinerant personal and professional backgrounds, political rat cunning, narcissistic qualities and an entrepreneurial eye for a financial chance. Both had been bruised by the legal system and politics.

Both share an unshakeable belief in their own versions of the truth; they shed relationships like snake skins, and know how to walk a fine ethical line. And both are as thin-skinned as Donald Trump, taking offence at perceived slights.

Hanson has slapped more people and organisations with gag orders, bans and threats than most politicians. The first time media were banned for daring to do their jobs was from the One Nation gathering at the Ipswich Showground for her concession speech when she ran for the seat of Blair at the 1998 general election. It's continued in a crime-and-punishment cycle since.

Similarly, Ashby's history is one of professional sensitivity to perceived slights that most politicians and others in the tough game would be inclined to shrug off as merely part of the hurly-burly.

Apart from the legal assault on Slipper, Ashby took Nationals MP Barnaby Joyce and then Foreign Minister Bob Carr to the Human Rights Commission in 2012 when the Slipper drama raged. Joyce had sinned by declaring Ashby 'only slightly less dodgy than Slipper'. Carr landed in the dog kennel for tweeting that Ashby seemed 'more rehearsed than a kabuki actor'.

The pair also share a fondness for political conspiracies in which they star as victims. Hanson has long bleated that the political system was designed to cheat her; that politicians are out to get her; that her personal relationships have exploded because of villainous behaviour by the other parties.

Ashby has a similar bent. Questions raised about his motives in the Slipper business angered him, and he carried it with him into his next life. When he became Hanson's pilot, he refused to tell inquiring journalists where the plane was parked. 'There are a few people that probably want to take both of us out, so we've got to be a bit cautious where we put it. There's probably someone who wants to shove sugar in the fuel tank.' Apparently they were both so important that evil-doers wanted to take them out in equal measure.

That and many other flashes and signals should have belled the cat for Hanson's loyal foot soldiers back in the bunker. But it didn't, and the ole familiar tune cranked out.

Party treasurer Ian Nelson kicks himself for not checking out Ashby from the get-go. Extraordinarily, Ashby's name hadn't clicked with him or others in the Queensland branch who were ignorant of the new recruit's sordid not-so-distant past with Slipper. Nelson vows he would have sent him packing had he known when he came knocking, cheap printing be damned. 'I was there to watch Pauline's back, and when I had time I was going to vet people before they got too close to Pauline,' he later told the ABC. 'But I absolutely failed miserably on that one.'

Another brash, bright, manipulative bloke had bulldozed his way into Hanson's world. She has carbon-copied her closest advisers for decades. They're always male, always pitbull aggressive, and have the political people skills of rottweilers.

Despite her strident insistence she's the boss, and that it's her party and she'll do what she wants and to whom, her devolution of a large slice of her authority and control to a succession of hard-nosed male lieutenants is an unbreakable pattern in the times she's been leader. In so doing, she repeatedly ditches party loyalists to clear the way for her and her current partner-in-conspiracy's duopoly control of the organisation.

If, in the most generous of worlds, it was possible to believe that Ashby was once starry-eyed and naive, his saddling up with Hanson certainly knocked it out of him.

*　　*　　*

Hanson and Ashby were cagey and unusually defensive from the start about where exactly he fitted into the One Nation organisation. By mid-2015 he was stuck to her like a fly to sticky paper, calling himself her spokesman. But don't dare ask him or her if he's a One Nation employee, or what is his real role, or who's paying him if he's not on the books.

He dismissed a question from the Victorian *Herald-Sun* with the retort he worked for free. Another reporter, from BuzzFeed, was monstered by Hanson after innocently asking if her sidekick was on the One Nation payroll. 'It's none of your business,' she snapped, rehashing her stock answer to questions demanding transparency about her and the organisation.

'So you better make sure with what you report on this because it's not your business or anyone else's business whether James Ashby is on the payroll or not. I told you he works closely with me.

He is my pilot. Now anything past that I am not going to disclose. So if you write anything, you make sure you write the truth because if you put anything there that is not, I have solicitors who are very supportive of me and I'll have you for defamation,' she threatened.

How any scribe is supposed to write her version of 'the truth' is hard to guess when she won't respond to questions.

Ashby must have been quite the self-funded individual if he worked for free, and the party must have had an impressive stable of bankrollers propping up the organisation. It's not cheap to run an election campaign, and Hanson's bid for a Queensland Senate seat kicked off in July 2015, a full year before the election.

Hanson was now crouched in her favourite position, that of defensive indignation, when questioned by journalists about how her campaign was being funded; indeed, how she was earning a crust. She did not take a salary from One Nation and lived off the money she made in business, she responded testily, and anyway: 'How I support myself is no one's business.'

\* \* \*

Hanson and her new sidekick took to the skies in a Jabiru 23-D on the ambitious year-long tour of Australia they christened the 'Fed Up' campaign. The motto had a strong whiff off Hanson's personal lament about her constant defeats: 'Don't Give Up, We Haven't'.

Ashby told the *ABC* he'd sourced the plane for Hanson in Australia because 'Pauline's all about keeping things local'. The plane was emblazoned with the name of her party, bearing a caricature of her beaming face waving a fluttering Australian flag. Just that month she'd rebadged her party yet again as 'Pauline Hanson's One Nation', another clear indication she was firmly back in control.

Sometimes, she was happy to talk to the media—as long as the questions were tame and she didn't have to account for herself or answer silly questions about accountability and funding.

'As I have travelled around the country, people are telling me they are fed up with losing the farming sector, they're fed up with foreign ownership of our land and prime agricultural land, they're fed up with the threat of terrorism in our country and the free trade agreements that have been signed, which are not in our best interest, and foreign workers coming in to Australia . . . So hence the "Fed Up" tour,' she explained one time when spruiking her campaign.

The little light aircraft would later be the star exhibit in a muddy tale of hidden benefactors and ownership; but for now it was just a plane, and they were just a couple of committed campaigners spreading the good word and warning Australians of the hidden and ever-present dangers of government policies.

The pair criss-crossed Queensland with their binoculars peeled for stray votes in the regions. Their first campaign destination was a Reclaim Australia rally in Rockhampton as they puttered from here to there across the state, campaigning, inter alia, against Sharia law, halal tax, Islamisation and for free speech.

In what seemed a bizarre move for a person with a hostile attitude to the media, Hanson allowed film-maker Anna Broinowski open access to her campaign. She'd also previously allowed Fairfax's Margo Kingston to trail her during her road-crash campaign to win Blair in 1998. Hanson detests the media, but she loves the limelight. She considered the odds, and the limelight won.

Broinowski chronicled how well Hanson's anti-Islam theme worked on her remote and regional tour. At this time the Syrian war was pumping out refugees at a rate that saw them inundate neighbouring countries in catastrophic numbers; the hollow misery of their pathetic odysseys, seeking a better life elsewhere, was highlighted by the confronting image of a little Syrian boy, Alan Kurdi, washed up on a Turkish beach. The rivers of compassionate tears that spread from Australia to America prompted swift global action. Even the hard-hearted Abbott responded with an announcement Australia would accept 12,000 Syrian refugees.

But there was no such waterworks in the little plane cruising across the clear blue skies of Queensland. 'Their parents shouldn't be bringing them out on boats to put them in that situation,' Hanson flatly told Broinowski. 'I'm not a bleeding heart—my job is to look after the people here first and foremost. You can't save the world. It's time these countries got their acts together.'

Hanson isn't, nor was she in the two years she was an Independent MP between 1996 and 1998 in a parliament dominated by Coalition MPs, in a position to 'look after the people here'. Her pompous affectation of importance and influence is what keeps her appearance of relevance alive.

Every time Hanson took Prime Minister Abbott to task for accepting the Syrian refugees, her Facebook 'likes' jumped dramatically. Broinowski noted Hanson's excited pride at the hundreds of spikes that followed a TV appearance where she ranted that everyone 'better be prepared, because a lot of people are going to suffer if we open the floodgates to let them [Muslims] in. We have never had such problems as with the Muslims.'

Just as she had taken sackfuls of fan mail home to read and re-read following her 1996 maiden speech, her following these days also entranced her. The number of social media posts she garnered became her new fascination. Her eyes shone as she read some of them 'with quiet pride' to Broinowski's camera. She boasted about the anti-Islam slogans Ashby regularly posted on her page on the One Nation website. Look at this, everyone: 'I did a post on this [anti-Islam] in May: we reached 4 million.'

Hanson repeatedly and stubbornly refused to meet any moderate Muslims proposed by Broinowski. She would not talk with any religious or academic Muslims about the peaceful religious teachings followed by nearly all their adherents, nor would she visit suburbs with high Muslim populations. She didn't feel safe, she demurred: 'With their belief to kill those who are non-believers, do you honestly feel that you can trust every Muslim out there?'

This is Hanson's shtick, her stealthy modus operandi. She cannot afford to be educated or swayed against her blind prejudices. Her disciples rely on her sticking to anger and voicing their indignation about the changing face of Australia. She is the ventriloquist who mimics their fears in her strained and cross voice. Giving oxygen to countervailing facts or argument would only dilute her message.

She knows her audience, and is ruthless about raising their rage level with fallacies that stoke their fears. It is human nature to find something or someone to blame, and Hanson is canny at identifying a vulnerable target.

Expressing fear for her own personal safety in a world of heightened terror attacks and alerts, she carried a message of anxiety and resentment with gusto as she criss-crossed Queensland cajoling support. Reasoned arguments are for academics, not for Hanson. Offering solutions is passé. It's all about the grievance and the anger.

Back in Canberra, Hanson's blitz was barely registering on the political radar. 'Here she goes again,' was the sentiment—until it was, again, too late. Besides, the usual turmoil was afoot, this time in Coalition ranks. PM Tony Abbott was confirming what everyone had known since he snatched the Liberal Party's leadership baton from Turnbull in 2009: very few people, inside or outside the parliament, liked him. Even fewer liked the way he ran the government or the country.

The prime ministerial churn had started up again after an absence of just two years. The last time had been in 2013, when Rudd returned Gillard's favour and heave-hoed her out of the prime ministerial chair. And hadn't that played out well in the Sunshine State—even though Kevin was one of their own, they weren't prepared to help him back into the prime ministership.

It was September 2015. As Hanson winged her way around the state ramping up her rhetoric about mainstream politicians ignoring ordinary Australians, the very slick, very Sydney, very wealthy former merchant banker, Malcolm Turnbull, shoved Abbott out of the headmaster's seat.

Hanson was on the ground to offer a sympathetic ear to the voices of anger and frustration venting about the remote, self-obsessed clowns in Canberra playing leadership footsies again. When news of Abbott's dethronement flew north, shouts from the little plane cruising across the skies over Queensland could be heard. *Hallelujah!* And it wasn't just because the prime ministerial overthrow fed into her narrative about political navel-gazing at the expense of the worries of ordinary voters.

Hanson still harboured mortal rage against Abbott for his role in her jailing. 'Heaven help this country if Tony Abbott is ever in control of it. I detest the man,' she had said at that time. He did get control, but not for long. But now he'd got his come-uppance— God's in his heaven and all's well with the world.

Ashby also had his grievance with Abbott. In a teary appearance on *60 Minutes*, he had once accused the Mad Monk of knowing full well about the sexual harassment allegations he would launch against Slipper before he'd taken the action. He told the program that Abbott's 'attack dog', Christopher Pyne, had lent moral and pledged financial support to the action with Abbott's knowledge. Both men had pooh-poohed these claims, leaving Ashby beached and alone.

Adding lustre to the Canberra PM switch was the knowledge that a suave bloke, who'd have trouble rubbing shoulders at the local pub in regional Queensland let alone separating a cow from a bull in the paddocks out bush, was taking over. It doesn't get much better than that.

It seemed to matter not that, in November, in the middle of this unofficial 'Fed Up' campaign, the Slipper tragi-drama slipped into its second season. Ashby's mum's home was raided by federal police on the hunt for documents relating to possible collusion with Mal Brough over the illegal copying of Slipper's diary. Brough's home was also searched.

Pfft. Hanson either didn't notice or didn't care . . . Or maybe she didn't read or listen to news. Why would she? After all, she created most of it, and what she didn't, didn't matter.

\* \* \*

The campaign that must have been fuelled by hot air was spreading its wings into other states. Hanson was clocking up more miles in the cockpit in a week than Amelia Earhart, but she had no intention of disappearing off the face of the electoral map. This wasn't 1998; she was tougher, and determined to succeed after the marathon effort she'd put in over the years. She and Ashby winged their way to branches all over the country, attending rallies and meetings and stirring the pot of community division.

Their anti-Muslim, anti-immigration line intensified in tandem with global unrest and events. She was congratulated with loud cheers at a rally in the regional Victorian town of Bendigo when she lauded her local candidate Elise Chapman for standing up against the building of a mosque. She was greeted like a rock goddess in city centres from Brisbane to Perth as she reminisced about the old Australia and slammed deaf big party politicians.

She talked with nostalgic Trumpian delusion about an Australia that never existed, conjuring up whimsical visions of home and hearth on quarter-acre blocks, of plentiful employment and booming manufacturing industries, of prosperity and safety for all. She nurtured and amplified fears about 'them' taking jobs, robbing Aussie kids of school places, thieving first-home opportunities from struggling home-grown young people and bringing terror to the streets.

And don't, for the love of God, criticise her. She's the poster girl for the Forgotten Australian. She's the Mother of Australia, remember. She'll react like a cornered tigress if you question her. It doesn't matter if the questions come from journalists, party colleagues, other public figures, even family. Her way is to be loved and adored.

*   *   *

Ashby was navigating the horizon for Pauline and seizing the controls of the office on the ground. It didn't take long before he was interfering in the selection of candidates and exerting power over the party's strategy and daily agenda.

Ian Nelson sent him an email in February 2016, warning him against overstepping his authority. 'Don't you ever speak to anyone about a possible candidate for this party unless you discuss it with the executive,' he stated. 'Do not meet with anyone unless you clear it with me first. You have been in this party for a very short time. Respect our constitution and rules.'

This didn't suit Her Mistress's Voice, who was in thrall to Ashby. Pretty soon Nelson found himself on the outer. So did others who'd devoted years to the cause while Hanson was picking up an indoor tan beneath studio lights and lucratively standing as an Independent candidate for office.

They didn't matter anymore. The message was what it was all about, and Hanson and Ashby had it sorted.

Their year-long campaign was working a treat. On 2 July 2016, twenty years and four months after Hanson first blazed her way into federal parliament, she was on track to return. She was loved, she was redeemed. She could feel it in her bones: she was back.

# Chapter 9
# THE VOICE OF THE PEOPLE

YOU HAVE TO HAND it to her. It took her twenty long years after the publication of the *Bulletin* magazine poll predicting a landslide result for a Hanson-led Senate team to fulfil that forecast.

She returned in a cloud of righteousness laced with smug self-satisfaction. She'd done it. She'd outsmarted those who'd been wronging her for twenty years and thwarting her selfless ambition to stand up for 'the people' in the people's palace.

When she left the parliamentary chamber in 1998, she defiantly declared: 'I'll be back!' A chorus of derisory chortles from major party MPs rang out: 'No you won't!'

Yes, she would. And yes, she did. But not without help. It wasn't just Ashby's advice, nor the headwinds of a year-long campaign and strong community anger at the perceived neglectful ways of big party politicians that she amplified and exploited. She enjoyed considerable media support, even though she would die in a ditch before admitting it.

Commercial TV stations, particularly Channel Seven's *Sunrise* program, gave her a platform in the months leading up to the election. *Sunrise* hired her as a paid commentator to waffle on about subjects she knew nothing about, and which she didn't bother to research before lecturing viewers. Seven had a soft spot for Hanson, having given her a prize berth in its first season of *Dancing with the Stars.*

Another Queenslander, Kevin Rudd, had previously exploited the powerful electoral advantage of regular appearances on *Sunrise,* the #1 rated infotainment brekkie program. The monstrously egomaniacal pretender, in a long run-up to his 2007 electoral victory, had shoulder-charged his way into the psyches of middle-class voters via his cheesy appearances on the show, alongside the equally wide-grinned Liberal leadership aspirant, Joe Hockey.

Hanson's debut, in what became more than a dozen very influential election lead-in offerings as a commentator on *Sunrise,* was a backhander to refugees in the wake of the November 2015 terrorist attacks in Paris: 'We've got to be very cautious in the people we bring into Australia. Yes, I'm very concerned about refugees. They've come in through Syria to France and they have suicide bombers. They're out there to destroy, to kill people, to murder people. Look, I don't want to spread fear. Don't shoot the messenger . . .' And a call to someone or other to alter one of civilisation's oldest biblical books: 'We need to revise what the teachings are in the Qu'ran. It is about the killing and beheading of the non-believers.'

Her social media likes went off the charts.

In January, *Sunrise*'s paid commentator offered lucid advice to parents about vaccinating their children. Stated the program favourite, who had been promoted with her own slogan 'the redhead you can trust' since she first joined the stable in 2013: 'I think the whole thing to do with vaccination should be a common sense debate. I have my kids vaccinated, but I tell you what! I think twice about it these days and if the government wants to be government, they should have thought about it years ago.'

In the same month numeracy and literacy testing in schools, and the teachers who attempt to help kids cobble a sentence together or add up a few simple sums, copped a blast: 'One in four teachers aren't passing the tests themselves. They can't read or write. How can we put them back in the schoolroom and teach our kids?'

A bluster about the housing crisis followed the next month, and the disgraceful cost of private health cover. Critics of Eddie McGuire's tasteless remarks about recently deceased sports journalist Caroline Wilson—who joked he would have paid $50,000 to see her drown at a charity ice-water dunking event—were lectured to 'toughen up': 'Some of these journalists, I'd drown half of them,' an unsmiling Hanson told the two journalists aiding and abetting her.

A month before the election, flag-burners and protestors were the target. They were 'disgusting', and their behaviour was a 'direct result' of the policies of multiculturalism.

When does a paid commentary gig become a political promotion? *Sunrise* executive producer Michael Pell awkwardly tried to explain it to news.com.au. He argued that Pauline didn't receive special treatment and her role was nothing out of the ordinary: 'On the odd occasion Pauline was asked to appear on the show solely as a political guest to discuss her own campaign, she was not paid.'

Rival breakfast program *Today* also gave her a run in the paddock after the Paris attacks. In characteristic Pauline style, without evidence or based on any knowledge, she stated: 'These refugees may be cells that have been brought out, who have been planted ISIS . . . to become refugees who will end up in Australia, on Australian soil . . . people of Australia don't want more Muslim refugees in Australia who may be ISIS plants.'

Writer and commentator Osman Faruqi was one person prepared to stand up against the decision by the commercial television
networks to give her a platform for her views: 'Hanson isn't an
expert on terrorism, international conflict or radicalisation,' he wrote
on SBS's website. 'She's a right-wing candidate for election adept
at maximising the opportunities afforded to her by commercial
networks keen to attract viewers in a contested marketplace. There
is absolutely no public interest defence for the decision to provide
someone with such appalling views a megaphone immediately following a terrorist attack.'

Whether or not she was paid for the *Today* appearances was not
something Hanson cared to share. In Hanson's playbook, transparency has always been for everyone else. 'What business is it of
yours or the public?' she snipped at BuzzFeed, which put questions
to her during the campaign. 'And you know what—whether it is
or not, I'm not saying whether I am or not. I don't see it is any of
your or the public's business whether I am paid or not. There's a lot
of appearances that I make on TV I can tell you, I don't get paid.'

All the other Senate candidates would have traded every rubber
chicken meal they were forced to consume at campaign events at
local clubs, as they slugged and sweated their way around their electorates, in exchange for just one of those slots. Paid or not, Pauline
was able to mainline her political messages thinly disguised as news
commentary straight into the veins of working Australians.

And it wasn't just *Sunrise* and *Today* giving her a leg-up. For all
her whining and howling about being denied a voice, Hanson has
aired her views across numerous friendly platforms for years.

She has been given fawning treatment by the king of Nasty
Old Man Radio, Alan Jones, who broadcasts on the 2GB network
to the largest breakfast audience in Australia. His key over-
fifties demographic is more inclined to a dislike of establishment

politicians, in particular those to the left of centre. Jones has for years lionised her as the voice of the people.

On *Sky News* she has been the calendar girl for its stable of election commentators and an anchor point for the right-wing commentariat who shout at viewers after 6 p.m. They include monotonous monologist Paul Murray, who fills in an interview with others by answering their questions for them; Andrew Bolt, for whom Hanson has always been 'ahead of her time', didn't matter what time she was running for office; and oh, there's Alan Jones again. His 24/7 anger must mean he doesn't sleep because he also holds down a late shift on Sky TV.

Then there's the embittered, failed political adviser who was thrown a lifeline by News Corp—Peta Credlin, the manager of Tony Abbott's revenge campaign.

None of these right-wing warriors have paid heed to the reasonable advice once proffered by South African human rights activist, Archbishop Desmond Tutu, who was fond of quoting his father: 'Don't raise your voice, improve your argument.'

This crew of righteous after-dark yelpers, margin-dwellers in lonely pockets of the News Corp empire, have one characteristic in common: their harrumphing indignation at everything that doesn't fit into their world view is far greater than the logic of their arguments. Courtesy of the power of the News Corp kingdom, those hired to bleat the Murdoch line of the day to small Sky audiences are recycled through the empire's online and newspaper outlets; this provides them with more influence and a far bigger audience for their irrelevant anger outbursts than they deserve.

In the lead-up to her Senate triumph, the electoral value of Hanson's paid and unpaid promotional spots was pure gold. As Paul Kelly in *The Australian* noted on 16 July 2016: 'In this campaign she was the beneficiary of truckloads of soft free media time and interviews based on the fraudulent excuse that she says what many people think—and hence deserves uncritical publicity.'

\*     \*     \*

But the biggest leg-up came from Prime Minister Malcolm Turnbull, who took a double dissolution election gamble that exploded in his face. Also, his tone-deaf pre-election declaration that Hanson wasn't welcome back in Canberra gave her vote a boost.

One Nation's then national secretary, Saraya Beric, reported a spike of 10,000 'likes' a week on Hanson's Facebook page after this intemperate comment. Her voters don't like out-of-touch city politicians telling them who they can or can't have representing them. The forgotten and ignored masses were quietly waiting there, with pencils poised, to make a mockery of the PM's pronouncement at the ballot box on 2 September.

For a smart bloke, Turnbull at times has surprisingly insensitive political antennae. He ignored both polling that showed One Nation was a threat, and the fact that double dissolutions halve the quota needed for candidates to be elected. But none is as blind as the politician who refuses to see and, in one of the more misguided political decisions of the last decade—quite an honour, given the double-figure number of nominees for the accolade—Turnbull chanced his arm on a double dissolution.

Aiding her return was a marathon eight-week campaign, a showcase of trite slogans and empty sound bites that reminded voters why they so loathed big party politicians.

The campaign turned political strategy on its head. Astute political operators know not to unleash swarms of wannabes into neighbourhoods for much longer than the 33 days constitutionally required from the announcement of an election to polling day. Unlike Turnbull, the cluey among them appreciate that the default position of the Australian voter is dull anger with the political class. When voter disenchantment is running high, it's a roar.

Quite why Turnbull thought Australia's large brigade of turned-off and tuned-out would consider eight weeks of shallow song-and-dance campaigning a welcome intrusion into their lives is a political mystery. Angry voters watched the same electioneering TV on repeat; were subjected to never-ending grandiose election announcements; got angry as hell as a tizzy chorus line of all-talking, non-hearing message-prepped major party politicians sashayed across the political stage for eight long weeks. They promptly voted for renegade fringe-dwellers. Top of the list was Hanson, who'd been out there carpet-bombing for one long year.

Turnbull had become increasingly blind to voter mood since claiming the prime ministership from Abbott. His popularity, he hoped against all evidence, would override the entrenched political wisdom that short and sharp is best. He'd also become so obsessed with the wearyingly monotonous game of being stalked by the deposed PM and his cronies that his political radar was broken.

In his mind, the rationale for the double dissolution seemed logical: he wanted to be rid of a bothersome Senate, dominated by a grab-bag of mercurial Independents who repeatedly thwarted his government's agenda. Unfortunately for Turnbull, he and his advisers dramatically misread the public mood.

The more Hanson zoomed across regional Australia in her curiously funded private jet on her Fed Up campaign, cajoling the angry and antagonistic to kick the major political parties, the more votes she picked up. But the more Turnbull campaigned, the less he was liked.

And while Labor Leader Bill Shorten gained some traction with his ferocious criss-crossing of the country, donning hi-vis vests, gladhanding in shopping centres and railing against the government's 'Big Business' agenda, Labor's primary vote remained abysmal.

The big parties were on the nose, and the long campaign became a joke. One tabloid newspaper invented a drinking game to while away the time and highlight the repetitive absurdity of the modern political message spruiked by big party candidates. If voters had downed a shot for every time PM Malcolm Turnbull roared the government's 'Jobs and Growth' slogan, as the newspaper's tongue-in-cheek game prescribed, rehab centres would have closed from over-crowding. Voters who didn't have jobs, and whose only experience of growth was the size of their mortgages or debts, got shitty and insulted.

As the weeks dragged on, Labor and the Coalition remained in the popularity doldrums while One Nation, Nick Xenophon Team (NXT), the Greens and a hodgepodge of other Independents gained followers.

*   *   *

Turnbull ignored another important message thrumming like a permanent hangover through published polls and Coalition research: voters had had high hopes for him, but were now disappointed. They had been left scratching their heads. Where was the conviction politician they knew, who had so resolutely stuck to his guns through the climate change wars that it cost him the leadership to Abbott in 2009? Where was the bloke who had flaunted his social conscience on the ABC's *Q&A*, oozing a charming mix of authority and bohemia in that trademark leather coat?

He was well-liked and respected by both conservative and Labor voters. They expected him to lead the way he talked when he was positioning himself for the prime ministership. When he finally got there, they expected him to be fearless and to deliver for what the vast mainstream of electors represent—the ideological middle ground.

His original presentation to weary Australian voters—as a PM who would offer respite from gladiatorial politics, who talked optimistically of Australia becoming a forward-thinking, can-do nation—had been received as hungrily as rain on a drought-affected paddock. His vision to turn a negative, inward-looking Australia into an outward, agile nation struck a chord.

But the realities of an angry, Rudd-like Abbott and his vengeful army dogging his days, combined with a bolshie Senate, had served to nobble Turnbull's courage at pivotal points in his government's first term. He'd reacted with whiplash speed to any mutterings by the vexatious minority rump huddled in an angry little group on the right flank of his party room, earning him rare praise from Abbott at one stage. He had become a 'more orthodox centre-right coalition leader', Turnbull's predecessor said approvingly, instantly alienating a vast tract of voters who thought he would be a centrist leader leading a broadly representative, inclusive government.

Disappointment is potent in any relationship; toxic between a political leader and voters. The knowledge that electors were dis-illusioned with him should have informed Coalition policies and guided Turnbull on the election trail as he struggled to become the brave leader that voters thought he was, and as he attempted to find the common touch so beloved since Bob Hawke.

But it didn't. Watching footage of Turnbull in a crisp shirt in a pub downing a beer and sprouting inane slogans was like watching an embarrassing reality show. All you could do was turn your head away in dismay.

His strategists must surely have figured that the undecided vote, along with a steadily growing enthusiasm for minor parties, would determine the election. Supporters of the defunct Palmer United

Party were casting around for an alternative; the growing numbers of protest voters were looking around for a place to park their votes.

But if Turnbull's advisers hadn't noticed this, the Hanson camp had. She'd been out there with her antennae twitching to the mood. She was coiled like a cobra, waiting to strike again at the national parliament.

\* \* \*

Counting for the senate on the night of 2 July 2016 had only just begun. But at the euphoric One Nation election party, held in the suburb of Booval, west of Brisbane, she was on fire. Who cared that only 2 per cent of the vote had been counted?

'I'm the person that's going to come in, like the cleaner. If they don't clean your house properly you get rid of them, and you have a clean sweep of the broom.' So pronounced Senator-elect Hanson.

She was clad in One Nation's virulent orange T-shirt, blue and white lettering shrieking the party's name. The head-turning outfits she'd donned on election nights, back in the day when she was trying to pivot the spotlight back her way, had been despatched to the back of the closet.

No need for that sort of prop and nonsense anymore. The working-class gal from Ipswich was back now, representing the battler. She would've been back earlier had not the corrupt electoral system and her nasty opponents conspired to keep her out. 'I've been working on this for the last eighteen years since I lost the seat of Blair—not because people didn't want me, but due to preferences,' she angrily told journalists.

She immediately started issuing warnings to the incoming prime minister—even though, at this stage and for a nail-biting time, who would actually win this election was unknown—letting it be known she'd follow her usual pattern of consulting widely only with herself. Maybe her adopted son James too, though she doesn't say that.

'I don't need to listen to anything!' she yelled at Channel Nine interviewer Lisa Wilkinson. 'I know what the people are thinking and how they are feeling. So let's get this country on track!'

Labor Senator Sam Dastyari was on a Channel Seven election panel. Like all media outlets, Seven had cameras parked at election victory/wake parties across the country in party headquarters and in electorates that offered the most viewer interest. As always, Hanson's was top of the pops and they crossed to her. She was surrounded by adoring supporters. Dastyari, a broad grin on his face, cheekily asked her if she was up to visiting western Sydney to share a halal snack pack.

Hanson shuddered and wagged her finger in what she thought was Dastyari's general direction. She'd always been missing a key piece of Aussie DNA: a sense of humour. 'It's not happening, not interested in halal, thank you,' she said crisply, raising her voice. 'I'm not interested in it. I don't believe in halal certification.' And anyway, she added confidently, '98 per cent of Australians' oppose it.

Evidence? Source? It was characteristic Hanson, a variation on the theme of faking it until you make it. Hanson doggedly refuses to dabble with facts. They've not important. It's the sentiment, the attitude, the support her bombast attracts that matters.

In these days of social media—Hanson's favourite platform— her utterances spread like the black plague. But at least that scourge had a source—most of her utterances don't.

She's the voice of the people. A video soon appeared on her Facebook page spelling out the new regime. She won't be a 'punching bag' for the media. 'So what I'm saying: get your act together! I could be in Parliament for up to six years. I wouldn't mind a working relationship with you. But if you're not going to give me a fair go, don't come knocking on my door, because you ain't going to get an interview out of me.'

Cop that, ratbag media! You need me more than I need you. Voters and supporters, beware! Speaking solemnly down the barrel of the camera, she warned: 'Unless you see me live on TV or hear me live on radio, don't believe a thing you read in the newspapers.'

Sadly, that would rule out reporting her absence in the unfortunate event her plane had an emergency landing in a rugged, forgotten part of Queensland, then. Okeydokes.

Senate voting is notoriously torturous; it can take days. But waiting has never been in Pauline's DNA. Most candidates consider 2 per cent of the vote counted nowhere near enough of a sample on which to claim victory. But she went even further and boldly predicted she'd snag another Queensland seat.

She'd been there and done that so many times that her wildly optimistic predictions were usually as predictable as the chiming of Big Ben, but as accurate as a cheap two-bob watch.

This time she was right.

More than 250,000 Queenslanders gave Pauline Hanson's One Nation party (PHON) their first preference vote. When the count was finally done and dusted, she came in third on raw votes, bested only by the big party politicians who sat atop their party tickets. So great was the popularity of this latter-day Joan of Arc in her home state that she brought another unknown from Queensland with her, the eccentric Malcolm Roberts, thanks to the quota system in which running buddies snag surplus votes.

Roberts himself polled a fabulous 77 primary votes. You'll never hear a peep from Hanson that this aspect of our electoral system is corrupt, where a nobody with numbers that would embarrass an extended Irish family can sit in parliament and make decisions for 24 million Australians.

Two other PHON candidates joined the Queensland pair, one each from New South Wales and Western Australia, and the Turnbull Government was now going to be forced to rely on her party's vote in the Senate.

But it wasn't just Hanson and her motley mob that had capitalised on the growing trend away from the major parties at this election. The minor parties and Independents had recorded their highest-ever vote; the majors had recorded among their lowest ever.

In the Senate, more voters opted for the smaller parties and Independents than for Labor—a dubious first for Australia's oldest political party. Around one-quarter of all voters—many of them feeling sidelined by the modern Australian economy and ignored by major party politicians—opted for any other party than Labor or the Coalition.

On this still harbour night at the Turnbull family's Point Piper dress-circle pad, which doubles as the prime ministerial Sydney residence, teeth were surely heard grinding and clenching: *Didn't the Australian people hear me when I said that Pauline wasn't a welcome presence on the political scene? Why isn't anyone listening to me?*

Hanson meanwhile was trumpeting that it was because big party politicians don't listen to 'the grassroots' anymore that the minor parties are achieving such impressive voting numbers. Hanson plays this sentiment like she's the James Morrison of politics. And now she's going to ensure her tune is heard.

Sort of. She doesn't like accountability, and she doesn't like to be questioned about her policies. She doesn't like to explain; she likes to vent.

\*　　\*　　\*

'You, you're standing here having a go at me because I stand up for my culture, my way of life and my country. Every day that I went to school, I saw the Australian flag raised and it was instilled in me the pride who I was to be an Australian. And yet I stand here before you and want to bring that back to my country and to the floor of parliament, and you stand there and criticise me because I don't want anyone else to destroy that.'

She'd called a press conference in Brisbane two days after the election to crow about her return to parliament, and journalists had the impertinence to ask her about her policies. She wasn't happy about that one little bit. Questions were criticisms designed to silence her—she wasn't going to put up with it.

'What I'm saying is let's get back to the Australia where we as a nation had a right to have an opinion and have a say. Clearly, the way our nation is going is not in the right direction and my opinion and my policies were clearly accepted by the Australian people just last Saturday.'

While the return of PHON to Australian politics and the floor of the Senate was an undisputed fact and her vote in Queensland was particularly impressive, across Australia Pauline Hanson's One Nation had only received 4.29 per cent of the primary vote. It's a springboard for growth, but a long way from being described as clear acceptance by 'the people'.

Pauline's own personal durability and the endurance of her party in the nation's political fabric at this point in history was going to rely on PHON becoming a professional political outfit run along the lines of our other big parties: a democratic, accountable structure; decent candidate vetting procedures; reasonably consistent policies. Given Hanson and the party's chequered past, that was one mighty ask.

PHON's four senators would be joined on the crossbenches by a glorious assortment of Independents. The headache Turnbull had hoped to be rid of when he called his double dissolution election had quickly turned into a migraine.

# Chapter 10

# MISTRESS OF FAKE NEWS AND ALTERNATIVE FACTS

UP IN THE CLOUDS on level 36 of Waterfront Place, Brisbane, the view of the city and river takes your breath away. On a crisp, clear day, the floor-to-ceiling glass of the Commonwealth Parliamentary Offices affords an outlook that few in the suburbs beyond the fringe of the city laid out below will enjoy during their working lives.

Prime Minister Malcolm Turnbull has a suite of offices here for when he visits, but he still maintains an electorate office in Wentworth, in Sydney's Eastern Suburbs. Home Affairs Minister Peter Dutton, a Queenslander and former cop, has an office here too.

Ministerial and Parliamentary Services is the department responsible for running the Commonwealth Parliamentary Offices, located in every capital city. Interstate and out-of-town MPs and senators use the offices, and suites are limited. Only a few MPs take up permanent residence on the floor in the clouds.

The state of Queensland has twelve senators in all, and nine of them have their electorate offices in the 'burbs, choosing to remain connected to the locals who gifted them the privilege of high office. But Pauline, the voice of the people, has her permanent office in the classy mahogany and brass waterfront office block, high above the ordinary working class, alongside the elite of Australia's ruling class.

It's for my security, was her plaintive pitch to Ministerial and Parliamentary Services. That's a curious reason, given the offices are manned only 8.30 p.m. to 5 p.m., and anyone can ride the lift to the 36th floor where just an intercom and a set of glass doors separate the ratbags from the MPs.

Malcolm Roberts joined his leader on the lofty floor. The advocates for the forgotten Australians were set for battle on behalf of the strugglers.

\* \* \*

One Nation's New South Wales senator elected at the 2016 poll was Brian Burston, whose main office is in Toronto, a lakeside suburb of Lake Macquarie on the state's north coast. He's an old party hand who's weathered the fire and fury of the two decades of the party's rise, fall and renaissance, and the ups and downs, ins and outs of its mercurial leader.

He was in the party's hierarchy from the start, and also worked for David Oldfield in the New South Wales Parliament. Burston became collateral damage in Hanson's spectacular falling-out with co-founder Oldfield. But he came back on the scene in 2003, and has remained remarkably loyal since.

Pauline was very proud to have the former teacher in engineering drawing and lecturer in teacher education at the respected Newcastle University in her team; his intellectual firepower was promoted to gilt-edge the party's credibility during the 2016 campaign. He referred to his remarkable life story of 'poverty to politics' in his maiden speech. If a learned bloke was a key player in One Nation, then it follows it couldn't be branded a party of misfits and a magnet for oddballs and Walter Mittys, as many of its critics have maintained over the years. The party attracted respectable types.

Then Fairfax journalist James Robertson did some digging. Newcastle University had no record of Hanson's number one New South Wales lieutenant ever being employed by the university. The senator initially maintained a wall of silence in response to Robertson's emails and texts seeking answers, the standard One Nation practice in handling difficult questions. Burston subsequently stated he had worked for the technical college that had been located on the campus.

The journalist had tried for clarification prior to print with Burston's adviser Peter Kelly, who sits as an Independent on Ku-ring-gai Council in Sydney's northern suburbs and is a One Nation member who variously calls himself Dr or Professor. Kelly has a rich background: with no undergraduate degree, he claims a doctorate from an unaccredited university incorporated in Florida and Gambia; he holds a professorship from the 'Poseidon International University'; and one of his career highlights was advising an Asian sultan on the implementation of Sharia law, a valuable skill to offer a party that is violently opposed to Islamic law.

The CVs of Burston and his spokesman are part of the rich tapestry of experience and credentials One Nation brought to the federal Upper House in July 2016. Burston, being part of the inner circle, is in lockstep with his leader about the way she runs the party; he backs her on major policy utterances, particularly when it comes to the infidels. 'We're a Christian country, I know we have some Jews as well . . . but the Muslims, they kneel five times a day and it's not how we are in this country,' he told News Corp in his first post-election interview.

He was confident that the mass of defections, resignations and character assassinations that rolled out in staccato time after the 1998 Queensland election of eleven One Nation newbies wouldn't happen again. 'They ran dopes, unemployed, inexperienced, not all that intellectual . . . we're more cohesive than the previous bunch,' he explained to Fairfax's Damien Murphy. 'We're a more intelligent bunch for a start.'

Malcolm Roberts, Hanson's Queensland running mate and One Nation's second senator elected from that state in 2016 on the strength of her vote, has been described in terms far removed from 'intelligent'. Crackpot and dithering pretender are among the more generous of the adjectives applied to the One Nation candidate who reaped just 77 primary votes.

Born in India in privileged circumstances, Roberts was briefly a coalface miner in Australia in the 1970s before earning an engineering degree and shifting to management; he spent his down-time furiously writing letters to a host of surprised recipients, espousing conspiracies that would impress spy thriller writer John le Carré.

One such sedition reported by Roberts was that Australia's eminent scientific research organisation, CSIRO, had colluded with the United Nations to produce corrupt reports on climate change. A variation on this theme is that the UN attempts to impose global government through climate policy. Major international banks are also behind the 'climate change scam', and there's 'not one piece of empirical evidence anywhere' to support the man-made climate change 'hoax'. He's a leading light in the super-fringe Galileo Movement, a consortium of hyper-sceptic climate change deniers.

Another philosophical underpinning for Roberts was the sovereign citizen movement, which sees governments as illegitimate and encourages citizens to ignore laws and taxes. He once signed a lengthy, batty letter of demand to 'The Woman, Julia-Eileen: Gillard., acting as The Honourable JULIA EILEEN GILLARD', starting each of his 28 declarations with 'I, Malcolm-Ieuan: Roberts, the living soul'.

One noted: 'I, Malcolm-Ieuan: Roberts, the living soul, has not seen or been presented with any material facts or evidence that compels me, Malcolm-Ieuan Roberts., the living soul or any other free man to be a member of a society and believe that none exist.' Using hyphens and multiple commas is a signature tactic of the sovereign citizen movement, which believes governments try to enslave their citizens through grammar.

He demanded Gillard sign a contract exempting him from the carbon tax. If she refused, then he wanted $280,000 in compensation. Another demand was to provide evidence that 'the Commonwealth of Australia CIK 000805157 is not a corporation registered on the United States of America securities exchange, is not a society and is not a trustee in the public trust, and believe that none exist'.

In 2015, ABC's *7.30* obtained a report by the New South Wales Counter Terrorism and Special Tactics Command revealing that Australia's growing population of sovereign citizens had 'the motivation and capability to act against government interests, and should be considered a potential terrorist threat'. The Federal Bureau of Investigation in the United States classifies sovereign citizen extremists as domestic terrorists, and the Department of Homeland Security rates them as America's number one domestic terrorist threat.

Staff employed by MPs and senators who might have access to sensitive information, even at a low level, undergo rigorous ASIO security interviews to gain a clearance to view classified documents. Not so MPs and senators. Section 6.3 of the Australian

Government Personnel Security Protocol states that 'Members and Senators of the Commonwealth, State and Territory Parliaments' do not require a security clearance to have access to classified security information.

When asked by the ABC in August 2016 if he was a sovereign citizen, Senator Roberts replied shortly: 'No, I'm not.'

Dispossessed farmer Rod Culleton was the other member of the fab four of One Nation newbies, choofing across the Nullarbor from Western Australia. His time on the pink leather was to be short and not particularly sweet; he followed a familiar nasty path to those who fall out with the supreme leader, but he started out with high hopes and ideals.

\* \* \*

Despite their luxe surrounds on the top floor of Waterfront Place, from the outset sightings of Hanson and Ashby there were only as frequent as swallows in spring. They spent a lot of time out and about among the proletariat, angrily campaigning against the policies of the government.

When they were in situ, One Nation's central Brisbane command exerted control over the party's parliamentary troops as tightly as a hangman's noose. Pauline's parliamentary rebirth had been a difficult one, and from the outset the chief and her lieutenant saw no reason why the power of her brand—based, they believed, only on the pull of the leader—should be shared too widely.

The history of PHON showed that maybe this wasn't the way to go if political longevity was the goal. Autocratic rule sits outside the comfort zone of most individuals attracted to One Nation. They are rebellious, angry, anti-politician, and have a lot to say about a lot of things. The party's track record of defections, sackings, bust-ups over centralised control and legal shenanigans shows that its members don't take too kindly to being corralled. Hanson doesn't care.

From the start, Ashby controlled access to the boss and took on an almost presidential role as party spokesman, sometimes fronting the media instead of Hanson. He's the party's eyes and ears, and Hanson's chief of staff and media minder. For someone whose career was in the doldrums only a year before, his comeback to a position commanding a remuneration package in the vicinity of $150,000–$200,000 was almost as stunning as Hanson's.

After a brief settling-in period and a few meet-and-greets between the One Nation senators and their cross-party colleagues, Hanson and Ashby took control of access to government decision-makers, particularly the Prime Minister. But such was Hanson's view of her own standing, Turnbull had to be seen to be knocking on her door.

She met with the PM in Sydney in the last week of July, and told her supporters in a video blog she was satisfied she had his respect. She stressed that the meeting wasn't at her invitation. 'He asked for it, and I attended . . . what it all came down to was I did most of the talking, and I raised the issues with him.' He was gracious, she said; he even offered his frontbench ministers to her as advisers so she would know what was going on.

Ashby immediately got a hot line to the Prime Minister's office and to contacts in other key ministers' offices, such as Finance Minister Mathias Cormann. One Nation party room meetings became brief; Hanson and Ashby did the negotiating with government power players and told the others how to vote.

At the beginning, One Nation's Whip, Senator Burston, was a reluctant attendee at the weekly cross-party Senate whip meetings where upcoming legislation is presented and discussed. Without that knowledge senators are flying blind, not knowing what legislation or amendments are before the House. A minor party whip doesn't get a pay loading for taking on this responsibility; but performing it well is for the good of the party, the nation and informed decision-making.

At first Burston himself went along to these meetings; then his chief of staff, Peter Breen, stood in; then no one went and the new senators were largely ignorant about the goings-on of the new business of the Senate, for which they are each paid a starting annual salary of just under $200,000. As time went on, Burston's attendance jumped back—to intermittent.

Labor took a decision to ignore Hanson and Ashby. They would tell them their position on upcoming legislation, and that was that. 'We don't negotiate with her,' says Labor Senator Anthony Chisholm, fellow Queenslander and former ALP secretary and campaign director for that state. 'From the outset we said we'll brief them on our position, but we won't engage in any negotiations or deal-making. We took it as a principled decision that we don't negotiate with One Nation.'

Besides, says another Labor senator, Ashby is untrustworthy. 'I made the decision that he's too dangerous to have any dealings with. When I first got elected he made an approach to me, but I decided not to deal with him. Anyone who has dealings with him has been burned, and I didn't want to put myself in that position.'

Ashby had barely kicked his shoes off under the desk on Level 36 before he started barking orders outside the parliamentary realm. The first few months were a flurry of activity strongly reminiscent of an era that party stalwarts hoped had evaporated in the mists of time.

First up, media. Ashby insisted he'd do it all. Press releases from One Nation were so last decade. Social media and a Hanson video blog became the primary source of feeding supporters and the chooks in the media. Journalists have always been enemy number one for Hanson, unless you're lurking in dark corners on Sky nights, or shout like Alan Jones, or work for the trash glossies or are a fawning presenter on Channel Seven's *Sunrise.*

Journalists in the federal parliamentary press gallery, in particular the ABC, are blood-sucking vampires, unless momentarily you're not and you're allowed in the door. By and large, Hanson and Ashby see the political press as the enemy who won't give them a fair shout, even though there is no evidence to support that view. They don't subscribe to the notion that scrutiny and accountability are essential for a healthy democracy.

Jones is Hanson's blueprint for honourable media behaviour. In his first post-election interview with his favourite persecuted heroine, he purred: 'I just want to congratulate you on the fact that you are a very courageous woman. And you haven't changed one bit from the day you first began . . . you may be a lady whose time has come.'

\* \* \*

Mrs Hanson pinned a special brooch to her jacket when she gave her first speech in the Senate on Wednesday, 14 September 2016, her second 'maiden' speech in the Australian parliament. The brooch didn't have any particular significance; she thought it finished off her outfit.

'I go back to watching my mother, how she dressed,' she told the ABC's Caitlyn Gribbin in a behind-the-scenes look at the returning parliamentarian's special day, before the national broadcaster was cast yet again into media purgatory by the One Nation leader. 'She had gloves, a hat and a brooch, and she always dressed up and took pride in herself, and I like to think that I do the same.' Mum has always loomed large in Pauline's personal and political psyche; the tough Norah Seccombe raised her daughter to respect her culture, the laws of the land, hard work, and to be wary of the 'yellow' people that wanted to rule the world.

This time around there were no nerves, there was no equivocating, and no beseeching to Ashby to defer the speech, as the nervous newbie had entreated her first minder, John Pasquarelli, in the run-up to her maiden speech in 1996, delaying its delivery by six months.

She was now firmly in control and firmly on message. She'd had a year on the hustings before the election to hone her message and pitch. And she felt she'd got it right. Hadn't 593,000 Senate voters opted for her teams nationally, the fourth highest party vote across the country? She wanted to talk to her fans sitting mainly in Queensland (250,126 votes, easily trumping the Greens on 188,000); NSW (184,000); and Western Australia (55,026, trouncing the Nationals' 34,618).

Time to feed the fan base.

First up, she spoke in her well-rehearsed role as a national martyr. It was the system that had destroyed her in 1998, when her stellar parliamentary career was abruptly cauterised after she had sat for just two years in the House.

> My electorate boundaries were changed, forcing me to stand for the new seat of Blair. Also with the introduction of full preferential voting, this cost me the seat.

It sounded almost informed, but her facts were wrong. Full preferential voting hadn't just been introduced in 1998; it had been introduced in 1918.

> It has taken numerous elections, countless legal battles and doing a stint in maximum security on trumped-up charges—of which

former speaker Bronwyn Bishop stated I was Australia's first political prisoner—to find myself here.

The conviction was overturned, but the Queensland Crime and Misconduct Commission and lawyers with an interest have never been able to find any evidence that the charges were 'trumped up'. Hanson omitted from the narrative that concerned prison authorities had put her in the maximum security wing at Brisbane Women's Prison for her own protection. Asians and Aborigines— the people she'd demonised in her 1996 maiden speech—were over-represented in the general prison population and had every reason to give her grief.

Hanson's constant use since 2003 of the term 'maximum security', with its spectre of grubby, sparse conditions and 24/7 isolation in an abject, narrow cell has been squarely aimed at garnering the sympathy vote. But she wrecked her own storyline in a radio interview during the election campaign, painting a picture of a carefree holiday at taxpayers' expense.

Conditions were 'pristine', she told one of her radio cheerleaders, 2GB's Ray Hadley: 'There was air conditioning, exercise bikes, a personal trainer . . . we had fantastic meals, our washing was done for us, we just had to keep our cells clean. There was a library, television in our cell, education facilities . . . people on the outside who haven't committed a crime don't have these facilities.' What's more, it was 'disgraceful' she opined, because the set-upon taxpayer was footing the bill.

As for her alleged wrongful imprisonment, 'There's a lot of women who are doing a lot more time for a lot less,' Debbie Kilroy, founder of the group Sisters Inside, retorted at the time. Her fans nevertheless love the victim story.

Some call it persistence and tenacity. My daughter describes it as a Johnny Farnham comeback. I call it standing up and fighting for what you believe in and not allowing the bastards to grind you down. So, to all my peers in this place and those from the past, I have two words for you: I'm back—but not alone.

That's five words, but let's not quibble.

It has been 20 years and four days since I last delivered my first speech in this house, a speech that shook a nation, woke up many Australians and gave hope to those who thought no-one was listening. That speech was relevant then and it is still relevant today.

'Shook a nation' is correct. Australia's Race Discrimination Commissioner, Tim Soutphommasane, told the ABC that the Human Rights Commission had found that Hanson's original anti-Asian comments had unleashed violence and division in the community. This was a sentiment echoed by Australia's Chinese community, which launched a social media campaign after the 2016 election to counter Hanson and One Nation's 'intolerant and racist views'.

Speaking at the launch, Chinese Australian leader Dr Thiam Ang said organisations representing Asian communities had documented a significant increase in the number of people of Asian heritage being verbally and physically abused by strangers following her 1996 maiden speech. Sydney's then-Deputy Lord Mayor Henry Tsang accused Hanson of 'splitting the nation'.

Hanson's 'maiden' Senate speech continued to unfold as a tour de force of unverified, unsourced assumptions and scare-mongering aimed at needling the jumpy nerves and short anger fuses of her fan club base.

The problem is we have not had leaders with the foresight or the intestinal fortitude to cast aside political correctness. They have failed to discard old treaties and agreements that are not in our best interest and have signed new ones giving away our sovereignty, rights, jobs and democracy. Their push for globalisation, economic rationalism, free trade and ethnic diversity has seen our country's decline.

The OECD consistently places Australia as among one of the top performing developed economies, due to government trade liberalisation and economic policies over the last three decades. As Hanson talked, Australia was on the cusp of setting a world record by ringing in our 100th consecutive quarter without a technical recession.

> This is due to foreign takeover of our land and assets, out-of-control debt, failing infrastructure, high unemployment or underemployment and the destruction of our farming sector.

The farming sector at the time Hanson talked was at its most profitable for years, and continues to grow. In its report on agricultural production 2016–17, the Department of Agriculture and Water Resources reported a record year of production, with the gross value of farm production valued at more than $63 billion.

> Indiscriminate immigration and aggressive multiculturalism have caused crime to escalate and trust and social cohesion to decline. Too many Australians are afraid to walk alone at night in their neighbourhoods . . .

The Australian Institute of Criminology reported no increase in crime between the early 2000s and 2016. In some areas, such as robbery and common assault, the number of incidents decreased. Domestic violence remains the number one crime against persons. Hanson ignored the inconvenient truth that the profile of a perpetrator of this particular crime, as concluded by the Royal Commission into Family Violence using data collected over a decade, is that of an Australian-born white male, most likely to be mid-thirties and unemployed.

Hanson attempted a new twist in meaning to the headline statement in her 1996 maiden speech—that Australia was in danger of being swamped by Asians. She meant no disrespect to Asians, she said; she was delivering a 'slap in the face' to Liberal and Labor governments, which had 'opened the floodgates to immigration, targeting cultures purely for the vote . . .'

Governments since Federation have devised immigration programs to build the Australian economy and society, a historical necessity for our nation to become anything other than a cluster of under-performing towns. Since the abolition of the White Australia policy in the 1970s, governments and oppositions have united in bipartisan support for a non-discriminatory immigration policy— that is, the source country is not factored into the selection process.

Successive governments have responded to skills shortages, bringing in workers from whatever cultures and nations offer valuable talents to enrich our growing economy and society. Australia has periodically opened its arms to the human consequences of conflicts, regardless of geography or the nationality of sufferers.

Next up, the new Asian bogey.

Now we are in danger of being swamped by Muslims, who bear a culture and ideology that is incompatible with our own.

The 2016 census found that Muslims comprise 2.6 per cent of Australia's population, or 604,000 out of a total population

MISTRESS OF FAKE NEWS AND ALTERNATIVE FACTS

of 24.4 million. Catholics make up 22.6 per cent, or 5,291,000; together with others who identify as Christian, the total Christian pool is a shade over twelve million, about half the population. It's fair to assume that in the event of a Holy War, we'll have the numbers.

Notwithstanding, Pauline soldiered on in Trumpian style about the assault Muslims are inflicting on Australian culture.

> I love my country, culture and way of life. My pride and patri-
> otism were instilled in me from an early age when I watched
> the Australian flag raised every morning at school and sang the
> national anthem; watching our athletes compete on the world
> stage, proud to salute the Australian flag being raised to honour
> them as they took their place on podiums.

At the Olympics held in Rio the month before her speech, Australian competitors born overseas, or who had parents born overseas, won medals for Australia. Half the women's Rugby Sevens team that won the inaugural gold medal in that sport, for instance, were born or had parents born overseas. They took their places on the dais as medals were hung around their necks, and passionately sang the national anthem. Do they count?

> It is about belonging, respect and commitment to fight for
> Australia. This will never be traded or given up for the mantras
> of diversity or tolerance. Australia had a national identity before
> Federation, and it had nothing to do with diversity and everything
> to do with belonging.

Australia's identity before Federation was built on the slaughter and indiscriminate relocation of the country's Indigenes to make way for white settlement and the establishment of penal colonies full of disgruntled Poms and political prisoners from Ireland. And the Chinese helped build the country too, working the goldfields; another inconvenient truth.

It's unclear if this is the identity Pauline yearns for the nation to reclaim; perhaps she is confused about timing. If she meant the White Australian policy, it was introduced after Federation, in 1901.

> Tolerance has to be shown by those who come to this country for a new way of life. If you are not prepared to become Australian and give this country your undivided loyalty, obey our laws, respect our culture and way of life, then I suggest you go back where you came from. If it would be any help, I will take you to the airport and wave you goodbye with sincere best wishes.

Since 1949, when the rights of citizenship were first conferred on immigrants, five million have taken the pledge of citizenship. It involves study, diligence, commitment, and often a renunciation of citizenship of the place of birth, if that country doesn't allow dual citizenship—an emotionally difficult decision.

The current non-religious pledge—one of two choices—states: 'From this time forward, I pledge my loyalty to Australia and its people, whose democratic beliefs I share, whose rights and liberties I respect, and whose laws I will uphold and obey.'

In a 2011 research paper, the Australian Institute of Criminology reported that 'migrants have the lowest rates of criminality in Australia, followed by first generation Australians, with the remaining Australian-born population having the highest rates of criminality'. Indeed, those from other countries who have made Australia home will experience a greater incidence of violence during their lifetime from people born here than the other way around. In other words, the home-grown are the baddies.

Australia is now seeing changes in suburbs predominantly Muslim. Tolerance towards other Australians is no longer the case.

The prevalence of 'predominantly Muslim' suburbs is minuscule. In this context there's no evidence to support the contention that 'tolerance towards other Australians is no longer the case'. Associate Professor of Geography and Planning at Sydney's Macquarie University, James Forrest, analysed the last census and concluded: 'The geography of Muslims is . . . much less segregated [than other ethnic groups]. They are a much smaller proportion of Australia's 11 metropolitan and major urban areas. But they are almost entirely absent from many neighbourhoods and suburbs.'

Muslims constitute half the local population in only one suburb and 82 of 33,337 neighbourhoods (he classifies a neighbourhood as having an average population of 430 residents). This amounts to 0.025 per cent of Australia's clusters.

The remainder of Hanson's speech continued in the same vein, making false statements and erroneous claims. It was a fraudulent call to arms to the blinkered and ignorant, based on distortions. Hanson is the mistress of fake news and alternative facts.

The new Queensland senator rounded out with another reference to her 'false' imprisonment, and singled out her family and steadfast friends for helping her triumphant return. In particular, long-serving loyalist and party treasurer Ian Nelson ('special thanks for never giving up'); party secretary Saraya Beric ('you have been invaluable'); 'dear friends' Bill and Renata (she omitted the surname, but they were identified in press reports as Bill and Renata McNee); and the man of the moment and kindred spirit,

James Ashby (who the establishment also 'kicked about unfairly', just like her).

The bovver boots were now on the other foot, and don't dare question the post-truth facts she'd just laid out. On the defensive at a community forum in Rockhampton a few days later, she snapped: 'If anyone wants to have a go at what I said, I'd suggest go and read the speech. Everything I said in it was factual, and especially about Muslims, Islam and the impact it's having on our country. I won't back down from what I believe in.'

Not even in the face of clear and unequivocal evidence to the contrary. This is quintessential Hanson. Over the years she has not only diligently refused to be educated about the veracity of the issues she so righteously spruiks, but she refuses to accept it when she's confronted with evidence she's wrong.

This quality was first highlighted to a mass audience in 1996, on prime-time Sunday night TV, when *60 Minutes* reporter Tracey Curro read figures to her clearly debunking her claims about Australia being 'swamped' by Asians. 'Let's look at some actual numbers,' Curro said after Hanson repeated her specious assertion that 40 per cent of all migrants to Australia over the previous decade had been from Asian countries. 'There are 866,224 Asian-born Australians out of a population of over 18 million. Is that in danger of being swamped?'

A slight pause. 'I don't believe those figures,' Hanson said.

Curro: 'Well, these are from the Department of Immi ...' Hanson cut her off. 'As far as I'm concerned, those are book figures. I don't believe those figures.'

# Chapter 11

# A BUSINESS DISGUISED AS A POLITICAL PARTY

AFTER THE ELECTION dust settled, James Ashby tried to assume charge of hiring decisions in the senators' offices and in the party structure. He decreed there'd be no jobs for the boys, but in the blink of an eye Hanson's brother-in-law, Greg Smith, replaced loyalists who were forced to walk the plank.

First to be frozen out were the 'invaluable' office manager Saraya Beric and faithful treasurer Ian Nelson, both of whom had been singled out for loving praise and thanks in Hanson's parody of a responsible first Senate speech. In October, Nelson tendered his resignation from the party he'd loved and devoted much of his life to for years, declaring Ashby a 'maggot' after the Hanson sidekick started interfering in party business and in pre-selections. Hanson would later attack Nelson as a 'lonely . . . bitter and nasty man. I have no time for him.'

Beric had no choice but to resign when it became clear that, for whatever reason, she was on the persona non grata list. Hanson later nastily remarked that Beric had been vying for a job in her parliamentary office 'which I told her she wasn't capable of doing'.

Hanson must have had a rapid change of heart about Beric's skills. She'd leant on her in the months leading up to the election, when the professional musician set aside her career to work sixteen hours a day managing the One Nation office, candidates, online and social media and IT. All for a miserable $800 a week and the love of the party. Beric strenuously denied asking for a job in the new senator's office, and later told journalists Hanson never bothered to have a conversation with her about the future after the election.

In quickstep time, Ashby and Malcolm Roberts were added to the party's executive, without seeking the endorsement of party members, which in the new age of PHON enlightenment was supposed to happen. To many, including Nelson, this was the final revelation of what had been Hanson's long-standing modus operandi.

'Pauline seems to think the One Nation political party is her own personal property,' he said at the time. He added: 'Anybody who stands up to Ashby is gone. That's what happened to me, that's the way it is. It's a full-on dictatorship at the moment.'

This is blueprint PHON under Hanson's leadership. Devotees enter the bunker full of fervour and loyalty but are inevitably chewed up or spat out, departing disillusioned, deeply angry and often deeply scarred. Unlike signposts on an Irish country road, all signs indicating who's to blame for this sorry state of affairs have only ever pointed to one door: Pauline Lee Hanson's.

Ashby quickly started populating the inner sanctum with uniquely One Nation 'experts'. At the Rockhampton community forum, he brayed to the attendant throng that Hanson had hired 'one of the world's leading economists', who'd been advising US presidential hopeful Donald Trump.

'We have just taken him from the Trump camp, so he's come on board with us, so that's pretty exciting and we need to build credibility on the economics front!' Ashby enthused. All requests by journalists for information about the elusive world-class econo-mist were ignored for months. He was a phantom figure, hiding in the shadows. When Darren Brady Nelson was finally revealed, it turned out he wasn't quite what he was cracked up to be.

The dual Australian–US citizen was something of an employ-ment drifter with a string of relatively short-term gigs to his name in the US, including writing for small-fry organisations with weird names like the Heartland Institute, based in Illinois, and the Center for Freedom and Prosperity, which Philip Dorling from the Australia Institute found had lobbied for support for offshore tax havens. Nelson had worked for the Trump campaign for two months in a junior position, but never met the bloke.

Staffers working in the offices of major party senators say that no One Nation staffers except Margaret Menzel, who worked for Culleton, and Ashby seemed to know anything about parliament or procedure. But Ashby's knowledge wasn't even flash: he'd only had a scant four months' experience garnered from his brief time working for Speaker Peter Slipper before he slapped him with legal action.

*     *     *

Rod Culleton hated banks, and wasn't a fan of the law either. He entered the Senate in July 2016 trailing a complex web of legal stoushes against banks and other creditors relating to his foreclosed farm and business in Western Australia. One of his legal troubles related to a conviction for larceny in New South Wales over a $7.50 tow truck key, incurred when he claimed he was 'protecting his property' in a fracas over a move to repossess his truck.

Another theft charge hovered, sparked when he allegedly stole another key, this time to a hire car being used by receivers trying to seize a farmer's property during a protest in his home state.

Hanson first met Culleton at an anti-bank rally, and after a few more meetings begged him to stand for the party. A basic knowledge of the Constitution and cursory investigation into his affairs should have raised a red flag that maybe he mightn't be eligible to sit in parliament. Bah, no matter. The technical requirements of running for office weren't high on the checklist for candidates. Culleton had guts and passion, and she reckoned he was the gun guy to represent One Nation from the west.

Before launching into a passionate attack on bankers and the legal system in his maiden speech on 12 October, Culleton tipped his dusty hat to his leader. 'I pay tribute to my party leader Pauline Hanson, the PH in One Nation. A good PH balance will grow a healthy Australia, and this "hung parliament" promises to do exactly that. Being a Nationals voter for 35 years, I am honoured to be a One Nation senator representing my constituents in WA.'

Questions about his eligibility were already hovering over him like flies on a carcass in a country paddock when he rose to his feet: his larceny conviction carried a possible maximum sentence of five years' imprisonment. But he wasn't worried—he was appealing the conviction, and he had his leader's support, for sure. He hadn't put his hand up for the job; she'd asked him. Repeatedly.

Anyway, he told journalists confidently: 'Pauline Hanson would stand by me as an Australian person, not just because I'm one of her candidates.' Uh oh. In the election campaign hurly-burly he must have missed making elementary character checks on her or googling her history of fractured relationships.

In August the larceny conviction was annulled in a New South Wales regional court, but the magistrate said it would still have to be heard before a court at a future date. 'Ripper!' yelled a delighted and very confident Culleton outside the Armidale Court House. The action had been 'a joke' anyway.

His problems were far from over, however. Despite the later annulment, he had actually stood for election as a convicted criminal and bankruptcy hearings were still in the ill wind. Selective speculation began to be planted in media outlets that the government might refer him to the High Court, as well as other senators whose eligibility at the recent election was under scrutiny.

Culleton didn't know it, but he was on borrowed time. And the problems he did know about worried him. He had started to see Hanson in a different, depressing light—he discovered that the face Hanson presented to her adoring fans was different to the one she revealed behind closed doors.

His disillusionment had begun when Attorney-General George Brandis held a meet-and-greet for the newbies during the first sitting week in the last week of August. The Prime Minister dropped by to air-kiss and charm. Hanson was suitably air-kissed and charmed, having already met him after the election—at his invitation, she noted emphatically at the time. After Turnbull murmured a few words of greeting, she spoke up. In his book *Rogue Nation*, Royce Kurmelovs reported Hanson gushing: 'Prime Minister, One Nation supports you, tell us what you want us to do.' Two others in the room have confirmed his report.

Culleton was shocked and aghast. Hanson's fiery anti-politician, anti-establishment platform—magnified in her federal campaign slogan, 'Fed Up', and matched with a squawking entreaty to put the bastards last on preferences—was a con. She wasn't going to shake them up, as her supporters wanted; she was going to join them.

Culleton was also confused and agitated by the top-down approach to decision-making meted out by Hanson and Ashby. He was frustrated that the One Nation team wasn't informed about impending legislation, or able to debate it in the party room. This, he decided, wasn't what he signed up for, and he started to isolate himself so he could fight on the issues he thought they were all united against.

*   *   *

In early November, the Attorney-General rang Culleton to say it looked like he may have to be referred to the High Court. Senator Brandis told ABC's *7.30* that the Western Australian One Nation senator in the spotlight was 'decent', an 'honourable' person who found himself in the middle of an 'unwitting constitutional maelstrom'. Culleton felt sure Hanson would support him, regardless of the distance that had grown between them. They were all in this together; they were a team.

On 7 November, the Senate met to vote on whether Culleton and Family First Senator Bob Day should be referred to the High Court. Hanson rose to her feet; she hadn't told Culleton what she was going to say.

'I have always stood for honesty, integrity and what is the truth,' Hanson told the chamber. 'I have fought for eighteen years to be on the floor of this parliament as a representative of the people, and I cannot sit back and disregard what may have been a wrong judgment. But I will leave it up to the court to make the final decision.' With that, she sided with the government to send to the High Court the question of Culleton's eligibility to sit in the parliament. Hanson had pushed him over the cliff. His own leader had ambushed him, he told other party senators.

A few days later, a furious Ashby chucked his mobile phone at Culleton's chief of staff, Margaret Menzel, after she refused to follow a directive. What a storm in a teacup, Hanson fumed after the incident was reported in *The Australian*. He chucked the phone underarm—what's the big deal? The woman who once sobbed when describing her alleged abuse at the hands of one of her husbands couldn't understand what the fuss was all about. After all, Ashby missed his target. And it was an underarm throw, she repeated.

Until the government dug deep and agreed to foot the costs for his legal defence, after Hanson refused to extend party funds, Culleton shambolically represented himself before the High Court. As a bonus pre-Christmas present, he was declared bankrupt and that was yet another decision for him to challenge before the courts.

Hanson never turned up in court to support him. But the Member for Kennedy, Bob Katter, did—bush bloke to bush bloke, you support your own. It was a lesson in loyalty for Hanson; but the history of the One Nation leader is that fidelity and loyalty have never been high on her list of must-cultivate attributes.

Culleton quit One Nation on 18 December. Hanson had let him down and betrayed party policies, he said, and she and Ashby were too controlling. What had particularly boiled his blood was her crab-walk away from a Royal Commission into the banks. It had once been adopted as a PHON signature policy, reflecting the obsession of many of her bush supporters. It was Culleton's raison d'être for standing for office.

'Policy decisions have been run in the morning media, with no consultation, discussion or agreement from the party room, and personal attacks and undermining, un-Australian behaviour towards myself and my team has been ongoing,' he said in a resignation statement. 'I can no longer tolerate the lack of party support for my positive initiatives, including the recent abandonment of PHON's pre-election commitment to a Banking Royal Commission.'

Hanson's 'public rants against me have also been accompanied by demands for my resignation and control over diaries, office management and staffing by senator Hanson and her chief-of-staff James Ashby. The irrational dictates have caused only disunity and distrust.' True to form, Hanson retaliated that he'd been 'a pain in my backside, to tell you the truth. I am glad to see the back of him'; and, ironically, 'He is ego driven and he loves the media.'

On 3 February, the High Court finally gave Culleton his marching orders. Family First's Bob Day was also sent packing. Good riddance, Hanson would have said privately. She'd have been doubly pleased to see the back of him, given that he had resigned from her party and now PHON could get its fourth Senate spot back.

Ashby had known what was coming. Holding court in front of other One Nation staff at the Watermark restaurant in Townsville on 21 December, three days after Culleton resigned from One Nation, the party's controller received a call on his mobile from Attorney-General Brandis.

After a few hail-fellow-well-mets, he hung up and breezily boasted to his lunch mates that it had been George on the phone. Fill those glasses, boys and girls! 'It's official, Culleton is out!' he squealed. Quizzed later in Senate estimates by Senator Derryn Hinch about whether he had been the caller on the phone, Brandis demurred. He may have rung Ashby; he simply couldn't remember, but he didn't dispute it may have been. Throughout his political career the Attorney-General had periodically suffered from bouts of amnesia, a most unfortunate affliction for the chief law officer of the land.

Still, how very cosy if it was him on the blower. The Liberal Attorney and the One Nation power-broker, exchanging bonhomies and confidences. It was going to be a really good year. Here's cheers and happy Christmas. Clink!

\*   \*   \*

The year 2017 was looking good. It offered Pauline the promise of two state elections that would be possibly lucrative and power-building. The first would be in Western Australia in March, and a Queensland poll was widely tipped for the end of the year. It was time for Pauline and Ashby to fill the coffers again with a spot of campaigning, leading a cabal of candidates.

Sure, there were a few issues to sort federally, what with the Culleton mess and the pesky irritation of her job in the Senate that Australian citizens were paying her handsomely to fulfil. But where there's a will, there's others to make it her way.

First up, Western Australia on 11 March. But the leadership of the long-established One Nation WA (Inc.) were furious. Hanson had been trying to shut their state branch down and replace it with the party reincarnated in her own name, but State Director Brian McRae and President Lyn Vickery weren't playing ball. She'd managed to have it de-registered a few years before; but it was still incorporated, and it still had members and a hierarchy.

She'd rebuffed McRae and Vickery's pleas to unite with them in the national interests of the party. No dice, boys. She wanted them to shove off. She didn't want another One Nation player on the scene, even though One Nation WA (Inc.) had remained steady for nearly fifteen years while Hanson was off doing her bit as a professional Independent election candidate and celebrity TV star.

In December 2016, she lodged papers with the Western Australian Electoral Commission to register Pauline Hanson's One Nation. McRae and Vickery challenged the registration on the grounds that the party names were too similar. Dang! The pair became annoyingly and vocally resistant to Pauline's plans.

Electioneering was the real stuff Hanson loved—on the road, gladhanding and being adored. No matter that, as usual, she was taking a last-minute run at an election without vetted candidates, policies or knowledge of the state.

McRae posted a relatively mild open letter on the One Nation WA website in early December, disassociating the old party and branch from Pauline's latest push.

She dismissively told *The West Australian* that McRae and Vickery were just 'a couple of ratbags', a derogatory term similar to other bitter slurs she has hurled at abruptly de-friended colleagues and others who, for whatever reason, had displeased her.

She'd been trying to close their incorporated body down 'for years', Hanson moaned, a stretch given she hadn't been back in One Nation for years. McRae, who along with Vickery had given her help and logistical support since the heyday of the late 1990s, could only shake his head and ramp up the questioning. One Nation WA geared up to fight the interloper.

She stamped her stilettoed foot. It was so annoying! The ratbags weren't going to give her an easy passage, or slink away cowered by her abuse. Any similarity to episodes of this comedy–drama aired in other states over many years was entirely coincidental.

It quickly became open warfare, fought out in the pages of *The West Australian* and on the old party's website. Another McRae missive, posted on 6 January, echoed a now far-too-familiar cry from the party faithful. It read in part:

We in One Nation WA (an Incorporated Association) have for a long time tried to have the national body of the party managed in an open and transparent financial and executive style for the benefit of ALL MEMBERS so that we could feel confident of being part.

Pauline Hanson's new party is not owned by its members but is more accurately a BUSINESS controlled by its 'Leader'.

In addition, Hanson's preference for chopping off heads without consulting members or setting up some form of disciplinary committee is hardly democratic or constitutional. Rather it is what we expect from banana republic dictators.

Another attribute expected of such demagogues and potentates is a complete lack of financial reporting. Which begs the question:

Just when did Pauline Hanson's One Nation members see, or have access to, their party financial statements?

The question must therefore be asked: If not about money and total power, what possible reason would she have for trying to close the only ONE NATION branch (in fact a State Division) which holds the Incorporated status recommended by both the Australian Electoral Commission and the Western Australian Electoral Commission?

Vickery told *The West Australian* a few days later he believed the only reason One Nation WA (Inc.) had been sidelined was because One Nation was 'a business disguised as a political party, and they could not control an incorporated association protected under the umbrella of state and federal legislation. And they couldn't get their hands on the bank account.'

Accusations were levelled by the old party hierarchy that the national leaders of the new party had tried to seize its bank accounts; had unlawfully used membership data; had passed sham motions to shut it down; and had consistently refused to provide evidence of its constitution or financial records. Hello, echo chamber!

The bolshie duo was bothersome to Hanson, but not too worrying. The Western Australian Electoral Commission washed its hands of the internecine blue, and registered PHON. It was now full steam ahead to set up a new branch of the national closed shop that was Pauline Hanson's One Nation, to pluck a few candidates out of nowhere and to take a run at the state legislature.

In readiness, Hanson had already contacted a couple of devotees from back in the day to reprise roles they'd occupied two decades before, as president and secretary of the state branch—86-year-old Ron McLean and 79-year-old Marye Daniels. They were wide-eyed optimists who loved Pauline; she'd stayed at their place many times over the years. She was just like a daughter, really.

The pair also loved One Nation, having graciously pumped $100,000 into it when things were tight. They were the sort of loyalists political parties pine for, and reward with lifetime memberships and gala thank-you dinners.

'When she rang us up to say she was giving it to us, we were really very proud, and we asked her what changed her mind, and she said "Marye and Ron, you're the only people we can trust in WA,"' Daniels proudly told the ABC. 'She's never changed. She's always been there for the people of Australia and she's always said more or less the same thing all along,' McLean added. A delighted Daniels chimed in: 'She's such a good girl. I can't think of anyone over the last twenty years who's been so devoted to this country!'

The pair was given responsibility for collating a list of possible candidates—nominations were flooding in, they enthused. Naturally, Hanson would have the final pick, just in time for nominations. Meanwhile in the backroom, Pauline and Ashby busied themselves dreaming up their unique business blueprint for the way candidates would fund the campaign.

Imagining the interview process is a wonderful pastime: *Hi, how's things today? Before James and I talk to you, can you flick us $150 for the privilege of being interviewed, so we can see if you're up to scratch to represent the party? Ta.*

*OK, you're through! Now write a cheque to One Nation for the $250 nomination fee. What, to the WA Electoral Commission? No, don't worry, we'll do that.*

*Can you make sure you look out in your email inbox for an invoice from us for your campaign expenses over the next little while? Won't be much—$3000, $5000 tops. Chump change.*

*Oh, that little condition in the small print in this contract? Just says you'll pay a $250,000 administration fee if you're elected as one of us and you defect. Nothing to worry about, you won't, right?*

*What, that other bit that states you'll only get 75 per cent of your expenses returned through public funding, capped at $10,000 or 75 per cent of the maximum reimbursement amount, whichever is lesser? The rest goes to the party for, you know, stuff, campaign stuff.*

*Sign here. Now. Yep, right away. Great! We'll be in touch from the Queensland headquarters. Good luck!*

The uproar from candidates at the heinous $250,000 charge was dropped following resistance. It was a reinterpreted trick from One Nation's dark early days. It didn't fly then either. But you never know if you're going to luck a few suckers, so 'keep on keeping on' is as good a motto as any other.

Fifty candidates were chosen to proudly don the Pauline Hanson's One Nation cap and stand at the 11 March poll in both the Legislative Assembly and Legislative Council.

\* \* \*

The road show quickly hit a number of concrete bollards in predictably dramatic fashion. Candidates railed against the hijacking of their social media accounts by head office, the interference in their advertising, the barked commands floating out of the Queensland and Canberra central commands.

Ashby's Queensland-based company was supposed to be supplying the printed materials, and candidates complained they weren't materialising. And they were expensive. When pre-poll voting opened, how-to-vote tickets weren't available.

Hanson didn't help by freewheeling a few thought bubbles, from admiration for murderous Russian dictator Vladimir Putin to trotting out discredited anti-vaccination theories and getting herself in a twist over federal GST payments to the states.

But most of all, a candidate boil-over erupted over the treason-ous preference deal Hanson and Ashby brokered with the Liberal Party: the Liberals would preference PHON in its Upper House regional seats, in return for One Nation preferencing the Liberals above Labor in the Lower House.

Only in January Hanson had given a guarantee to candidates that there'd be no preference deals. They had principles, y'all know—for heaven's sake, they were anti-establishment! One particular problem with the deal was that One Nation was supposedly opposed to the Liberal Government's electricity privatisation policy.

By the time polling day dawned, five PHON candidates were on the scrapheap after either walking away in disgust or because they'd been sent to Siberia for unknown sins.

First out of the blocks was surveyor Stephen Piper, candidate for Geraldton, who strenuously denied the accusation by party oper-atives that he was being dumped for sending intimidating emails and texts to another One Nation candidate.

Next up, Sandy Baraiolo and Dane Sorensen in quick succes-sion. One Nation state leader Colin Tincknell stiffly informed the media the pair were being let go because they had 'failed to reach the required standards'—a dictatorial catch-all that allowed the supreme leader full rein to execute anyone he or she liked, for whatever reason.

Baraiolo's particular crime was that she 'refused to follow direc-tion and refused to work as a team', accusations she scoffed at. She'd helped other candidates with their social media and had a reputation as a strong community worker. After being given her marching orders, she stated pointedly: 'I think if people googled my name they can see what I do within the community. For me it's about giving back with honesty to my community.' She believed her real crime was that she had criticised the preference deal and advised One Nation supporters to direct their preferences where they liked.

Following her into the cold because he too failed to support the roundly criticised preference deal was Lower House candidate Dane Sorensen, who labelled the campaign 'shambolic'.

Step up Ray Gould, the candidate for Kalamunda. He told the ABC he was giving it away because of the dishonest preference deal: 'I've had enough. It's a lot of work when you haven't got the support of your party. I'm talking to voters and they say: "We like Pauline Hanson, but she's done a deal with the Liberals and she can't be trusted."'

Quitting on the eve of the election, law and order campaigner Margaret Dodd complained: 'I have only been a member of PHON for four weeks and in this short period I am of the opinion that this party is more adherent to a dictatorship than a democratic organisation, and lacks principles. PHON in my eyes are not about the WA people and their future but for personal power for Senator Hanson, who will do and say anything to achieve her goal at whatever cost.'

The gold star award for pitiless, shameful treatment is awarded to Hanson for her awful treatment of her idealistic, faithful aides, Ron McLean and Marye Louise Daniels. Without warning or explanation Hanson, Ashby, WA leader Colin Tincknell and one other arrived on their doorstep on 20 February; they announced that they were 'reassigning' the shocked pair's duties, and demanded all their files from twenty years of devoted service.

McLean was told he was disendorsed as the number three candidate on PHON'S ticket for the Upper House. It was a spot he had no hope of winning from, so his sacking was gratuitously cruel punishment for sins unstated. The ageing couple were banished from the kingdom, their lives and finances in ruin, their confidence in the human race shaken. They believed it was because they spoke out against the preference deal.

The feisty couple hired Perth lawyer John Hammond to represent them in an age discrimination case. Hammond told journalists at a press conference the week before the election: 'They had been told that their conduct wasn't up to scratch and that's why they've been booted. We haven't been told what that conduct is. They haven't been called upon to give any answers as to any concerns One Nation have.' The couple was 'devastated', he said.

'It's totally wrong, what Pauline Hanson and the One Nation party have done.' A shell-shocked Daniels told *The Saturday Paper*: 'She's been my buddy. We sat in the lounge room in our nighties and had a glass of wine, like girls do.'

One candidate who lived up to the required standards, despite hitting the headlines for the wrong reasons, was David Archibald, the party's hopeful for the seat of Pilbara. A 2013 article he had written for *Quadrant* magazine surfaced and was quoted in the media; it described single mothers as lazy women who raised lazy and ugly children. He pontificated that they shouldn't get welfare just because they were 'too lazy to attract and hold a mate'. They were 'undoing possibly three million years of evolutionary pressure', he strangely asserted.

This was surely a candidate any party would be scrambling to grab, but bad luck: Pauline had him, and she was standing by her man. Pre-empting possible calls for her feller to be stood aside, she tweeted on 1 February: 'To all the fat lazy politicians & fat lazy journalists in the fat lazy media playing fat lazy, PC, identity politics—the answer is no.'

What question she was responding to would be best reserved for an after-dinner parlour game with plenty of throat lubricant close by. In Pauline's world it's okay to slander and shame single mothers—the other type, of course, not like her—but don't dare question her right to make deals that sell out One Nation principles or you'll be belittled, frozen out, discarded, dismissed. And often end up broke.

\* \* \*

Pauline Hanson's Western Australian sojourn ended in a pathetic whimper. Punters, disgruntled at PHON and Pauline's rank amateurism and sell-out preference deal, tanked polling predictions that the party would snag a double-digit vote. PHON received less than 5 per cent of the state-wide vote, no Lower House seats and three Upper House berths. Their tactics helped Labor across the line to form government.

Everything and everybody, except Pauline herself, was to blame. Deploying marvellous linguistic contortions to avoid taking any responsibility, she averred that it was the uneducated swill that was to blame: 'It's been the biggest topic, people ask me about preferences and they don't understand the voting system, the preference system, the preferences. I'd like it to be introduced into the educational system. I think that's where most of the damage has come from,' she spluttered to the media.

On another occasion, it was the fault of Colin Barnett, that wretched Liberal ex-Premier; it was not because she'd asked her voters to direct preferences to the party as a whole: 'All I heard all day and leading up to this election [was]: "Why are you sending your preferences to the Liberal Party?" I don't think it was the Liberal Party, I think it was Colin Barnett. The people here did not want Colin Barnett—he should have stepped aside.'

Within One Nation, the recriminations and blood-letting spilled immediately. Their failed candidate for the Lower House seat of Fremantle, Warren Duffy, laid the blame squarely at Hanson's door and probably won't ever again get another candidate's cap: 'Too many un-thought comments, comments misunderstood from Pauline commenting on federal matters rather than on West Australian matters,' he told the ABC.

Fiery sacked candidate Dane Sorensen fired off an email to the candidate team and head office: 'What I would like to see us all take away from this is the utter conviction that we were absolutely duped and used—certainly by one James Ashby but sadly, it appears, also by the lady herself. This is the person who demanded that it is "My party and you'll do as I say"—as such, the owner of the party must take responsibility for what she allowed and/or directed to happen.'

A thin-skinned Ashby fired back: 'Wow, you've surprised me with such eloquent words Dane, unlike the multiple foul-mouthed calls, where words like "cunt and fuck" spewed from your vile mouth. Don't ever contact me again you self-righteous, deranged man.'

Sandy Baraiolo thought she'd get into the group email action too, sending off to her former candidate fraternity: 'It's my personal belief candidates were placed in as many seats as possible for monetary gain for the party only.'

For good measure, Ashby also received an email: 'You, James, should be ashamed, you're nothing more than a bully and this is not a good trait in a person. You spew vitriol at any one who cares to stand up to you. I have been on the end of your tirade a few times. Just remember many a person has been taken down by the written word, I did absolutely nothing wrong and you became a monster to me.'

But the best word goes to Lyn Vickery, who let forth with a written technicolour yawn on the One Nation WA (Inc.) website, penned with savage ferocity the morning after the election. If words could be coloured in blood-red anger, these would be:

People across one third of the land mass of our great country will awaken this morning to the realisation that a brainless self serving bull in a china shop from Queensland massively helped demolish any chance of economic recovery in Western Australia for the next four years.

While Barnett was roundly considered as arrogant and aloof and the whole electorate saw his government needed a sound kick in the pants, many thinking voters still broadly realised the need for a state government with a real chance of dealing with the consequences of the end of the mining boom.

Enter Pauline Hanson, the wonder woman with hair of red, forked tongue, and claws to match. Fully charged with the energy of some mad catalytic nuclear reactor filled with squawking rage, a quavering voiced Hanson tore at everything in sight in her personal quest for power and fame. Every political issue and unfortunate politician was fair game for her negative unhinged vitriol, but in the final analysis she offered no economic plan for recovery, not a single set of audited figures . . .

She came here intent upon two things. Firstly to tear down and destroy a long serving state government in the vain hope she could further financially feather her own nest—PHON is a business and fan club, not a true political party. Secondly, to feed her own increasingly deranged and severely damaged ego.

That's just an extract. Those who have been burned by Hanson don't take it lightly.

# Chapter 12

# THE BEATING HEART OF QUEENSLANDERS

AFTER THE CULLETON debacle the political blood sport de rigueur for the political and media classes became lining up in the cross-hairs potential dual citizens who might be found to run foul of Section 44 of the Constitution. Greens Senator Scott Ludlam set the next hares running, resigning in July 2017 because he'd accidentally forgotten he was born in New Zealand. Unsuspecting dual Canadian–Australian citizen, fellow Greens Larissa Waters, quickly followed him.

It was so much more fun for political apparatchiks in the major parties to now hunt down the duals than concentrate on the business of government. MPs started falling like dominoes.

One such was PHON's Man from Queensland, Senator Malcolm Roberts: living soul and sometimes sovereign citizen; international climate conspiracy theorist; man of considerable, often incomprehensible mystery; new BFF of the party leader and, according to many who know the dynamics of the relationship, one of her key advisers.

Roberts delivered his maiden speech in the Senate on 13 September 2016. One year and nine days later, on 22 September 2017, High Court Justice Patrick Keane reckoned he shouldn't have been there in the first place, but the final decision would be left to the Full Bench. The clock was ticking.

Roberts had spent months slipping and sliding around the truth of his birth in India and his claimed renunciation of British citizenship. The snakes and ladders of truths and fallacies were spellbinding. The arguments he offered to try and persuade everyone of his Australian-ness were as winning as the verities of his climate conspiracies.

When laying out his crackers climate change theories to the Senate in his maiden speech, he boasted: 'Like Socrates, I love asking questions to get to the truth.' Alas, his Socratic zeal was MIA when it came to his citizenship status. He strenuously offered the notion that he'd only ever been Australian, had never thought he was anything else, so everyone should have a good lie-down and let him get on with the business of conspiracies.

One persuasive argument he volunteered was that he'd sent an email to the British Consulate. A wee problem emerged via the seditious ABC: it was sent to a non-existent email address. Another problem was the plaintive question contained in his email's subject line: 'Am I still a British citizen?'

He remonstrated that he'd later sent another email to the consulate stating that, if indeed he was a British citizen, then he renounced it. No need for other messy paperwork. Then media unearthed his name on a General Register Office's list of British nationals born overseas between 1818 and 2005. Oops. His fact-packed response was to sign a statutory declaration, the most convincing part stating: 'I can confirm I am not a citizen of The

United Kingdom, nor am I a citizen of India. I am a citizen of Australia only.' That'll fly with the High Court.

But drat! BuzzFeed dug up documents showing he'd travelled on a British passport as a child. It was looking a bit messy, so he took the friendly media route and lobbed onto *Paul Murray Live* on Sky. He said he would not produce documents for other media, because everyone knows what the media and the twitterati do with documentary evidence. Instead he shuffled a few papers around that he said were proof positive of his true-blue creds, and didn't actually say much because Murray did all the talking.

After a detailed interrogation, which involved more paper-shuffling and leading questions that the host himself answered, His Honour Justice Murray pronounced that on the forensic evidence provided he was 'one million per cent' sure Roberts was not a dual citizen. Roberts had also answered enthusiastically in the affirmative when Murray posed his final question/comment: 'I'm very confident in everything that I've seen. Are you very confident if anyone wanted to challenge you?'

Just in case, Roberts had another ace up his sleeve that would end this nonsense once and for all. 'He is choosing to believe that he was never British,' Roberts' spokesman, one Sean Black, soon to be arrested for rape and criminal assault charges, explained to *The Guardian*. 'He is preferring to believe that he was never British because he has no allegiance or exercised any citizenship arrangement.'

But just in case, Roberts' legal team had a unique argument. It was almost irrelevant that he was born overseas; he was a natural-born Indian, 'whatever that means', his lawyer Robert Newlinds SC intrepidly argued. He criticised the Commonwealth for trying to discriminate between people born in Australia and those born overseas. It was 'un-Australian' to try and stop someone born overseas from sitting in parliament. It was an audacious argument to put on behalf of a senator representing an anti-immigration, anti-multicultural party.

If that wouldn't convince Your Honours, then Senator Roberts had more ammunition that would seal his legitimacy in the Upper House. He confidently hopped into the High Court witness box in early October to present his irrefutable evidence to the Full Bench. He'd 'always felt Australian', he said with firm voice, and he was 'entitled to put out of his mind that he was a British citizen'.

Astonishingly, the Full Bench of learned jurists were as unconvinced as Justice Keane, and on October 27 gave him and four others found to be dual citizens a permanent leave pass from parliament. Senator Roberts again became just Malcolm Roberts: the living soul, masterful purveyor of alternative facts. He was on the hunt for another career; his parliamentary colleagues prayed that it would be in a galaxy far, far away.

\* \* \*

Maybe not. Within hours of the High Court handing down its decision, Hanson and Roberts fronted a bank of cameras and a healthy gaggle of journalists at Canberra's Parliament House. Hanson was emotional, teary.

'I've lost a great man in Malcolm Roberts,' she croaked. He was her 'backbone'. 'I'm devastated. Absolutely devastated with losing Malcolm. I tell you what; it will take a mighty person to fill this man's shoes because I think he's unique. I think he's been a person on the floor of parliament who brings so much to this parliament, and I think that is lacking in some many others, of our other colleagues.'

The crowd fell into astonished silence. Not much anyone could say to that. She went on, a buoyant Roberts nodding next to her:

'Federal Parliament may have lost Malcolm Roberts, but Queensland has not lost Malcolm Roberts.' Drum roll: 'Malcolm will be standing for the seat of Ipswich in the upcoming state election!'

Never one to let slip by an opportunity to trot out a few alternative facts, the new state candidate refused an invitation to apologise for dissembling about his citizenship. But he did regret it; he'd been wrong, 'but it was genuinely my belief—and the High Court has confirmed that'.

No, it didn't. Their Honours emphatically stated in their judgment that: 'Senator Roberts knew that he did not become an Australian citizen until May 1974 and at the date of his nomination for the Senate, Senator Roberts knew that there was at least a real and substantial prospect that prior to May 1974 he had been and that he remained thereafter a citizen of the United Kingdom.'

The voters of Ipswich, Pauline's old stomping ground, were in for a wild campaign ride on the distinctive Roberts information highway. And they didn't have to wait long.

Queensland Premier Annastacia Palaszczuk called the election on Sunday, 28 October, a day after Hanson had packed her port with red blazers and fancy gowns for a parliamentary delegation to India on 'an important trip to build trade relationships', Ashby announced. The election would be held on 25 November, a date that had been predicted monotonously for months. But apparently this had gone unnoticed by Hanson, et al.

The Queensland senator was not amused. She tweeted: 'Seems a cowardly Anna Palaszczuk decided to wait until I was out of the country to cancel on her grandma & call a snap election!' Seems a misinformed Hanson forgot to check her Twitter account before hitting send: a pic of the Queensland Premier and her grandma, who she visited before going to Government House, was all over social media.

Election speculation had been ratcheting up for months, swirling in both Queensland and Canberra. It had become so silly that the Premier had to give a day-by-day blow of her intended movements in the days leading up to her announcement. She had informed the twitterati—her tweets were read like tea leaves by journalists and political operatives searching for election-date clues—that she'd be seeing her gran early on Sunday morning. Hint, hint.

The following day, Hanson sniffed to reporters at a press conference at the Australian High Commission in Delhi: 'Being able to campaign through the state is very, very important, so I think it would have been beneficial for her to have me out of the country for eight or nine days.'

She was no less modest when she touched down in Australia seven days later and was met at Brisbane airport by a media crush. 'They're going to realise they truly have a campaign on now I am back in Queensland!' she gushed. With that, off she popped to climb aboard her campaign vehicle, which she and Ashby had dubbed 'The Battlers Bus', which was suitably christened with a bottle of cheap bubbly helpfully provided by a TV crew.

The astute political tactic faithfully practised by the major parties—that the path to electoral success is to claim underdog status—was not for the dynamic duo of Hanson and PHON's Queensland leader, LNP turncoat Steve Dickson.

Hanson had over-hyped her chances in Western Australia, and she hit the replay button here. She and Dickson couldn't help themselves, offering wildly optimistic forecasts of One Nation's probable kingmaker status, inflating expectations of a glittering seat tally. Their statements became the main barometer against which mainstream media and commentators judged them.

Dickson kicked it off, stating that One Nation was 'assured' of holding the balance of power. 'We need grown-ups in government,' he maintained. On another occasion he whistled up a tortured analogy to describe how One Nation would view balance of power negotiations. 'It's like drinking water,' he explained. 'Without it, you die. At the end of the day, you're going to have to come and have a drink. We're holding all the water.'

Freewheeling the party's chances in front of the microphones and cameras another day, he mused that One Nation, the decisive 'pox on both their houses' party, would consider ensuring one of the majors could govern. 'I think there's a very good chance we could end up with the balance of power, and that is basically the equivalent of a senate,' he bravely suggested. The party would 'work with anybody to run the Queensland government, because I believe that's what we all should do.'

His federal leader was no less bullish about the party's popularity and chances. 'This is going to be one hell of a campaign, because I think the people of Queensland are fed up with the major polit-ical parties,' she told *Sky News*. 'I think it is time for One Nation, and honestly I think this is going to be bigger than 1998.'

Honestly, maybe not. Better pointers than hubris should have told her so. The published opinion polls in the months leading up to 25 November were not supporting an Olympian seat haul. The party's popularity had been in the 20 per cent range at the beginning of the year, but it had been dropping since, hovering pre-election at around 15 per cent. And then there were the usual campaign disarray and candidate problems that frayed credibility.

Impressively, by the time Palaszczuk visited the governor the headcount of sacked or resigned PHON candidates had risen to eight. They disappeared into political obscurity for a variety of reasons: homophobic statements on social media; denying the reality of the Holocaust and/or the 9/11 terrorist attacks; or, for those who walked away, the exorbitant personal financial cost levied on candidates by the party for the honour of running. Western Australian candidates could only sympathise.

\*   \*   \*

One candidate to vanish early was Andy Semple, who by November 2016 had been confirmed as the candidate for the idyllic Gold Coast seat of Currumbin. Semple's pre-selection process involved an interview for a few hours in Brisbane conducted by party secretary and seat candidate, Jim Savage, and Hanson's brother-in-law and newly installed Queensland Treasurer, Greg Smith.

On 18 December, Semple and 29 other state candidates had a pow-wow before being proudly paraded before the Brisbane media. At the closed-door meeting, Smith informed candidates they'd have to cough up $3500 for campaign collateral—pamphlets, corflutes, a few caps and T-shirts. He didn't mention that Ashby's printing company would be undertaking the work.

Semple, who'd been in business as a financial adviser and stockbroker for decades, raised questions about the cost. He knew what advertising materials cost; he regularly used printing companies, and the 'ask' seemed excessive. Savage defended the price. Ashby was in the room, silent.

At the end, Hanson briefly gave her standard stump speech on the usual issues of immigration, etc. 'She can talk with a degree of passion,' Semple recalls. 'My observation was that she's great at making a headline, but there's nothing behind it.' They all filed out for the media cattle call, beaming brightly for the cameras. Semple followed up his verbal questioning of the price of campaign materials with an email to Savage.

The next day he received a text from Savage asking him to delete an old, little-noticed tweet he'd posted months before. It was harmless enough, even if to some it was in bad taste—a picture of someone wearing a joke T-shirt with the letters LGBT under simple graphics, indicating that these letters were an acronym for the Statue of Liberty, a Gun, a glass of Beer and a pair of 'Titties'. 'Mate, the comment on your Twitter account needs to be deleted. James and Pauline not happy at all. The one about the LGBT stuff and picture of a pair of tits. Not kosher,' Savage texted.

Semple knew where all this was heading, so he pulled the pin before the hierarchy could make it even more difficult to continue. He texted Savage back: 'Then I withdraw my candidacy, Jim. I believe in free speech. Sadly it appears PHON does not.'

It puzzled Semple: here was a party led by someone who loudly championed free speech, allegedly taking mighty offence at a fairly harmless tweet that had been posted months before. Any connection between the timing of Semple's questioning about Ashby's printing deal and the leadership's thin skin over Semple's ancient tweet was entirely coincidental.

Another candidate who fell on his sword, blaming the 'lefty media' and 'pathetic haters', was Mark Ellis, who was standing for Macalister. The former Queensland copper was one of the notorious 'Pinkenba Six', one of six police officers charged in 1994 with kidnapping three Indigenous teenage boys from Brisbane's Fortitude Valley and leaving them 12 kilometres away in Pinkenba. Despite admitting what they did, the charges were sensationally dropped after the magistrate found the boys had 'gone willingly'.

When the media discovered his past, Ellis claimed he received death threats and abuse. He said he was bowing out. Entirely coincidentally, he announced this just 24 hours after *The Guardian* had run a story that he'd threatened the life of Mihalis Kalaitzidis, a former employee of his business, Gatecrash Security, after the university student and part-time worker failed to show up for a shift and wanted to quit.

'Fuck you. I'm gonna kill you. Fuck you. You're a cunt . . . I'm gonna fuck you up cunt,' pinged one message from Ellis's personal Facebook account. And: 'You're dead to me. I know where you live . . . call the cops. I don't care . . . See you.' Ellis initially denied to *The Guardian* the messages came from him, but he then conceded: 'It might be (me), it might not be, I don't know which.'

Trying to sort out what is acceptable behaviour for a One Nation candidate and what is not is a mind-bending exercise in inconsistency and illogicality. The Western Australian candidate experience showed that if you make derogatory and insulting comments about single mothers, for instance, it's A-OK. If you make fun of domestic violence, it also appears to be A-OK— you're one of hers.

Hanson defended a classy post on the Facebook page of the Cupids Cabin Adult Shop in Townsville, which is owned by candidate for Thuringowa, Mark Thornton. 'Good sex should be in the gray area between tickle fight and domestic violence,' the post advised.

'If I think something is wrong, I will do something about it, but in this case it's not wrong,' Hanson angrily retorted to questioning journalists. Anyway, it was all the fault of the Channel Seven reporter: 'You purposely came on the [campaign] bus here to get a gotcha moment with any of our candidates, and that's what you've gone after: well I'm fed up with it!'

\*   \*   \*

Hanson awoke with her usual blind optimism on 25 November. This was to be her next triumph. This would mirror—nay, maybe surpass—the halcyon days of the late nineties: of 1996, when she'd won the seat of Oxley, and 1998, when she'd guided her fledgling party to an eleven-seat win at the Queensland state election.

Unquestionably: she was in a much better position this time around! She'd brought three other party candidates along with her into the Senate at the July 2016 federal poll—wasn't that a strong sign of belief in a resurrected Pauline Hanson's One Nation party? She could sense that the ole train was a-chugging again. She could hardly wait for the results.

By 9 p.m., hanging out with supporters in Dickson's residential garage in Buderim, the beer was losing its fizz. PHON walked off with one seat, a far cry from the 1998 seat haul of eleven. Its state-wide vote was 13.7 per cent, 10 per cent lower than the 1998 result. It spoke to Hanson's permanent state of hubris that she thought her star power could somehow triumph over the party's lack of focus, direction, strategy and flawed candidate selection process, and deliver a kingmaker number of seats.

Dickson fulfilled the predictions of a number of polls that his career as the One Nation leader in the state legislature was doomed. Naturally Hanson hadn't believed the polls; she felt she knew the mood of voters. A few days before, she'd responded to journalists asking about her state leader's probable future: 'Steve Dickson will win his seat. I'm positive. I said to you I don't care what the polls say, it is not, no, sorry . . . I have been around this electorate and I know that Steve Dickson is going to win. I am positive about that.'

She had been just as positive that the living soul sometimes known as Malcolm Roberts would win Ipswich. One Nation's previous Senate and state election voting figures for the area suggested he could be in with a half-decent shot.

But, alas, not so for the climate change denier and accidental senator, whose brief Canberra career had been due solely to him surfing shakily into the national capital on Hanson's leftover votes. The electors of Ipswich had now decided they didn't want him and the seat remained safely Labor.

This lack of popular support for either a federal or state career, however, proved no impediment to Roberts' optimistic view of his future parliamentary chances. With his trademark quizzical, open-eyed death stare, the ex-senator, ex-state candidate immediately announced he would leave the door open for a run back to the national capital. He was supremely confident of his own abilities, and Hanson continued to hold him in high regard.

Stranger political things have happened. Voters should keep a weather eye on the political horizon for a little angry puff of dark smoke billowing out of Queensland come the next federal election. After all, Ashby has all but anointed him. 'He will certainly have my support there—so Malcolm, regardless mate, Queensland wins by having you on the frontline there, so thank you,' Hanson's minder prattled on Channel Nine's election panel.

One thing's for sure: Malcolm-Ieuan: Roberts., the living soul won't be lying down like an old dog while there's more conspiracies to air on the national stage.

\* \* \*

After the dust settled, a good look behind the lonely single seat count, measured against the backdrop of the major parties' tally, put the froth back in One Nation's stubby. PHON had defied its lack of strategic focus to actually do well, notwithstanding the paltry one seat victory.

Even though Labor, against predictions, won majority government, both it and the LNP recorded a dismal combined primary vote of a historically low 69.4 per cent. In particular, the LNP—occupying the paddock PHON was trying to trample on—dropped to 33.69 per cent and just 39 seats, a canary-in-the-coalmine pointing to the possible result in the next federal election.

In the final wash-up, PHON secured a respectable 371,000 votes or 13.74 per cent of the state-wide primary vote. Its primary vote averaged 20 per cent-plus in the two-thirds of available seats it contested. In its non-city heartland, its best result was a whopping 34.4 per cent, and its candidates ran second in primary votes in 23 of the 61 seats in which it ran.

Within weeks of confirmation of the state election result, a cocky Ashby was boasting to Jamie Walker of the *Weekend Australian* that the party would contest every Queensland seat at the federal election. In the same edition of the newspaper, on 30 December, a quarterly demographic analysis of Newspoll showed the federal government's vote in Queensland had slumped to 32 per cent, which would cost the government twelve seats in that state.

The Coalition holds 21 of the 30 seats in Queensland; such a state loss would ensure a national electoral car crash for the Turnbull Government. But One Nation's ability to snag those seats is hampered by its ramshackle organisation and campaign structures that barely exist.

It beggared belief that Hanson was out of the country when the widely anticipated election was called; even more staggering that the party was caught short on both candidate selection and good quality candidate appointments. A year before the November election the good money even then was on the election being held exactly a year hence. Hanson crowed they'd have candidates in place in all seats within twelve months to take on the big parties. They didn't, and went on to feign outrage at the totally predictable timing of the announcement.

The party organisation (for want of a better description) also had no strategy for maximising the One Nation vote and seat tally—for example, focusing its efforts only on vulnerable remote and regional, former National Party stronghold seats that were, and are, ripe for the plucking. If they had done this, or did it in the future, their influence could be significant.

Old-school Nationals, who were never fans of merging their party with the city-based Liberals a decade ago, know it. Many believe the merging of the two distinctly different parties left vacant the vast and nationally important arc of regional and remote seats, previously dominated by locally grown Nationals, for the return of destructive sharp-eyed chancers like Hanson.

They were even less impressed when LNP Leader Tim Nicholls and the state campaign team faffed about over whether it would form government with One Nation in the event of a tight result. While Nicholls dithered, Palaszczuk took the high road, declaring that Labor would rather go into opposition than do a deal with the devil party. Compounding its error, while the LNP strenuously denied doing a formal deal with One Nation, it preferenced Hanson's party over Labor in 50 seats, alienating moderate Liberals in its city electorates.

One Nation didn't return the favour. The party put the two majors second last on nearly every one of its how-to-votes, saving the lucky last spot for the hated Greens. The party's lofty goal was to unseat sitting MPs, regardless of which party the candidate represented.

In the end, despite Hanson's instruction to her voters to put big party candidates last, they ignored her. An analysis of preference flows shows that One Nation voters gave 65 per cent of their preferences to the LNP. But in the outer-metropolitan seat of Redlands, for example, One Nation's 17 per cent primary vote was almost evenly split. This meant LNP MP Matt McEachan—a bush poet, former motorbike riding instructor and crack LNP strategist, who'd worked on federal and state campaigns for a decade—lost his seat. He'd been in for only one term.

'The LNP, me included, wore the opprobrium of a deal with One Nation,' McEachan says. 'We didn't do a deal, but we wore the cost of a preference arrangement that helped Labor. Nicholls categorically ruled out any kind of deal with One Nation for preferences, but what he didn't rule out was forming government with them. That was a mistake'.

McEachan is scathing about Hanson and One Nation, but he says that, so long as the major parties shy away from promoting their beliefs more forcefully, One Nation will remain on the scene. 'I saw and heard comments over and over: "Screw them both, vote One Nation,"' he says. 'It was more just a kick up the bum, without having any real intent of affecting the state or policies. One Nation don't really have any political ideology or philosophy for people to cling to. What does Hanson stand for? Look at what she says—days apart, even—she's contradictory. Look at what she said as a Queensland senator, campaigning for more GST funds for WA.'

He adds gloomily: 'But for anyone voting for One Nation, that doesn't matter. The lesson for us is to ensure that we embody the culture that we say we have—that we fight for individual liberties, that we promote reward for effort, that we promote property rights.'

Former long-serving senator and nominal father of the Queensland Nationals, Ron Boswell, concurs. He'd been privately warning LNP strategists and MPs to take Hanson head on, to hold her to account for her thought bubbles, debunk her ill-thought-out policies and deny her preferences.

He knows the rhythms and the beating heart of Queenslanders, and he could hear them en masse stirring to Hanson's call. 'I've never seen anyone successfully do a deal with One Nation and win an election,' he muses. 'The one thing you can't do is leave Pauline Hanson alone. You have to attack her.'

The smart operators at Katter's Australian Party had her measure too. While Hanson scatter-gunned candidates across the state, KAP restricted its sights to regional seats it saw as winnable, fielding just ten candidates. Despite receiving only 62,600 votes, or 2.32 per cent of the state-wide primary vote, three KAPs took their place in the new parliament.

Snagging his second term, Bob Katter Jnr seized a massive 66 per cent of the primary vote in his seat of Traeger. Even though KAP swapped preferences with One Nation, they fight for the same constituency; but unlike One Nation, they're good at the game of politics.

Bob Katter Snr, the long-serving federal member for the vast Queensland seat of Kennedy, keeps a keen eye on Hanson federally and the party's growing influence in Queensland. One of the most eccentric characters in parliament, he is nonetheless a whip-smart campaigner. He lives and breathes the heave and ho of regional and rural people.

He was elected in 1993 as a National Party MP, blew up the friendship over policy differences in 2001 and vaulted to the crossbenches, where he remained as an Independent until forming Katter's Australian Party in 2011. He remains on the green cross-benches in Canberra as its titular national leader and only federal representative, entertaining his colleagues with rambling dissertations on anything, everything and nothing in particular, usually jammed into one contribution. But a strong political brain thrums behind the oddity that is Bob Katter, and his constituents have not deserted him in 25 years.

As a party, KAP offers what Hanson can't: serious, evidence-based policies, real-world experience in farming and business, and strong and consistent conservative social and family values. The KAPsters and their loyal and growing supporters are the finger in the dyke holding back the One Nation water-burst in remote and regional Queensland.

They know it, and they've got their sights on bigger and better things, knowing that Hanson and her unpredictable inner circle will never offer their level of consistency of purpose and performance.

\* \* \*

Fraser Anning took Malcolm Roberts' place as a One Nation senator for a couple of hours on 13 November. The Queensland election was in full battle cry, but louder bellowing could be heard in the One Nation party room. Anning had been number three on the PHON ticket at the 2016 election, commanding a stellar vote of nineteen, the second-lowest primary vote of any candidate running.

Even by One Nation's standards, the unravelling of Anning's tenure as one of its elected representatives set an impressive new record for speed and turmoil. Who did what to whom is another One Nation game of Cluedo, to be played after dinner with the Irish whisky close by. Nah, grab your cocktail makings and mix yourself Pauline's favourite cocktail, the ginger bitch. It suits this game.

The various bits of the puzzle went like this. Anning arrived at the One Nation party room on the morning of 13 November, polished and primped and ready to take up the legislative cudgels on behalf of his many voters. At the door, his staff were prohibited from entering. He went in alone, regardless. 'As soon as I got into the room, I was verbally attacked,' he said.

'This was profoundly shocking to me as I had been a friend and supporter of Pauline for over twenty years. I tried to answer as best I could, but the attack was so vitriolic that I was obliged to simply walk out.' His alleged misdemeanour was conveyed by senators Burston and Peter Georgiou—Rod Culleton's replacement from Western Australia—who pattered after him to his office. It had something to do with staff and disloyalty, a catch-all that means Pauline or Ashby have been offended by something or other.

The staff in question had previously worked for Roberts. Anning says Ashby disliked them—one in particular, who had previously complained about Ashby's aggressive behaviour—and Pauline wanted them all gone. Anning didn't think it was right to be dictated to about staff recruiting, or to be told to sack good workers who he knew to be loyal.

He says he thought that was that—they'd agree to disagree, and he'd remain loyal to Pauline. Sitting in his new office, he glanced at the TV and saw breaking news: he was an Independent. 'This was news to me,' he said. 'Without even contacting me, Pauline had unilaterally kicked me out of the party. I must say I was stunned. What a way to treat someone who'd been loyal to her for over twenty years.' He'd just joined a club of people that would need to hire an airport hangar if they wanted to hold get-togethers.

But to Pauline's story. She released a statement an hour after he'd been sworn in stating that Anning had 'abandoned' the party to sit as an Independent, adding snidely 'until something else comes along'. She 'believed' that the former staff of Malcolm Roberts had tried to encourage Anning to join Cory Bernardi's Conservative Party. She was unimpressed when Anning refused to stand aside to allow Roberts back into the Senate, or to bend to her will when she dangled pre-selection for a state seat as a possible, inferior, fallback option to him taking up his rightful Senate spot as next on the ticket.

Anning is adamant he was 'expelled by press release'. Whatever the truth, Hanson and Ashby's hot tempers resulted within a few hours in the loss of one precious Senate vote. Sorry, Shirley, but ego can be a very big, very dirty word.

# Chapter 13

# AND THEN THERE WERE TWO

THE MIRAGE THAT one nation is bigger and more influential than it is and has more popular appeal than it does is part of PHON's bag of tricks to force an appearance of endurance. But the members flocking to the One Nation cult are mainly imaginary friends. If the party is seen to be storming across the nation gathering recruits and posing a threat to governments, then it stands to reason it is, right?

And if the people don't want you, what do you do? Hype it up anyway. Pauline threatened to run candidates in the March 2018 Tasmanian and South Australian elections but neither state seemed to want her.

In May 2016, Tasmanian PHON was up and running via Facebook. In December it announced it would storm the citadels of Tasmania's parliament at the next poll, not due for at least fourteen months. In January 2017, the call went out for potential candidates to 'get on board'!

The following month the party's national executive secretary, Rod Miles, told the *Sunday Tasmanian* that PHON would be raring to go in all five electorates, even if the election was called within two months. PHON's support was then at a modest 6 per cent. In May, opinion polls showed that support had halved. The party was registered in December. Pauline would shortly vet candidates for the election.

But the only engine that fired up was in the headquarters of the Jacqui Lambie Network, which offered voters looking for alternatives on the right flank a selection of candidates. After its bravado statements and predictions, One Nation couldn't even present a single runner at the blocks.

Not one to let such a dismal lack of voter enthusiasm douse her optimism, Pauline enthused at a doorstop in Hobart in May 2018 that she'd 'dearly love' to stand candidates there in all federal Lower House seats at the next election and put pressure on the federal government.

She wasn't there to stand up for either party; she was there for 'the people', she asserted erroneously. The statement clearly contradicted the voting record of her team federally.

One Nation's performance in South Australia was also abject. Before Christmas 2016, Hanson announced she'd be registering the party in that state and targeting the next election, set for March 2018. Steve Burgess, who had been PHON's lead 2016 Senate candidate in South Australia, was excited about the number of phone calls from people eager to join the nationalist political family.

Nine months later, the party had missed the deadline for registration with the state Electoral Commission, which is six months out from an election. A cynic might have been inclined to the view that the deadline for registration was accidentally-on-purpose overlooked due to lack of interest.

Opinion polls had been showing that South Australians—a naturally centrist state that had birthed the Democrats and the

Nick Xenophon phenomenon—had little interest in a right-wing Queensland senator and her flock.

* * *

The One Nation leader demonstrated the disconnect between Pauline the parliamentarian and Pauline the hustler on the hustings when she voted in support of the Australian Building and Construction Commission's (ABCC) building code in 2017.

As an outraged ACTU posited in a dissection of the policy: 'The code will remove many critical rights for workers, including the right to bargain for minimum apprentice positions in agreements and for priority to be given to local unemployed workers in new roles over temporary migrant workers. The ABCC and the Code attached to it, actually outlaws a union's ability to negotiate for more apprentices in the industry.'

ACTU Assistant Secretary Scott Connolly bemoaned: 'This will cost local jobs by allowing big construction companies to bring in more temporary workers through visa programs . . . This is a vote against apprentices. This is a vote which will deepen the crisis in youth unemployment.' There was no difference, he seethed, between Hanson and a senator from the Liberal National Party.

Hanson would later crow that she'd been responsible for the government's decision to scrap 457 visas for skilled migrants, which allowed businesses to import valuable skilled workers in short supply in Australia. Never mind that her support for the building code legislation meant she'd prioritised temporary migrant workers over locals in the building and construction industry, which is one of the biggest employers in the country. And never mind the fact that the change had been mooted well before Hanson returned to parliament.

She is nothing if not consistent in her inconsistency. The most high-profile example was her dizzying succession of somersaults over the government's signature corporate tax cuts.

First up, support: 'With company tax, yes, I do support a cut there because small businesses have to be supported,' she announced on her Facebook page in March 2017. 'We have to drive this economy. We have to give people the confidence to actually want to go into industries, manufacturing, create jobs, and the farming sector as well. This hopefully will flow on and it will help industries and manufacturing.'

Next up, opposition: 'The government persists in the false claim that company income tax rates drive business investment,' Senator Hanson wrote in the battlers' broadsheet, *The Australian*, in February 2018. 'This is ridiculous—all it does is undermine my confidence in the government and its advisers.'

But her confidence wasn't that undermined. The following month, on 20 March, she declared she now had 'an open mind' on the tax cuts that only weeks ago were 'ridiculous'. She was impressed by Trump's corporate tax cuts, she said. The framework and conditions of the United States tax package are vastly different, but that's a by-the-by to Hanson.

Seven days later, on 27 March, she was enthusiastic. 'One Nation will be supporting the government's corporate tax cuts . . . let's pass these company tax cuts!' she enthused.

She had busied herself putting together a random laundry list of wishes and wants, including, amongst a raft of other measures, a new coal-fired power station and a dramatic cut to immigration, in return for her support. She wanted it signed in blood by the ever-patient Finance Minister, Mathias Cormann.

Then along sauntered the towering figure of the By-election Bogey, a creature that makes politicians wilt at the knees and dump that week's steadfast principles. The slew of five by-elections was prompted by a string of resignations over the course of a few weeks in early May; one for family reasons, and four because sitting MPs fell foul of Australia's archaic constitutional bar on MPs holding dual citizenship.

One seat up for grabs was Longman, a classic Queensland middle-income provincial seat. Labor's Susan Lamb was forced to announce her resignation as its MP on 9 May because of her dual UK citizenship. Lamb had long been perceived as constitutionally vulnerable: her explanation—that her family's dysfunction had prevented her from accessing the documentation she needed about her parents' circumstances—had convinced few, even some on her side of the political trenches, although they said nothing. The blackand-white world of constitutional law is tone-deaf to family feuds.

One Nation had been responsible for putting Lamb into parliament at the 2016 federal election. In a targeted attack against the LNP's sitting MP, Wyatt Roy, One Nation had directed its preferences to Lamb—the only seat in Queensland where Labor had received PHON preferences. The decision delivered nearly 57 per cent of preferences to Lamb, destroying Roy's superior primary vote advantage.

It hadn't escaped notice at the time that Roy wasn't James Ashby's favourite Queenslander. The young MP had at first assisted Ashby, but then deserted him during the Slipper business. Ashby had been furious, and he doesn't react kindly if he feels mistreated.

With the announcement of the by-election imminent, Hanson and Ashby were aiming to be the kingmakers again in Longman. If they performed badly, the hit to the party's credibility in its heartland state would be tough to overcome.

A ReachTEL poll commissioned by the Australia Institute a day after Lamb resigned on 9 May made Hanson's heart race quicker, for all the wrong reasons: One Nation sympathisers in that seat seriously, intensely, didn't like the company tax cuts.

Hanson had already been under relentless political pressure from a razor-sharp Labor attack over what they claimed was her sell-out of battlers in support of big end of town tax relief. Labor's assault zeroed in on the $17 billion windfall the big banks would reap from the package, accusing Hanson of deserting her people whose lives had been blighted by the banks.

It hurt. At the time, banking executives were slithering in and out of the dock at the Financial Services Royal Commission, 'fessing up to heinous gouging of customers, deceit, fraud and other customer-unfriendly practices.

Time for action. Or rather, retraction. Again.

She didn't bother first telling Finance Minister Cormann of her next change in tack. She gave an exclusive interview to Struggle Street's least-read rag, *The Australian*, which on 22 May published her curious string of thought bubbles for the day. She followed up with a rambling press conference in Canberra, offering up a number of contradictory positions to justify again supporting the corporate tax cuts. These included the strange excuse that measures she'd negotiated, and which depended on the passage of the legislation, hadn't been delivered before the passage of the legislation.

'It's not good enough,' she cried. Her opposition was her 'final' decision. Until the next final position, that is.

Two days later, on 24 May, Speaker Tony Smith let off a stink bomb in parliament when he announced the by-elections would be held in nine weeks, on 28 July, the day set down for one of Labor's biggest talkfests, its triennial national conference.

Only the party luvvies cared about that. Voters in four states—Queensland, Tasmania, South Australia and Western Australia—were now facing a protracted period of electioneering. The only saving grace was that, instead of an Australia-wide scourge, the song-and-dance act would be restricted to five seats.

But in the national parliament and in the Cabinet room, those seats would determine and frame daily politics and policy deliberations in the pursuit of electoral advantage.

On cue, three days later the next final position sauntered into public view. Pauline announced she'd yet again consider supporting the government if there was enough community support. She'd gauge that, she announced, by the thoughts of punters whom she invited to ring her office and tell her how to vote. In another remarkable coincidence, this backflip was the same day *The Australian* carried a Newspoll that asked leading questions and then found that 63 per cent of voters approved of the tax cuts.

Basic issues of tax policy have long confused the One Nation leader. In 2014, she was rooting for the abolition of weekend penalty rates because of what she stated was the impost on small business. When the government reacted to a Fair Work Commission decision to cut Sunday penalty rates for some industries by supporting it, she offered in-principle support. Then she abruptly torpedoed those positions after a backlash from her supporters.

A strong and principled stand depends on the day, the direction of the political winds and the mood of her faithful.

\* \* \*

Within sixteen months after the July 2016 election, Pauline had lost three PHON Senators—Culleton, Roberts and Anning, who had replaced Roberts when he fell foul of the Constitution's bar on dual citizens. Anning set a stellar record as the shortest-serving senator ever for any party.

In the March Western Australian and November 2017 Queensland elections Pauline lost a combined generous baker's dozen of candidates to expulsion or flight prior to the starters' guns being popped.

At the time of publication, another senator had bitten the dust. Brian Burston, who thought he'd been her friend of two decades' standing, had been in a fierce battle of wills against his leader. She wanted him expelled from the party. Improbably, given the electoral and other requirements around such matters, she demanded he give her back his Senate seat.

His sin was his decision to honour the original handshake agreement he and Pauline had made with the government to back the company tax cuts.

As he discovered, Rule One in Hanson's Senate playbook is that if you defy her will and want to exercise your Senate right to a free vote, you're a traitor and it's off with your head. Rule Two is that she will make other unsubstantiated accusations against you to reinforce her right to enforce Rule One.

On Sky News, she accused him of 'back-stabbing' her in the past, which a bewildered Burston emphatically rejected. A large roll-call of candidates and party faithful—among many others, former treasurer Ian Nelson and former secretary Saraya Beric— would also attest to the abrupt way Hanson severs relationships if she's displeased.

Rule Three is that she will flee the country when trouble erupts and, with any luck, she'll visit a high-profile anti-Islam activist at the same time. After issuing Burston a resign-or-else ultimatum, Pauline hopped on a plane to London on the taxpayers' coin. Her cover was a fact-finding parliamentary excursion to discuss, among other issues, counter-terrorism and online abuse—presumably how to stamp it out, not how to improve her efforts.

However, Pauline had at the top of her to-do list in London a wish to visit the far-right activist Tommy Robinson, founder of the hyper-nationalist English Defence League, who was doing time at Her Majesty's pleasure for various civic violations. In a video message on social media, she insulted every fair-minded Australian when she said she'd love to visit him and 'bring the messages from the Australian people to you, because I can tell you, you're not alone'.

The astonishing part of the Burston saga was that Hanson was prepared to reduce her party to a rump of two, thus losing critical Senate influence, because she couldn't control her rage that her authoritarian will was not able to cower a member of her team. In her furious letter demanding he resign and hand the seat back, she claimed she no longer had confidence he could 'work as a member of my team'.

Burston wasn't impressed. 'She is saying she's no longer got the confidence I'll agree with every single decision she makes, as president for life,' he told Ben Fordham, standing in for Andrew Bolt on his show on *Sky News*, PHON'S program of choice. 'I thought I joined One Nation as a democratic political party, not a dictatorship.'

And off he waltzed, into the ample arms of Clive Palmer. With jaw-dropping hubris, the multi-millionaire businessman, who'd spent more time in a courtroom than a boardroom since voters booted him from parliament in 2016 after just one term, announced he was resurrecting his political career.

In a Parliament House courtyard on the chilly morning of 19 June, Palmer proudly presented Burston as the Senate leader and, well, only senator representing Palmer's newly formed United Australia Party. Only an hour before, Burston had announced to the Senate that he'd be sitting as an Independent, raising reasonable questions if he'd misled the chamber. This craziness followed a week after the announcement that another PHON banishee, Fraser Anning, was joining Katter's Australian Party, Pauline's fierce competitors in regional Queensland. Ouch.

What was the divorce from Burston really all about? Pauline's party appears to have no rules regarding voting. Spokesman James Ashby told a media scrum after the July 2016 elections that PHON senators would be bound by the party's flimsy 'policy manifesto'; otherwise, they could vote according to their consciences and according to their constituents' wishes. There's no reference to corporate taxes in the party's so-called 'manifesto'.

The personality turmoil in the party is not an aberration, or peculiar to the recent re-emergence of Pauline Hanson's One Nation. Since PHON was established in 1997, thirty of its candidates have been elected to state or federal parliaments, but only eight have stuck with the team. Something has always been very, very rotten in the state of Denmark.

Those who have chosen over the years to blow the whistle on the dysfunctional practices nurtured by the volatile personality of its leader are isolated or discarded. More optimists and idealists fill their shoes until they too transgress and are flung aside. Burston should not have been surprised that the relationship he held dear for a few decades wasn't what he thought; he had been around her long enough to see the pattern.

By the time the fog rolled across the national capital, sending MPs and staffers scampering back to their home states for the long 2018 parliamentary winter recess, bets were being taken on how long her last team-mate, Peter Georgiou, would stick with the angry redhead. There were no long odds on offer.

Georgiou isn't particularly simpatico with his leader. The mild-mannered former sparky rebelled against Hanson's support for the government's public interest test on union mergers that would have blocked the marriage of the militant construction and maritime unions. Georgiou's opposition sunk the bill before the vote. Funny; she didn't ask him to resign.

He's not on board with her key beef that Muslims are in danger of swamping Australia, either. In March 2017, shortly after assuming the seat of his brother-in-law, the disqualified Senator Rod Culleton, the son of Greek immigrants told the ABC that Muslims should be able to live and settle in Australia like everyone else: 'If people want to come and embrace Australia and embrace the culture, like my parents did, and learn the language and integrate with the community, then I can't see it being an issue,' he said.

'If they're Muslim and they've passed the checks the Australian Government has on them, then I don't see it as an issue. That is different to my party's policy . . . everyone thinks differently of the party's policy.'

Following those comments, Georgiou appeared to go into solitary confinement. Whether he survives the Long March to the election due in 2019 as Pauline's only parliamentary foot soldier is not a bet astute bookies would take.

# Chapter 14

# REPRESENTING HER CONSTITUENTS

PAULINE HANSON TURNED her most ferocious gaze on a couple of hapless female bureaucrats from the Department of Agriculture. She was on a truth mission, seeking confirmation through a Senate estimates hearing for her vaguely justified opposition to halal certification.

'Now, it has been brought to my attention that under halal certification these cattle are actually still alive when their throats are slit,' she thundered at the civil servants, who looked blankly at each other. One silently beseeched the other: *Er, you want to . . . ?* Her colleague, stony-faced, stepped up to the task. Yep, she said solemnly, adding helpfully that the animals were stunned beforehand.

What they would have said if they weren't polite government employees was: 'Senator, the story of life is that breathing things are, by definition, alive before they're killed.'

Hanson's muddled questioning at the Senate's Rural and Regional Affairs and Transport Legislation Committee in May 2017 could be forgiven. After all, for the leader of a party that demands major politicians 'please explain', it was an unfamiliar forum.

PHON demands accountability. Transparency is one of its major platforms as it parades itself across the nation as the only party that can speak the truth to 'the people' and hold the major parties to account. But Hanson's appearance on this day was her first at any Senate estimates hearings since her election.

She'd skipped opportunities in October, three months after the election, and again in February 2017. She had simply been too busy elsewhere (a trip to Norfolk Island, dining with her Queensland leader Steve Dickson in the state parliament, that sort of essential federal business).

And since she was back in Canberra, she figured she'd give a few more bureaucrats the ole Hanson interrogation. But not on anything other than her pet peeves. Having made what was surely a killer argument against halal certification, off she motored to the Environment and Communications Committee to hammer the ABC about its treatment of her party. This is one of her very favourite themes.

She'd been noisily trying to muscle the government into cutting ABC funding to the tune of $600 million over the forward estimates—despite the respect it enjoys in her heartland of regional Australia—because she doesn't like the national broadcaster's critical questioning of her behaviour, finances and policies. She'd even threatened to withdraw her support for all the government's legislation until it complied with her demand, a unique approach to deliberative decision-making.

One particular investigation that riled her had been an incisive *Four Corners* story the preceding month that had raised serious questions about her accountability and ethics. Now she had a string of ABC managers, including Managing Director Michelle Guthrie, in front of her.

Forget asking about cuts to regional news services, or to other important public broadcasting services her supporters rely on in bush Australia, already suffering from years of government cuts. 'You might like to explain to me why One Nation was targeted in the *Four Corners* interview and also on the *7.30* report just recently,' the One Nation leader snapped.

Greens Senator Scott Ludlam, sitting on the committee, didn't wait for the ABC to respond, chiming in: 'Because it looked like you broke the law. Because you seem to have broken the law.' Adding for good measure: 'It's not targeting, it's journalism.'

Hanson doesn't believe in objective journalism, or facts. The 'public opinion of the ABC is very poor', she triumphantly told Guthrie.

Not so, said Guthrie. Studies showed that 80 per cent of people trusted the ABC's news coverage. Hanson's claim was 'not borne out by both the independent and the other objective surveys that have been conducted'.

Facts be damned. Getting no satisfaction there, Hanson's next target two days later was the Director-General of ASIO, Duncan Lewis. He was bloody well going to admit that Muslim terrorists were sneaking into Australia as refugees.

'I have absolutely no evidence to suggest there's a connection between refugees and terrorism,' he unequivocally stated in response to her questions. And no, Senator, there was also, categorically, no evidence that children of refugees were more likely to convert to radical Islam. And in response to your statement about Muslims and terrorist acts in Australia to date, only one of them could be identified as being by an extremist.

Oh, and ASIO did not have any security concerns about women wearing the burqa 'other than the requirement for individuals to identify themselves to authorities, and there are regulations in place for that'.

So far as Hanson was concerned, the head of Australia's top security agency was clearly speaking bunkum. At the same time as she was quizzing the country's spy chief, a post on her Facebook page bobbed up: 'Remember, there is only one religion across the globe blowing children up and cutting off infidels heads. That's Islam.'

Before Hanson was prodded into action, One Nation's lone representative at the May block of Senate committee hearings had been climate change denier Malcolm Roberts, whose only desire was to ferret out the fake scientists the ABC had secreted in its bunker who were sending out false facts to its gullible readers and viewers.

Like, perhaps, internationally renowned physicist Brian Cox who, in an episode of *Q&A* in August 2016, had in vain tried to educate Roberts about the basics of empirical scientific evidence.

In contrast to One Nation's invisibility, Nick Xenophon's team of three had attended 90 Senate hearings, and new senator Derryn Hinch had turned up at 30.

But there's nothing like a spot of public shaming to prod a politician into action. Two days before her first-ever hearings, Hanson had been outed in a few media outlets for her lack of commitment to pursuing accountability in government. Opposition Senate Leader Penny Wong tartly observed: 'Instead of spending her time trying to work out how to make money out of her members and the taxpayers, maybe Senator Hanson should do what she was elected to do and represent her constituents.'

Never one to step aside from a microphone, Hinch had also publicly marvelled at the grand opportunity Senate estimates gave politicians to 'live up to our electoral promise to keep the bastards honest'. As an innocent aside to a journalist, he murmured:

'I am surprised that Senator Hanson and some of her colleagues aren't here, and some other crossbenchers . . . But then, their attendance in the Senate when we are in session is also pretty cavalier.' For good measure, he added pointedly: 'Attending Senate estimates is part of our job. It's also partly why we will only formally sit for fifteen weeks this year.'

Shamed into attending in May, she decided she'd done such a top job she'd give it another fly in October, this time taking on defence chiefs at the Foreign Affairs, Defence and Trade Legislation Committee. 'Is it true that pump-jet submarines can only stay underwater for twenty minutes?' The One Nation senator had Rear Admiral Greg Sammut in her sights. Her task was to expose something very fishy about plans for twelve new vessels to be built by French shipbuilder Naval Group.

'I assure you they can last for longer than twenty minutes,' he responded, after regaining his composure. 'A pump jet is a form of propeller; it has no bearing on how deep a submarine can go, how long it can stay under water.'

Just how far under, he wouldn't divulge to the senator—it was classified because of operational security reasons, he assured her. Command Chief Hanson knew better: 'I don't think it's classified,' she snorted.

Hanson's credentials as the mistress of the authoritative high-voltage dummy spit, as someone who avoids follow-through or offering realistic solutions, had already clearly been on display during her parliamentary reincarnation this time around, just as it had been twenty years before when she sometimes regarded her attendance in parliament as optional.

For instance, before the estimates hearings in February, she'd kicked up headline dust with her angry denunciation of the 'atrocious, disgusting' $5.6 million pay package of former Australia Post head honcho Ahmed Fahour, gratuitously and irrelevantly adding a few insulting comments about his Muslim religion. But her stilettos did not ring out on the parquetry floor of Parliament House during estimates hearings when Fahour personally appeared before a committee on 28 February. Instead, Hanson scatter-gunned a string of angry questions/statements about him on her social media accounts for her fans.

She had better things to do than to ask for an explanation from someone whom she had very personally attacked in public. She needed to be out and about, raising the decibels of her empty anger. She needed to be pumping the eager hands of her loyalists, who mistakenly think she's in the thick of parliamentary battle, lifting political standards, probing government spending and looking after their interests.

Most MPs consider the estimates hearings the real work of the legislature's democracy in action. Hearings are held three times a year, giving MPs a rare opportunity to question ministers and their departments about government spending. Each of the eight committees has six senators, including a minor party senator, and any senator can ask to be co-opted to any committee. Up to four committees can sit at the one time, meaning each day of hearings offers a rich vein of parliamentary probing and discovery.

Ministers can fudge, but bureaucrats aren't that well trained in those political dark arts. There is no better way to get to the heart of government funding and program decisions, waste and political spending masquerading as community programs. And if they can't answer on the spot, there's the nifty tool of questions on notice so as to make them accountable in the future.

Incisive questioning can flush out secret data and hollow logs found to be full of cash. Ministers often alter programs and policies as a result of forensic questioning. It's not unusual to have two dozen senior and middle-ranking public servants lined up like crows on a fence waiting to be questioned.

Estimates can sometimes be off-pace and often frustratingly tedious theatre, but they are the beating heart of Australia's accountable democracy. A lot that passes for debate on the floor of parliament is theatre for the consumption of the cameras and to regurgitate in newsletters to constituents. MPs who ignore estimates aren't serious about the real business of parliament.

\*　\*　\*

The senate sits for only about fifty days a year, give or take, depending on what legislation ascends there from the Lower House. That other annoying bit of work that most senators diligently perform—attending estimates hearings—should add another twenty or more days to a senator's Canberra schedule of work, or four working weeks.

But it doesn't for Hanson. Why should she? Her time is better spent vigorously recruiting in the Struggle Streets of each electorate across the country.

If she fronted Senate estimates, it would be much easier to guess which way she and her team were going to vote on legislation. Not only had her party voted in favour of government legislation about 80 per cent of the time by mid-2018, but her supporters might be surprised to learn she's helped the government pass measures that mock her war cry that she's the protector of the left-behinds.

In October 2016 the One Nation leader told the *Australian Financial Review*—the organ of choice for business leaders, rather than the downtrodden—that she intended to back the government's $6 billion omnibus of welfare cuts. Such an action would have slammed low-income and welfare households. The measures included taking the axe to $2.9 billion in Family Tax Benefit supplements. It would have eliminated $1.3 billion in carbon tax compensation for future welfare recipients; it would have cut $1.2 billion in alleged 'double dipping' of paid parental leave and cut $600 million in other measures, including freezing eligibility thresholds and ending a pensioner's education supplement. It would have made young dole recipients wait one month before receiving payments; indeed, she declared that she personally would have been even harder on the under-25s: 'I'd make it three months,' she told the *Financial Review*.

By February 2017, with the measures still in negotiation with the other crossbenchers, Hanson back-flipped; not because she'd softened her heart, but because she wanted the 'generous' paid parental leave provisions further reined in. Women would exploit an extension to the leave scheme from eighteen to twenty weeks, she'd concluded, and she couldn't stomach that. 'They get themselves pregnant and [the government will] have the same problems they did with the baby bonus, with people just doing it for the money,' she told *The Australian*, without any proof or evidence there had been that sort of defrauding of the old scheme.

Her approach to policy making constantly springs from her own life, or her jaundiced, under-informed view of the lives of others: 'I've gone through a bloody tough life myself as a single mother and held down a part-time job. I had no assistance, no help from anyone,' she added.

Having your children minded by patient parents and in-laws, and at times by paid live-in help and by a turnstile door of husbands and boyfriends, apparently doesn't constitute 'help' in Hanson's world. Those details of her past life spoil her single-mum battler narrative.

Hanson's bitter attitude towards single mothers has been a staple of her political life. There is no insult too great for them in

Hanson's angry world. In her first maiden speech in the House of Representatives, in 1996, she demanded benefits be restricted to only the first child of a single mother. Twenty years on, she trilled the same tune in her Senate first speech.

One Nation's domestic violence and family custody policies are equally punishing to women. Hanson wants to all but disable the Family Court, vesting power in a ragtag of ordinary Australians to determine access arrangements. Both partners would automatically have joint access to children on the point of separation; an abusive husband would not be denied access, even if authorities had issued protection orders.

In the world view of the politician who had four children to two husbands, both marriages shotgun: 'Children are used as pawns in custody battles, where women make frivolous claims and believe they have the sole right to the children,' she claimed in her first Senate speech. Her second husband, Mark, once bitterly complained he was not allowed any say in his two children's upbringing following the couple's separation.

As far as those women who claim physical or other abuse are concerned, there'd better be some solid evidence: 'What needs to be addressed is domestic violence orders. Women—most of them are women—are going out and throwing them around left, right and centre,' she told the *Yahoo7* website in September 2017. With no evidence for this and showing even less knowledge of how domestic violence orders are issued, she soldiered on: 'If the partner wants to ring up and say, "I want to see my children," that's [a domestic violence order]. How ridiculous is that? Because they call it harassment.' At other times she has accused women of fabricating accusations of domestic violence because their partners had criticised their clothing colours. Her maiden speech was heavily sprinkled with derogatory accusations about single mothers.

Her Queensland domestic violence spokeswoman in the 2017 Queensland election, Tracey Bell-Henselin, managed to unite both major parties in opposition when she suggested women be required to prove they'd been abused through proof of injuries, medical files or documentation of a partner's criminal past.

For the feminists of One Nation, some information: the 2017 National Homicide Monitoring Program report by the Australian Institute of Criminology revealed that for the two years from 2012 to 2014, ninety-nine women were killed by their intimate partners—an average of around one a week. Women account for 79 per cent of all intimate partner homicides. In a separate report, the Institute also noted that women were five times more likely than men to require medical attention or hospitalisation as a result of intimate partner violence, and five times more likely to report fearing for their lives.

In another study into the endemic scourge of family violence in Australia, the Attorney-General's Department found that of those women who experienced violence, more than half had children in their care. At the 2011 census, 46,000 women were homeless, many with their children. Domestic and family violence is cited as the number one reason women seek specialist homeless services. Many women are on single-parent incomes.

But hey, Pauline Hanson's all about making sure the kids are looked after. Kids have a right to both parents, regardless of whether one has been deemed unfit by the courts.

We believe in family, she insists, ignoring her own experience of multiple fractured families and the experience of the women who look to her for support. But the kids—she'll look after them, make sure they get a good education, make sure they're not indoctrinated.

But there's no room for such medically and scientifically proven protection for kids as vaccinations against possibly deadly childhood diseases. Experts are not expert, in Pauline's world. Parents should make up their own minds, she repeatedly stated in 2017, despite overwhelming medical evidence that unvaccinated children can die, and also infect other children.

Australian Medical Association chief, Dr Michael Gannon, smacked her down, urging her to start 'behaving responsibly'. Vaccinations were 'the most important public health measure we've got', he said. 'This fatuous idea that parents can spend half an hour on Wikipedia and come to a greater understanding of the issues than their doctor and the accumulated wisdom of all the world's medical scientists is ludicrous.'

But vaccinations can cause autism, Pauline replied. Against this claim, the head of Autism Awareness Australia, Nicole Rogerson, responded: 'It shows just an absolute lack of knowledge to do with anything to do with childhood vaccination and autism, and I think she shouldn't comment on what she clearly doesn't understand.'

Nevertheless, 'One Nation is about protecting the whole family unit,' Queensland party leader Steve Dickson said proudly during that state's election campaign, with Hanson nodding like a battery-operated toy standing alongside him. Which brought him to the question of the Safe Schools program. He alleged darkly: 'We are having little kids in grade four at school, young girls being taught by teachers how to masturbate, how to strap on dildos, how to do this sort of stuff—that is the real problem in this country.'

The real problem in this country is that such crap is being peddled by Dickson and Hanson, who surely knew those statements were false. When Dickson finally tried to backtrack—following an uproar, including from those on the conservative side of politics—all he could offer was a grudging non-apology: 'I apologise if the specific words I used offended anyone.'

Setting aside the false statements about the program, Safe Schools wasn't funded for Queensland schools at this time. Commonwealth funding ceased in September. Hanson has never retracted or recanted her support for her Queensland leader's fabrications. She never does; she's always right, even in the face of ironclad, evidence-based research and official data that she's not.

\* \* \*

In the Australia presided over by Prime Minister Hanson, she would hold an expensive Royal Commission into 'whether Islam is a religion or an ideology'; would shut down 'Muslim' immigration, although she never says how this could be achieved; and would ban any further building of Islamic schools and mosques.

In the wake of the March 2017 terrorist attack in London, she tastelessly started a hashtag Pray4MuslimBan. Forgetting her allergy to vaccinations, she backed up the call to prayer by using an inoculation analogy: 'We have a disease, we vaccinate ourselves against it,' she opined. 'Islam is a disease. We need to vaccinate ourselves against that.' Through Christian prayer, presumably.

She'd also round up anybody looking vaguely suspicious and probably Muslim-ish, toss them in jail and forget about them. It's an interesting proposal in a democratic Australia, where tens of thousands of Second World War survivors from horrific concentration camps—including her first mother-in-law, Lydia Zagorski—have peaceably settled.

'Those on watch lists who are not Australian citizens need to be deported and those who are, interned to neutralise their possible harm to this country,' she wrote in an open letter to the Prime Minister in June 2017. 'I call on you to look seriously at instituting a moratorium on immigration of Muslims to Australia or, at the very least, greater stringency in vetting those wishing to come to our country. If laws need to be changed then so be it; if you need to consider a US-style ban, as proposed by United States President Donald Trump, then so be it.' The fact that successive courts in the US found Trump's proposal illegal is neither here nor there to the show-woman.

The radio strutter sometimes known, for good reason, as 'the parrot', backed her up: 'I'm saying if they're a suspect—and that's good enough—round them up, whether the evidence is there or not. I'm saying don't put these people in jail, where they will radicalise others. Intern them somewhere remote and leave them there or get rid of them,' Alan Jones said after her letter was published.

Another Pauline solution to an unverified threat is a ban on the burqa, despite the evidence presented to Senate estimates by that ignoramus, ASIO chief Duncan Lewis, that there was no point as burqa-wearers didn't pose a security threat. Three months after quizzing Lewis at hearings and promptly ignoring what he had to say, Pauline turned up in the Senate wearing a burqa she'd bought on eBay.

It didn't impress anyone in the chamber, least of all the Attorney-General, whose speech prompted a standing ovation. 'I can tell you, Senator Hanson, that it has been the advice of each Director-General of Security with whom I have worked, and each Commissioner of the Australian Federal Police with whom I have worked, that it is vital for their intelligence and law enforcement work that they work cooperatively with the Muslim community and to ridicule that community, to drive it into a corner, to mock its religious garments is an appalling thing to do and I would ask you to reflect on that,' an emotional Senator Brandis declared.

She didn't reflect on that. 'Doesn't the Australian people have the right to know that whoever sits in the chamber, that is actually the person they voted for?' she trumpeted later on 2GB. They do—which is why her New South Wales then-colleague, Brian Burston, had identified the woman under the black garb as the One Nation leader to the Senate's security guards before she entered the chamber, ensuring she could waltz in.

That was irrelevant to Pauline. As far as she was concerned, she'd deployed masterful logic and shown that anyone could wander into the Senate. She was damned pleased with the result. 'It's been an idea of mine to actually expose about the burqa,' she sort of explained to her radio audience.

A thoughtful academic piece published by the University of South Australia's Centre for Muslim and Non-Muslim Understanding put Pauline's stunt into perspective: 'For the people who want to ban the burqa, its appearance interrupts the vision of a mythical homogenous society in a bygone age,' it stated.

'The demand to erase the burqa is not an attempt to liberate oppressed women, but more likely an attempt to erase Muslim presence from public life. This erasure is perhaps couched in the language of public safety, combating cultural oppression of women and guaranteeing cultural integrity and civic peace, but what it is saying unambiguously is that Muslims should not be seen, let alone heard.'

The absurdity of the argument for a ban is also in the numbers of burqa-wearers. While figures are not counted in Australia, the paper stated that in France—where the Muslim population is higher as a percentage of the population—about 0.00005 per cent of the total population wears the religious headgear. That would equate to around twelve women in a state the size of South Australia.

'On what grounds should legislative effort and state resources be spent in targeting such a small group and imposing on them restrictions that are not generally imposed on other segments of the population?' the paper questioned.

Forget evidence. Evidence only confuses. As with Trump, if Pauline states it, then it's a fact. Climate change scientists, for instance, clearly speak crap. The overwhelming majority of the global scientific community—who have produced academically rigorous, peer-reviewed evidence of the existence of anthropogenic climate change—simply have no clue.

In 2016, accompanied by an entourage of 25 media and assorted hangers-on, including Senators Roberts and Burston, she went snorkelling off Great Keppel Island to prove climate change was a hoax. She'd barely donned the wetsuit and plunged awkwardly into the briny for the cameras before conservationists were noting with megaphones through media outlets that the site she chose was 1300 kilometres away from where coral bleaching occurred.

And oops, she snapped off some coral for the cameras in possible breach of regulations covering the removal of coral. And oops again, she forgot to declare the cost of the charter supplied by Freedom Fast Cats, estimated at about $4500, on her register of pecuniary interests. She added it following media questions.

Campaigning in rural Queensland during that state's election campaign in November 2017, she marvelled at the ignorance of the climate change science community. 'Climate change, it's all BS,' she told voters. 'It's a money making racket, and they brainwash the kids. Flying up here, I said the amount of trees and growth we have here is just amazing, yet they'll have you think that we don't have a tree up here.'

She doubled down in a snippy exchange with Greens Senator Sarah Hanson-Young on Channel Seven's *Sunrise* the same month: 'Climate is changing, but it's not from humans, Sarah—get this through your head.'

David Koch, who is often sympathetic to Pauline, interrupted to say that even the government's Chief Scientist, Alan Finkel, believed in climate change. She didn't care. She switched tack. People were sick of high power bills! That's all the proof anyone needs that human-induced climate change hasn't been scientifically proven.

*   *   *

Pauline's support for deep wounds to the welfare budget was just one of many legislative measures she's backed that, if known, would surely shock her supporters. Margaret Dodd, the candidate for the March 2017 Western Australian election who quit in disgust 24 hours out from polling day, sent a passionate email to other state PHON candidates explaining her position:

> Phon is supposed to be for the battlers, yet the PHON Senators crossed the floor supporting a cut in penalty rates, these people are low paid often casual or permanent part-time, who often need more than one job to provide for themselves, very few are full time workers with all the benefits that come with a steady full time Job.
>
> What is Phon doing about the 457 visa, overseas workers taking preference over Australian workers? This is not good for the economy as these workers send the largest part of their wage back to their country for their families.
>
> What has been done about the sell off of our farmlands and pastoral leases to foreign ownership, our food. What about our assets docks energy etc, all sold off to foreign ownership, our infrastructure. What about our natural resources, our mines.
>
> What is Phon doing about this globalisation which results in the filthy Rich getting richer and creating slavery as a workforce, Our people. What about the homeless, the unemployed, affordability of education, affordability of medical attention, affordability of power, gas and water.

Sorry—Phon did something about that, they voted with the liberals to cut money from the poorest and most vulnerable in our society, so much for fighting for the battlers. Phon do listen to the people as do all the other parties—in one ear out the other.

Hanson's parliamentary record has been poor when it comes to the concerns of her supporters.

She voted against a motion to increase the Newstart Allowance, a proposal that has significant support across the parliamentary benches but is not yet agreed to in the Cabinet room. She didn't bother to turn up to vote on a motion to condemn the Prime Minister for his neglect of northern and regional Queensland, her core support base. Nor did she vote on a motion to increase funding for homeless services for older Australians—again, this demographic is among her core supporters.

While motions don't have the same legal effect as legislative measures, they express the will of the Senate and are important in helping frame policies and committee work.

Surprisingly, Hanson missed an opportunity for some decent media bleating by also missing a vote on a motion (which failed) objecting to ABC's Triple J shifting its Hottest 100 hits from Australia Day, out of respect for Indigenous Australians. And after campaigning loudly against same sex marriage, she abstained from the final, successful vote.

A One Nation signature policy in the Queensland state election was to oppose further coal seam gas exploration in the gas-rich Cooper Basin, which had operated for 50 years and helped keep her state economy buoyant. Federally, the party's comprehensive three-line policy states: 'We will oppose the privatisation of water and any mining or CSG exploration on prime agricultural land, where it will have an impact on our environment and water supply.'

But when it came to the vote for a motion in November 2017, calling for the government to protect agricultural groundwater systems by imposing a moratorium on CSG projects in the richest agricultural area in New South Wales, around the Liverpool Plains, she voted against it.

She does take time out to wander into the Senate chamber for the really important votes, though. Conservative Party Senator Cory Bernardi moved a motion during the same month as the CSG moratorium, calling on colleagues to have a croissant with their morning coffee 'in solidarity with the defenders of liberalism and freedom'. The croissant symbolised the end of the Ottoman Empire's Siege of Vienna in 1529, according to Bernardi, but 'violence and oppression against liberal-democracy and other faiths by Islamists has continued into our own time'.

Hanson voted yes for the croissant. The overwhelming majority of her colleagues voted it down, probably opting for an Iced VoVo instead.

Luckily a few more bikies and drug-runners will be able to enjoy a croissant on the outside, courtesy of Pauline and her cronies. She voted against legislation that would have seen convicted firearm smugglers sentenced to life in jail, despite the Senate hearing persuasive arguments about the serious problems posed to ordinary Australians by the 600,000-plus illegal firearms on Australia's streets. This argument didn't hold water for the defenders of liberty and freedom in One Nation.

Malcolm Roberts—not yet booted out of the Senate for dual citizenship—took the lead on the argument for his party. The legislation came from 'the obsessive ongoing effort by enemies of freedom in this country to undermine the inalienable right of private citizens to possess firearms', the senator argued.

He must have hallucinated that he was in the Trumposphere. It isn't an inalienable right in Australia, nor did rights have anything to do with the intent of the legislation, but never mind. Roberts put the One Nation case that it was all the fault of the 'feral, pest-hugging collectivists in the Greens', who 'hate the idea of private ownership of firearms, just as they hate all other individual freedoms'.

One Nation went down in flames. The three amigos were joined by only one other senator, the nutty libertarian David Leyonhjelm, in voting against the bill. The 'burbs of Australia are now a bit safer, no thanks to Pauline and her team, with strict laws and punishments applying to trafficking 50 or more firearms or firearms parts in a six-month period.

\* \* \*

Out in the real world—where it matters because it's here she's seen and heard—Pauline has always been very loud about the real stuff of life that affects her people. Like the opening ceremony of the Commonwealth Games, in April 2018. She wasn't concerned about the businesses adversely affected by the government's exaggerated claims of gridlock, which drove domestic customers away; or the devastation to hotels and accommodation hot spots that, with horror, sat and waited for visitors who never arrived.

Hanson's beef was the presentation of Indigenous culture in the curtain-raiser. 'I thought it was disgusting, absolutely disgusting,' she said of the ceremony, which included Indigenous dancing, Indigenous hip hop artist Mau Power and didgeridoo-playing. She didn't understand rap and 'most Australians' didn't listen to didgeridoo music, she complained. 'As far as I'm concerned, that is not Australia.'

What's more, she yelled on Sky, she considered herself Indigenous. 'I have got nothing against the Aboriginal people, but I'm sick and tired of being made to feel as if I'm a second-class citizen in my own country. I'm Indigenous as far as I'm concerned. I was born here. This is my country as much as anyone else.'

It therefore went without saying that she then returned to one of her favourite themes, that Indigenous people get preferential treatment that nobody else gets. 'We have a lot of racism going on in this country—blatant racism that you will get the assistance and help purely based on your race.' So it's not that dispossession and poverty still afflict Indigenous Australians, who die at least ten years earlier than non-Indigenous because of poor health and social conditions; or because their mortality rate—the number of deaths per 100,000—is double that of other Australians; or because in states such as Queensland, Indigenous people still can't buy their own homes.

The provision of special government programs surely has nothing to do with the fact that the mortality rate of Indigenous children aged under four is double that of their more privileged brothers and sisters; or because the appalling rate of Indigenous suicide—up to 10 per cent of the Indigenous population—would be called a humanitarian crisis if it was in any other demographic; or because Aboriginal juveniles land in jail 24 times more than other young people.

And most definitely there is no causal link between these entrenched tragic outcomes and the dispossession, racism and paternalistic savaging of the family unit inflicted on Indigenous Australians by the colonisers of this great country.

No, it's racism pure and simple. Those privileged Aborigines are getting special treatment that the likes of Pauline—who enjoyed freedom, education, parental guidance and shelter when she was growing up—should also have been able to access.

# Chapter 15
# FLUSH WITH FUNDS

BY ALL ACCOUNTS—mainly hers—Pauline was a success-ful small businesswoman before she entered parliament in 1996. She'd helped her second husband, Mark, build up his plumbing business via which she bought, then sold, a few investment prop-erties. She bought a local Ipswich fish 'n' chips shop, building it into a successful business by often working seven days a week at the expense of the time she might otherwise have spent with her children.

There were a few money and staff issues that blotted her good record, however. After all, what small business doesn't have a few problems to deal with? She'd kept ignoring requests by a young staffer—who'd been with her as a dedicated employee for a few years—to be paid for hours of cleaning Pauline had requested of the obliging young woman prior to the shop's sale in early 1997.

The staffer, Jodi Blaine, was so incensed at the bullying tactics used to block her repeated requests for payment that she lodged a complaint with the District Industrial Inspector at the Ipswich court. The total amount owed was only about $40, but the investigation uncovered more examples of Pauline's poor behaviour as a boss. She was ordered to pay Ms Blaine $1462.67, which largely constituted arrears in wages.

But Pauline had been bred with a keen eye for money and commercial opportunity, and sometimes things can go a bit awry. Comes with the territory. She came from a large, hard-working, often struggling family; her parents had also worked around the clock in their outer-Brisbane takeaway business. They instilled in their youngest daughter an appreciation for the mighty dollar and, she says, hard work.

When she became an MP in 1996, the largesse extended so freely to the country's elected representatives must have boggled her. A six-figure salary; travel on the public purse; accommodation in five-star hotels when on official business. Federal backbenchers at the time were also gifted a generous $26,000 electorate allowance, with few guidelines on accountability except a vague requirement it be used in the service of the electorate. She could hire and fire staff, and not have to dip her hand into the till to pay them.

What an extraordinary life. It must have been almost too good to be true.

From the outset, Pauline made it one of her micro-management duties to keep an eye on staff salaries and payments, and control all other expenditures. She constantly queried staff on their claims for overtime, quibbling and challenging them. Recalling one particularly nasty encounter she had with Jeff Babb, one of her researchers, her first minder John Pasquarelli wrote in his memoir: 'It was almost as if she was jealous of him getting the extra money.'

In August 2006, Pasquarelli suggested to Pauline she use some of her electorate allowance, which was paid monthly, to purchase a TV and video for the Ipswich office. He priced a small combined unit for a modest $400. Pauline told him she'd think about it.

A few days later, a giant brand-new wide-screen TV in its own cabinet from a local outlet was delivered by a couple of burly blokes. It was paid for by a cheque from her office account. Pasquarelli, bemused, made a place for it in the office. When he fronted for work the following day, the TV had disappeared. In its place, in her office, sat a small second-hand TV and VCR.

The new one had gone to Pauline's ranch. 'Pauline had upgraded her TV and VCR with her electorate allowance which, to my way of thinking, contravened the spirit and expectation behind the granting of it,' Pasquarelli wrote in his memoir. Pauline has never disputed this account.

The Department of Administrative Services allocated backbenchers an extra $600 on top of the electorate allowance for the beautification of their electorate offices. Pauline's then-secretary, Barbara Hazelton, spent the money in July 1996 to fill the Ipswich office with a jungle of cheery pot plants of all shapes and sizes.

A few days later, Pauline asked Pasquarelli to help take some plants to her car. She made two trips home with the car brimming with the greenery. The procedure was repeated a few days later, and again twice in August. The air conditioning was killing them, Pauline told a disinterested Pasquarelli. The office, once a forest, now resembled a razed paddock denuded of all plant life.

In November, Pauline was a guest home gardener on Channel Nine's *Burke's Backyard*. Pasquarelli squinted a little closer at the TV. Those pot plants in the background sure looked familiar.

On 16 December 1996, the *Courier-Mail* blew the whistle on some unusual expenditure in the electorate office of the MP for Oxley, including the removal of the pot plants. By then, in what would become a set pattern, five angry staffers had left her employ, either voluntarily or because they were sacked. Any one of them could have leaked such juicy titbits.

The indignant new MP went on 2GB's Ron Casey program, establishing another pattern that would endure for the next two decades: try to only be interviewed by friendly, compliant media. She admitted to taking 'three' plants home—to save them from the deathly air conditioning, she added reasonably.

She then fired up, establishing yet another pattern: when under attack, attack louder, then deflect: 'Oh, for crying out loud—you know, the fact is that if the media runs through some of their old footage they will see that all the plants have been here all the time. So yes, there is this, you know, to pull me down, to discredit me whatever way they possibly can, and any way,' she told Casey.

Pasquarelli recalled in his memoir: 'It was becoming increasingly clear to me that the person who preached so fervently and frequently about the necessity for accountability in politics had, herself, quickly fallen victim to the insidious virus of double standards.'

\* \* \*

Pauline loves her name being on the ballot paper. Pauline Hanson's One Nation, Pauline Hanson (Independent), Pauline's United Australia Party. In her multiple lunges at parliament, Pauline has only been separated twice from having her name included in the title of the party she represented when standing for office.

Those times were when she was just another humble One Nation candidate: at the 2013 federal election for the Senate and in the January 2015 state poll in Queensland, when she stood and narrowly missed out after she had reclaimed the leadership. Six months after she was narrowly defeated in her home state, the party was again rebadged in her name.

The danger of putting the volatile redhead in charge again would have been a calculated risk for the party that had failed to spark for the years she was on the outer. Hers is a name ID that took two decades of her sweat, a lot of tears and much theatrical strutting to build. It is one that has served her exceptionally well in the rich and rewarding game of life, in all its many personal and commercial forms.

And her shingle on the office door offered electoral success not just to her but to many other parliamentary aspirants. Hopefuls who would otherwise have never had a shot at the political big time—a glittering example would be Malcolm Roberts—would go on to glide into parliament on her well-known and well-tailored coat tails. Yep, party people thought, let's roll the dice one more time.

But once Pauline's name is in the title, she assumes that naturally the party is her property. Democracy retreats as some quaint oddity to be practised by other political entities. If her name pulls in the crowds and money, surely it stands to reason that she owns the party and controls it? After all, it's rare for someone in the public eye—or even out of it, as Pauline was for so long—to have instant brand recognition at the mere mention of her Christian name.

But Pauline has this capacity; she knows it, and it's been her rationale for the way she's run the party when she's been the leader. Her name in some pockets has been electoral gold—in more ways than one.

Over the meandering course of her twenty-year pilgrimage towards a parliamentary berth, her political entities—including as Pauline the Independent candidate, and including the $1.6 million secured for the party's 2016 federal election vote—have reaped more than $8 million in taxpayer-funded election pay-outs.

Pauline has showcased her true small business smarts during her search for a seat. She's revealed an admirable ability to run no-cost, low-frills campaigns for herself, when she flew solo, and for the party, when she's talking to and leading them. These campaigns have delivered high taxpayer-funded returns.

She often declares her intention to run right on the deadline for nominations. That element of surprise—it's Pauline, back again!—allows her to gain maximum free media exposure, in turn alerting her rusted-on supporters to sharpen their pencils for the ballot box and largely dispensing with the irritation of mounting the sorts of expensive election campaigns favoured by other parties. Other small businesses could learn a thing or two from such a successful business model.

Her 1998 run at the Queensland seat of Blair netted her party $3,044,525.97, according to final Electoral Commission figures published in November 1998.

At the time Hanson and 'the two Davids'—Oldfield and Ettridge—tightly controlled all party monies through a complicated structure that was a showpiece of unaccountability. Under the party's unique constitution, only Hanson and the Davids could receive the public funding monies.

The 1998–99 annual return filed with the Australian Electoral Commission (AEC) by Ettridge—scrawled in his handwriting—revealed total receipts of $5,882,442.63, including donations and public funding amounts from the Australian, New South Wales and Queensland electoral commissions in payment for the federal, New South Wales and Queensland polls. The amounts also included private donations. The accounts were such a mishmash that Ettridge had to file amended returns multiple times.

The party's secretive structure and the possibility that in future further hefty dollops of federal funding would be tipped into coffers controlled by the troika sparked rare bipartisan alarm. Senior government ministers Tony Abbott and Philip Ruddock, backed by Labor's Shadow Treasurer Gareth Evans, unsuccessfully called for an independent investigation into the public monies distributed to PHON.

The party's complicated structure 'would do a tax-dodging lawyer proud', Abbott complained loudly and publicly at the time. It was an 'exclusive club', not a political party. Hanson and the two Davids brushed off the criticism, even though the lack of accountability and the concealment from party members of the trio's operations had already led to mass resignations by party members in Queensland.

Prior to the 1996 federal election, the system of public funding for political parties was through reimbursement-by-receipt for expenditure on campaigns. But the AEC introduced a change so that, following the 1996 election and beyond, parties received public funding automatically, dispensed on an amount paid for every vote above a percentage of formal first preference votes received.

In 1998, the amount was $1.62 for every vote cast above 4 per cent of the formal first preference votes received. Having instigated this change, the AEC wasn't in the mood to revert to the previous system.

The Commission responded to accusations of profiteering by One Nation with a masterpiece in bureaucratic understatement. In its subsequent report, it stated that it had been made aware of concerns about 'a particular party', and it noted that the intention of the public funding scheme, when introduced in 1983, was strictly to help political parties defray their costs. The current 'commentary' suggesting that a return to the reimbursement scheme would prevent profiteering was 'mistaken'. A lengthy explanation followed. The bottom line was that it wasn't going to budge.

At a state level, the $502,000 PHON received in public funding for the Queensland election had to be repaid after the party was de-registered in 1999, following the magistrate's court decision that it had been wrongly registered (this was a few years prior to Hanson's trial for fraud).

Pauline's life and times could have been so different if she hadn't treated the money as her own and refused a failed candidate's legitimate right to reimbursement of his campaign costs. One Nation hopeful, Terry Sharples, was incensed when he was denied reimbursement of $11,500 in campaign costs from the $502,000 received in public funding for the 1998 state election, sparking the action that led to her conviction and jailing. In an affidavit later to Queensland Police when he, too, was trying to recover funds from the party, David Ettridge attested that Hanson did not have any right to deny Sharples the money.

'The party's campaign committee was charged with the responsibility as a trustee on behalf of the ECQ for the disbursement of public money, not PHON party money, and Pauline Hanson had no legal right to interfere and retain Sharples' money in the PHON bank account,' he stated.

Campaign committee member Berwen Smith backed up Ettridge, attesting that Pauline instructed him not to pay Sharples. Pauline's former secretary, Cheyenne MacLeod, also stated in an affidavit that she had heard Pauline say Sharples would 'not get a cent' from One Nation. Nobody really knew what he'd done to spark Pauline's ire.

Despite what should have been overflowing PHON coffers at the time, Hanson launched the 'Pauline Hanson's Fighting Fund' on the John Laws program on Foxtel in March 2000, to raise money to repay the state Electoral Commission.

By August, half the money was repaid. Three months later, a further $252,000 was repaid. A few years after her original conviction in 2003 for fraud was overturned, she tried to get what she called 'her' money back from the Electoral Commission. She didn't succeed.

* * *

The party reaped another ripper pay-out following Pauline's unsuccessful low-key tilt at the Senate in 2001, this time of $1,471,549.23. By then, Ettridge and Oldfield had been blasted out of the PHON bunker and Hanson was the lone pilot with a loyal support crew. That's a lot of moolah for a party that was losing more members than it was gaining.

But then the show was dynamited from within. By 2002 Pauline was out of the party, and by August 2003 she was in jail after being convicted of electoral fraud. By November she was back on the streets after a successful appeal. What happened to the books and the bank balance is a question for the ages.

Not letting the grass grow under her feet, Pauline stood as an independent Senate candidate in New South Wales at the 2004 federal election. By now wearing the mantle of Australia's political prisoner, she received a respectable 4 per cent of the vote. She didn't win a seat but won the jackpot, pulling in public funding of $199,886. Hanson was automatically entitled to the full amount. Electoral returns showed she spent around $35,000 on her short, sharp campaign.

Then ALP National Secretary Tim Gartrell was furious. He knew how much it cost to run a proper campaign, and he was a stickler for the spirit of public funding, which is to enable the free exchange of ideas unfettered by a candidate or party's ability to privately fund its campaign. He took another run at accusations that Pauline was profiteering. He told a parliamentary inquiry following the election that the AEC should be given powers to investigate and, if necessary, force repayment in cases where individuals personally benefited from public election funding.

When Pauline's 'meagre' campaign spend had been deducted from her public windfall, 'it appeared Ms Hanson pocketed the balance, more than $164,000—not bad for a handful of media appearances during that campaign', he told the committee during hearings. 'It is of deep concern that an individual should derive such personal benefit from the electoral process. Public funding should not be used to gain private profit in this way.'

Politicians and the AEC didn't act. To this day, candidates and parties can spend as little as they like and still be paid a regularly indexed amount per vote cast if they receive above 4 per cent of the formal first preference vote.

\* \* \*

Time for Pauline to retreat to the ranch and the bosom of her loyalists in Queensland.

She stood at the November 2007 federal election as the only Senate candidate for Pauline's United Australia Party. The party had been established in June 2007 as a vehicle to torpedo her back into the Big House on Canberra's Capital Hill. The party, as usual, was run by a small clutch of starry-eyed Pauline devotees, eager to see her return to parliament.

The leader of the party of one, Pauline failed to win a seat in parliament. But the money gods smiled on the perennially unlucky candidate. Her 4.2 per cent vote entitled Pauline's United Australia Party to an impressive $213,095.49 in electoral funding. The windfall reimbursement landed in the party's principal working account in two separate tranches in December 2007 and January 2008.

In May 2008, party treasurer Graham McDonald noticed that $207,000 had migrated from the party's Suncorp account to another Suncorp account in Ipswich, Pauline's home turf. McDonald was so alarmed he rang his failed candidate about this unusual financial transaction, and taped the conversation.

A partial transcript of the heated call found its way into the Queensland *Courier-Mail* in 2009. When McDonald told Pauline the money belonged to the party, she flared up: 'I haven't put all this bloody hard work into this . . . for everyone else to have control over it.' She had bills to pay, she remonstrated; and besides, she had legal advice she could seize control of the dough.

McDonald later told *The Australian* that he blew the whistle because he was 'not going to go to the clink with her for knocking off 200-odd-thousand dollars': 'I told her: "You can't do it, it's party money." And she said, "I can, I will, because it's legal." So all those people who put their faith in her, she just wiped them.'

Within a few weeks of the phone call McDonald and his wife Jan, the party secretary, told *The Australian* they were sacked from their positions and expelled for allegedly bringing Pauline and the party 'into disrepute'. This would come as no surprise to so many before them: challenge her and you're shown the door.

A new management structure was installed comprising the trio of Pauline; Brian Burston, who would go on to become her New South Wales senator in 2016 and then her mortal enemy; and Pauline's good mate, Bronwyn Boag, who fortuitously was already the appointed party agent in control of nominating party bank accounts.

At the inaugural meeting that blessed the new committee, Pauline moved a motion that the original PUAP bank account be closed and all funds transferred into the Ipswich account. Burston moved another motion to pay Hanson $1000 a week plus expenses, backdated to June 2007 when the party was founded.

Pauline and Boag would remain signatories to the bank account and it would be 'at Pauline Hanson's discretion to pay accounts or expenses incurred on behalf of the party', the successful motion stated.

McDonald filed a complaint with the police fraud squad, handing over to them the tape of the conversation, and he reported her to the Australian Electoral Commission. The AEC shrugged it off; it had 'no knowledge about the money transfer'. A few years later, the fraud investigation was forced to wind up due to insufficient evidence; the new governing committee had advised the police that 'it did not wish to make a criminal complaint'.

Labor Senator and Special Minister of State John Faulkner had also tried unsuccessfully in 2008 to pursue the matter through the Australian Electoral Commission. He hit the same brick wall as McDonald. It was impossible to track just what had gone on, and the show moved on.

An exasperated McDonald told *The Australian:* 'Had she been running as an independent, fair enough. But to take the money from a registered party account and . . . to get herself back-paid to the time the party started . . . Well, I didn't think it was right back then and I still don't.' Neither Hanson nor Burston would respond to the newspaper's repeated questions, and neither has ever repudiated McDonald's account.

Flush with funds, in 2009 Pauline was back to try her luck at a state level, standing in Queensland as an Independent and pulling in enough votes to qualify for $21,649 in public funding from the Queensland taxpayer. In another two stabs at a seat—as an Independent at the New South Wales state election in 2011, and at the Senate again in 2013, this time as a PHON candidate—she failed to secure enough votes to attract public funding for the party (New South Wales by then had changed its system anyway, so that receipts needed to be provided to claim reimbursement).

Next up, the Queensland state poll in 2015. By now she was leader again and her star was in the ascendancy. Her vote ensured PHON received $65,512 in public funding. The times were clearly ripe; she could smell it. In 2016, as the leader of the by-now rebirthed Pauline Hanson's One Nation, the party spectacularly swept back into federal parliament with four senators and a healthy enough vote to fill the kitty with federal funding of $1,623,827.

* * *

Pauline has repeatedly insisted that public funding has gone to the party, that she has never personally received any money. She erupts with anger when questioned about funding. When she was preparing to run in the 2013 federal election, she reacted furiously to journalist Benjamin Law's questioning.

'Ben! This is garbage!' she shouted. 'Do you ask Tony Abbott how much funding he's going to get? Do you ask Kevin Rudd? Wayne Swan? Barnaby Joyce? I am frickin' sick and tired of this! I am not getting electoral funding. I stand with the party. Nothing goes directly to me.'

She categorically told *The Australian* during the 2016 election campaign: 'I have not claimed any money personally from any elections.' Only once, in an interview with Samantha Maiden in the News Corp Sunday papers in June 2016, before she won at the following month's federal election, did she leave a bit of wiggle room. 'That's cost me money to run. Do you realise at the last election the Liberal Party picked up $27 million? That Nick Xenophon picked up $600,000?'

As for the various ways PHON donations are recruited, sometimes there's a glimpse; or maybe not. Take the 2016 election as an example.

From late 2014 up until April 2017, Pauline's personal bank account was listed on PHON websites for donations under the heading 'Pauline Hanson Senate Donations'. Kind donors were to remit to a bank branch in the name of Pauline Lee Hanson in East Maitland, New South Wales, where Hanson part-owns commercial property.

A separate account registered in Queensland, the party's head-quarters, also appeared alongside to receive donations. Hanson's personal account was whisked offline after News Corp tabloids started snooping in April 2017. Former party treasurer Ian Nelson said at the time there was 'no way' in 'any way, shape or form' he or other party officials could monitor the activities of that personal account.

Hanson declared $2558 to her campaign from fourteen donors to the relevant authorities, but the return only covered up until 30 days after the July election. Her personal account was advertised for donations for eight months after that.

As per her distinctive approach to transparency and account-ability, Hanson refused to respond to media questions about monies donated to her personal account. However, she declared to the Australian Electoral Commission that she'd spent nothing on electoral or advertising material.

Fellow Senator Derryn Hinch noted at the time: 'If they had suddenly brought out a series of invoices to prove every dollar that went into her personal account went out again [for electoral expenses], you might be able to justify it, but it's a bit thin . . . Think back over the last twenty years and you start thinking about leopards and spots.'

\* \* \*

Since the 2016 election, there have been controversy, investi-gations by police and by various electoral commissions, and an avalanche of accusations of impropriety by disaffected members and candidates dogging Pauline and the team that runs the party named in her homage.

At one stage the federal police, the Australian Electoral Commission and the Queensland Electoral Commission were all running investigations at the same time. Two related to leaked, taped recordings of conversations involving Pauline, Ashby and party officials.

One recorded an alleged plan to make money out of PHON's Queensland 2017 state election candidates. Ashby's printing company would charge inflated prices for their campaign material, submit the overblown expense claims to the Queensland Electoral Commission and pocket the difference between the real costs and the inflated charges.

On the leaked tape, Ashby said he'd deny it if it ever came back at him. When the recording came to light, both Pauline and Ashby declared it had been an idea that was immediately knocked on the head. Party insiders disputed that. The Electoral Commission and the federal police investigated, but there was not enough evidence to take further action.

Another taped and leaked discussion related to an alleged plan to disguise the donation by Melbourne property developer Bill McNee of a light plane, with an estimated value of approximately $110,000. When she kicked off her 'Fed Up' federal campaign in July 2015, by flying to Rockhampton in the plane in question, emblazoned with the party name and a caricature of her face, she issued a media release headlined 'Hanson takes maiden flight in her new plane'.

The release stated: 'I am proud to announce Pauline Hanson's One Nation will be launching their new plane just finished being built by an Australian company last week. I am thankful to now have a plane as this will enable me to visit people around the state . . .'

Former party treasurer Ian Nelson described to *Four Corners* how he, Pauline, Ashby and McNee had discussed the purchase of the plane over roast lamb at Pauline's home in early 2015. He recalled Ashby kept saying that he was a pilot, and that Pauline needed a plane; and McNee responding: 'We'll have to get you a plane, then.'

Nelson recalled that, after it was bought and Pauline told him it was her plane, he urged her to declare it in line with donation rules. She told him: 'Don't worry about it.'

Hanson initiated legal action to try to stop the ABC from airing any further leaked recordings, but she then dropped it. As for questions by other pesky media, she crossly responded that the plane had 'nothing to do with the party'. McNee had bought it for James, she insisted.

The Melbourne property developer must be one of the most generous—and naive—donors going if he hands out planes to staffers. The very nature of a staffer's job—particularly if someone works for Pauline—is that it can be precarious and temporary. A plane donated to a party has usefulness well beyond the tenure of staffers, even the leader.

In May 2017 the Australian Electoral Commission launched an investigation into whether the plane was an undeclared donation. The investigation was still ongoing in mid-2018—coincidentally, the same time the party corrected another bout of the bookkeeping blues, amending its 2014–15 and 2015–16 financial disclosure declarations.

The 2014–15 record was amended to include a $57,720 donation from Vicland, which is one of McNee's companies. The 2015–16 return was changed to add $30,375 for the use of Ashby's allegedly private plane—243 hours at $125 per hour.

As sure as the sun rises over the hills of Queensland, a tailwind of controversy buffets Pauline wherever she travels, whether by 'private' plane or otherwise. She was forced to fend off accusations in the run-up to the Queensland November 2017 election that she was zooming around the vast state campaigning on the taxpayers' purse. A federal MP cannot claim political campaigning as a travel expense.

After a particularly hectic meet-and-greet in January with then-senator Malcolm Roberts in tow, Hanson fronted the nightly *Sky* program hosted by fan Paul Murray to put her case against her accusers. All of her travelling was in pursuit of her senatorial duties, she asserted.

'Everything that I'm doing now in Queensland travelling is, like, meeting the farming sector to do with the federal politics and, ah um, I went up to Townsville also to deal with the escalating crime that's actually happening there,' she said. 'So what I'm doing is on official, you know, parliamentary duties and businesses, like I go out to Chinchilla for the coal seam gas mining, the impacts it's having there, so I'm getting around and doing my job that I'm supposed to do as a senator, so we're having public meetings.'

She was back in the game of politics. After two decades of practice, she knew how it worked.

\*    \*    \*

Pauline Hanson didn't have a proper job during the eighteen long years she spent kicking around after being tossed from parliament in 1998 and her return in 2016. She had periodic payments for celebrity stints treading the boards, and lecturing to people at election time on TV.

In early 1997, she sold the fish'n'chips shop for an undisclosed sum. Documents provided to prospective buyers revealed a turnover in 1995–96 of $317,837, and relatively low staff payments of $32,333 for up to five full-time and temporary staff, plus government subsidies of $5454. It is reasonable to assume that, given those figures, the sale price would not have funded the retirement dreams of a 43-year-old single mother of four.

But the proceeds of that sale and piecemeal payments for celebrity stints appear to have been what financially sustained the astute small businesswoman, and helped boost her property portfolio and maintain an enviable lifestyle until she returned to parliament in 2016.

She has repeatedly stated she was a self-funded retiree in her wilderness years, and also that she self-funded her campaigns.

When she rejoined parliament in 2016 she declared as assets two unencumbered residential properties (Coleyville, Queensland), and one commercial property (Maitland, New South Wales as co-owner of a hotel). She had also co-funded an apartment on the Gold Coast for her son, Adam. She declared no liabilities, three savings accounts and one asset line, and shares in Webjet and AMP. The lone recipient of charitable donations was Meals on Wheels.

She was in such a financially secure self-funded position she was able to stump up $191,000 of her own money as a temporary loan to PHON prior to the 2016 election. She also told journalist Benjamin Law in 2013 that one (unspecified) federal election campaign had personally cost her $100,000 to fund.

She regularly took overseas holidays between runs at state and federal parliaments, and moved from house to house between Queensland and New South Wales when she was seeking office. It had been a very good life indeed.

* * *

At some stage in a person's life, there's a pivot point. A path is chosen. In February 2010, twelve years after her 1998 banishment from parliament and six years before her triumphant 2016 return, Hanson chose a certain path. She chose the unthinkable.

The proud patriot who had stood for so many elections on a passionate platform representing 'the people' and 'Australian values' was in the throes of voluntarily de-registering Pauline's United Australia Party, and was casting the net for a new country. She announced it would be Britain, land of her forebears, and it would be for good. Sadly, Australia wasn't her sort of country anymore. She was disappointed; it was no longer the land of opportunity. Or perhaps she meant no longer the land of opportunities for her.

Whatever the reason, in preparation for selling up and moving out, she invited her friends at Channel Seven's *Sunrise* program in April to take a tour through her multi-million dollar Coleyville ranch, which she'd be putting on the market. But prospective buyers had to be of a certain persuasion. She had 'no intentions of selling my home to a Muslim', or foreigners she didn't approve of, particularly Asians that lived offshore.

She was sorry for the subsequent backlash against the real estate agent, a local LJ Hooker franchisee, but 'if someone turns up to my doorstep that I'm not happy with, I won't allow them through my house', she told media. Unfazed that she had to take her place off the market because of the backlash, she jetted off.

After sashaying around Europe and the Old Dart for two months—average wage-earners would be so lucky—she returned home. Immigrants and refugees were over-running Britain and Europe, she said in horror.

Back to the ranch, then. Lucky the demographic of Coleyville was almost exclusively Anglo, according to Australian Bureau of Statistics figures at the time. Hanson directed her gaze back to her future in Australia. The country needed her. It was again time to contemplate the next chapter in the adventures of Pauline, the youthful self-funded retiree. There were plenty of elections left in the oldish gal, and she again set her sights on another low-cost, no-frills, high-return resurrection.

# Chapter 16

# PAULINE'S HOUSE OF CARDS

PAULINE HANSON HAS cleverly built her political brand as an anti-politician, as a truth-seeking champion for neglected Aussie battlers. She wants her fans to believe she's a fierce critic of the political status quo, which, she rants, no longer serves mainstream Australia.

Same for big party politicians. She would have us believe they've sold out the country to foreigners and undermined Australian values, when it's been her all along who's been doing it. She's hoodwinked her faithful devotees and hoodwinked mainstream politicians, who've pandered to her for decades.

Pauline has built her brand primarily to open another door back into that very world she rails against. The pull and power of being a chosen one in the political elite in Canberra has always been fundamental to Hanson's drive to restore her parliamentary credentials. Her anger has less to do with the plight of the overlooked average Aussie and more to do with personal revenge and misplaced victimhood.

Her skewed belief has always been that manipulative mainstream politicians and their manipulated electoral and judicial system robbed her. They and it conspired to end her parliamentary career after just two years. They and it jailed her. For eighteen long years they and it stopped her from fulfilling her all-consuming ambition for a political career.

Yet, if it were not for the benefits she has received from the very electoral system she claims fleeced her, she would never have returned to parliament trailing a few other PHON candidates behind her. Without the system, she could never have enjoyed a professional, commercially rewarding career for nearly two decades as a celebrity political candidate.

And thanks to two Coalition governments that have pandered to her prejudices, the system has allowed her to impose on Australia some of her insular, nationalistic policies that are not supported by the majority in this wide brown land built on the back of immigrants. Her unrelentingly loud opinions have only ever been attractive to a minority, but that didn't stop the Howard and Turnbull governments adjusting immigration and some welfare policies to placate her.

Her attitude to her job and to the institution that nurtures her epitomises who Hanson is: she sees no contradiction in angrily entreating her supporters to punish mainstream politicians while at the same time desperately, needily, striving to make herself relevant to those same politicians.

Her hero, Donald Trump, the world-class purveyor of alternative facts and narcissistic posturing, could learn a thing or two from Pauline.

She has continued to promote the fantasy that she's in the political game to help ordinary people and protect Australia from racial take-over and/or erosion of some vague but loaded notion of 'Australian values'. She relies on maintaining this perception by keeping alive the image that she's a battler, even though every shred of evidence points to the reality that she long ago ceased to be that person.

She can't afford to have that image tarnished. It's at the core of her appeal, and all her branding keeps the myth alive. She's permanently fed up, sick and tired of mainstream politicians, always standing up for 'the people'.

But the reality of her parliamentary record shows she does deals with the government that end up screwing the battler; she negotiates cynical preference deals that defy her anti-politician persona; and she only stands up for 'the people' when she's standing in front of them in campaign mode.

You can't tell the Prime Minister at George Brandis' original meet-and-greet for newbies that One Nation supports his government and stands ready to be told 'what you want us to do', as she did, and be considered an outsider.

You can't vote with the Coalition on legislation 80 per cent of the time and still promote yourself and your party as the independent spirit level in the Senate.

You can't cut crassly opportunistic preference deals with the Coalition in a state election and continue to stomp around the country declaring war on mainstream political parties.

At some stage even your most ardent admirers are going to realise that something's amiss.

\* \* \*

When she accidentally became a parliamentarian in 1996, Hanson had narrow, unmoveable attitudes, particularly on the red-hot issue of race, when her views were similar to those held by many who emerged from struggling small town Queensland in the Bjelke-Petersen era.

New PM John Howard didn't need the racially unfiltered new MP for the Queensland seat of Oxley. He had a comfortable majority and could easily have led from the front, instead of being led by her to change policies and tighten the parameters of our welcoming and inclusive society to accommodate her brash demands.

But her blunt force tactics had stirred a dormant White Australia soul in some pockets of alienated Australia. Turns out the final denouement of the White Australia policy in 1973 wasn't that final; it had merely been buried in a shallow grave, waiting for Pauline to come along and kick it alive. What she ignited rocked Howard's government, and he reacted like many politicians: he took a few pages out of her playbook.

But it wasn't that easy to stamp out her influence

Even those who didn't truck with her brutish race politics wrongly tipped their hats to her for speaking up; she became the flag-carrier for those who felt their voices were stifled, who'd been muzzled by political correctness. Yet despite her alienation from mainstream politics, which has been at the core of her enduring appeal, for all that time she'd been on the outside peering longingly back in.

She's never quite got over her need to belong to a tribe, just like the way she grew up in a large family. If she was honest, she'd admit that her heart has always been with the party that booted her, the Liberals. Her record speaks for itself.

They'd never have her back, though. They're too smart for that. They'll use her and her vote, as they did when securing her support for personal income tax cuts, but treat her like the Victorian-era mad aunt locked in the attic—feed and nurture her, but keep her hidden from public view. She's simply too hot to handle, too out of control, too Trump-like.

While most politicians duck and weave around the truth and play word games, Hanson is in a class of her own. Testing her statements against known facts and evidence has always been a futile exercise. She's long relied on firebrand rhetoric and stuttering passion to deflect any basic requirement for data and evidence-based argument to make a point.

To date her disciples haven't cared, so why should she? Back in the day, her enthusiasts mistook her blunt bigotry and fear-mongering as plain talking. Telling it like it is, without fear or favour, they reckoned. Good on her. She's one of us—not one of those slick politicians.

Twenty years on, and it's still the same old, same old. Pauline hasn't changed the blueprint, just the racial target. She still doesn't bother to think before she talks, or gather evidence before she pronounces. She relies on the emotions of fear and outrage, not empirical data.

She has no consistent platform of ideas or solutions. Her political life is one long ticker-tape parade of angry slogans and sound bites, embroidered by her rage that Australia is no longer the stuff of her 1950s fantasies. She repeatedly challenges people to produce evidence she's a racist, despite an abundance of evidence in her utterings revealing how incensed she is about sharing our continent with people of colour and race, whom she sees as receiving privileges that she hasn't.

Hanson doesn't offer solutions. Her policy manifesto resembles a protest flyer. What policies the party does have are vague motherhood statements, subtly fortified with racial overtones. The opening statement in the short four-sentence jobs policy, for instance: *Jobs for Australians first and foremost.* Or: *Introduce an apprenticeships scheme that will create jobs for Australians.* Does that mean only Anglo-Australians? Or does she include Asian Australians, African

Australians, Muslim Australians, or any of the other dozens of racial groups from which Australia's rich population is drawn?

* * *

The community view of politicians has dropped to such a low point that Pauline's anti-politician affectation and nationalist posturing are the best two things Pauline have going for her. These are matched only by her unerring ability to hoodwink her apostles into believing she has nothing else on her mind but their welfare.

Up until two decades ago, voters wanted solutions and we looked to our politicians to lead with vision, courage and determination in the interests of Australia. We believed they had our interests at heart.

The transformation of our collective view about our elected representatives from idealism about their motives to despair at their behaviour gave Pauline the opening she needed. But whether her vote can ever become anything other than a vessel for protest is doubtful.

She is good at stunts and can sometimes corral a few candidates to an election. In defeat, she trots out excuses to camouflage her lack of broad support and her party's lack of basic political smarts. The familiar lament is that One Nation was cheated by the major parties/done over by the system/ambushed by election timing/ outspent on its campaign.

The predictable bluster of excuses after candidates are sacked or quit in disgust can't hide the reality that the party is perennially incapable of recruiting quality candidates, or pre-selecting teams of candidates that can withstand character checks and Hanson's unique management style.

Whether the Pauline era in the time of Turnbull is as short and brutal as its counterpart in the Howard age, or whether it becomes part of the established body politic—another contradiction for the anti-politician party—depends only on the woman that runs the joint.

When Pauline blazed back into federal parliament, One Nation had existed in a number of states for two decades but Pauline Hanson's One Nation had only had two incarnations totalling seven years.

It's a telling reflection on her leadership style that, when she's in the driver's seat, the party is a riven, divided mess of personality clashes, bookkeeping chaos, mad thought bubbles, legal infractions and shambolic administration. But when the party doesn't host her name, it barely registers on the political radar.

She knows it. She is unhesitant about repeatedly referencing 'my party'. She, and whatever Manchu Court she has at the time, demand absolute control and authority; they run the organisation like a secret society, and have no truck with those who question or stand up to her. It's her way or the highway.

She confirmed that unbending approach when she engineered a change in the party's constitution in late 2017 to make her President-For-Life. In the unlikely event she decided she no longer wanted to rule, the changes ensured she had the iron-clad right to appoint her presidential successor.

As well, until such time as anyone dares challenge her, the 2017 changes gifted her the roles of senior executive officer, head of the national executive and registered officer of all One Nation divisions, meaning she could control the all-important public funding returns. This is democracy One Nation style. Vlad would be proud.

\* \* \*

If there's an appearance that Pauline's house of cards is held up by hot air, it's because it is.

PHON appeared to be at the lift-off stage of a glorious renaissance when Pauline and three of her team landed in the senate at the July 2016 election, helping to hold the balance of power.

But the more things change, the more they stay the same. There is no Pauline Hanson's One Nation. There is Pauline the personality cult, there are her disciples, and there's little else. For as long as she's in charge—and she gets to determine that—Pauline Hanson's One Nation is doomed to live its days as little more than a mirror for her vanity. The party is incapable of structuring into a decent political entity for as long as she hires and fires at whim.

Its candidate vetting remains as woeful now as it was decades ago, leading to mass sackings and defections during campaigns. One Nation's hierarchical and unaccountable party structure remains so 1990s, run tightly by Pauline and whatever politburo is around her at the time.

She's the queen of divide and conquer. Party officials, for want of a better term, are more often than not at each other's throats because of her. Loyalists and volunteers are forever doomed to help the party hum along and to consider Pauline one of the family before they inevitably find themselves brutally discarded without explanation or apology, left distressed and bewildered at the reason.

PHON has no national stable of hard-headed political strategists or experienced campaign architects. It continues to operate as a fringe rabble rather than the political force it has, despite itself, become. It suffers monotonously regular bouts of maladministration, investigations by electoral commissions for its dubious practices, and accusations of profiteering and gouging. It simply seems incapable of upgrading to become a professional political outfit.

The party lurches from crisis to crisis, chewing up devotees and parliamentarians, who enter the bunker full of fervour and loyalty and emerge on the other side, disillusioned and deeply angry.

The parallels between the party's star-burst rise in 1996 and super-nova explosion a few years later are eerily similar to her remarkable 2016 comeback and the possible demise within the parliamentary term of what should have been a winner-takes-all return.

Pauline only has herself to blame. She has the unique ability to shut her own door in her face. Some time during her journey from 1996 small-town politician to 2016 standard-bearer of the anarchistic right, Pauline became an overbearing, authoritarian professional campaigner offering little else than a permanent edge of scatter-gun fury.

The checks and balances of the system she superficially loves to hate, and the inbuilt bullshit detector of most Australians, were working against her political durability at the time of publication in mid-2018.

Despite her deepest cravings and the pessimism of voters about our two-party system, longevity in politics requires a bit more than a craven need for personal power and adulation.

# CODA

ON 28 JULY, Pauline Hanson's One Nation voters in Queensland put Malcolm Turnbull and his government on notice. Despite doing a runner on her supporters in the final week of campaigning, despite the usual questionable candidate, and despite the jailing during the campaign period of one of the party's key lieutenants, Sean Black, for the heinous crimes of rape and assault, One Nation reaped a menacing 15 per cent vote in the Longman by-election. It was just one of five national by-election contests held across Australia that day.

If mirrored in other Queensland seats at the general election, which the prime minister insists will be held on schedule in the first half of 2019, Turnbull and his team would be toast in Queensland alone, losing north of seven seats, most likely to Labor. One Nation would increase that state's Senate representation to three, maybe four seats. Pissed-off Queensland voters would again be responsible for ringing the death knell for another federal government.

Pauline Hanson was too busy playing board games and taking tea in fine China cups to turn up for the last all-important ten days of campaigning. While her candidate Matthew Stephen was batting back accusations of dodgy business dealings, she had chosen instead to rub shoulders with the well-heeled aboard one of the fanciest luxury liners going, the *Queen Elizabeth*, bobbing about the high seas off the coasts of Scotland and Ireland.

But her supporters didn't give a fig that her only presence was as a life-sized cardboard cut-out, grinning at voters at polling booths. As an insulting up-yours to her voters, it couldn't have been more breathtaking. Malcolm Turnbull or Bill Shorten wouldn't have survived the electorate and media backlash.

But Pauline is different. By and large the media shrugs its collective shoulders. And her diehard Queensland supporters would forgive her anything. They don't care what she does, no matter how out of sync her actions are with her image or her professed ethos. They cling to the misguided notion that Pauline listens, she cares, and she's unlike the major party leaders. Then there's the large bank of murderous protest voters. To them, it could be Pauline or a fisherman in Tasmania. Wouldn't matter. What counts is that they're not a major party leader. It's that lethal cohort of voters that both Malcolm Turnbull and Bill Shorten should be very, very fearful of.

Despite Labor's wins in four of the five seats, in the three key seats—Longman, Braddon in Tasmania and Mayo in South Australia—voters gave impressive numbers of votes to independents or, in the case of Mayo, to the centrist candidate, Rebekha Sharkie, who massively increased her primary vote. In the two other by-elections, in Western Australia, the Liberals didn't even bother to run candidates. But the Greens and other minor players put up a strong enough show to demonstrate that rebellion against the major parties is sitting pretty like so many time bombs across the nation.

One Nation's Matthew Stephen in Longman weathered a string of accusations about past dubious business practices to steal 15 per cent of the vote, 10 per cent leeching directly from the LNP candidate, Trevor Ruthenberg. In no political universe is it okay for a major party candidate aspiring to be part of the serving government to get only 29 per cent of the primary vote, as he did.

A hope for the major parties is that One Nation voters rarely follow the how to vote dictates of their leader. In Longman, they defied Pauline's screeching insistence that her supporters put Labor last; 40 per cent put Labor's Susan Lamb ahead of Big Trev.

The Super Saturday by-election results tolled a very grim warning for the government and establishment parties generally. They can continue to be deaf and blind to the obvious anger of voters who feel they aren't being listened to, and hand parliament and the country's stability to the erratic whims of a ragtag of independents and crazies; or they can listen, change their ways and maintain the integrity of our parliamentary system and our economy.

If the passing parade of political and ministerial spruikers, spinners and liars who polluted the media space the day after the by-elections was a guide, they still had their fingers in their ears and the blinkers propped high on their upturned noses. Much like her cardboard self, the real Pauline—who ever she is—must have cracked a big, wide grin. Or was that a smirk?

# ACKNOWLEDGEMENTS

WITHOUT EXCELLENT EDITORS, there'd be no books on shelves. None could be as good at their craft and all that entails—fine editing, support, guidance and patience—as the crew at Allen & Unwin, in particular Richard Walsh and Rebecca Kaiser. An enormous, heartfelt thank you.

Family and friends are my backbone. It goes without saying that I thank all my brothers and sisters and extended family who love and support me. At this time, I am particularly grateful to my Canberra-based sisters Cath and Bubs for their enduring love and support through good, bad and ugly times.

Without offending the blokes in my life, I extend particular thanks in this year of strong women to my extraordinary Canberra female pit crew, whose love and collective hoist is truly humbling. I am blessed by their unstinting friendship. Mao Zedong nearly got it right when he said women hold up half the sky; he just got the percentage wrong, which everyone knows is a lot higher.

This list is not exhaustive, but particular thanks for this project to Tess for her unwavering enthusiasm and wise words of wisdom—about everything, really; to Lou, whose thirty-plus years of friendship is a wonderful gift, as are our Friday lunches; lovely Lisa—an honorary Canberran whose journalistic eye is as acute as ever, and whose encouragement is unfailing; the effervescent Lynny (where would we be without movies to escape to?); quietly caring Kerie; and Lucy, for her friendship and feeding me crazy bits from the inexplicable twitterverse.

The constant hum of encouragement from Margie, Tritia, another Lou and another Lucy also kept me striding along, as did Mary in Melbourne and Leigh in NSW. Salutes to dearest Amanda, whose long, buoying friendship and daily phone calls I sorely missed as I knuckled down to the writing stage. She reads this with a critical eye and raucous laugh in another place.

Thanks to V in Parliament House for steady flashes of intelligence, almost before they happened; and to other behind-the-scenes helpers in and outside that bunker whose insights and information were invaluable.

Much gratitude to my Pilates studio, in particular Hannah, for ensuring my shoulders and neck were up to the typing challenge. Big hugs to my son Kieran for his love and support. And to my other boys, Les and Darcy, for hauling me out of bed before dawn for long walks; the unconditional devotion of a couple of big hairy four-legged fellers kept me marching ever onward.